Aspen
Handbook
for Legal
Writers

ASPEN COURSEBOOK SERIES

Aspen Handbook for Legal Writers

A Practical Reference

Third Edition

Deborah E. Bouchoux, Esq.

Georgetown University
Member, District of Columbia (active) and California (inactive) Bars

Wolters Kluwer
Law & Business

ISBN 978-1-4548-2520-3

Library of Congress Cataloging-in-Publication Data

Bouchoux, Deborah E., 1950-
    Aspen handbook for legal writers : a practical reference / Deborah E. Bouchoux, Esq., Georgetown University, Member, District of Columbia (active) and California (inactive) Bars. — Third Edition.
        pages cm. — (Aspen coursebook series)
    Includes index.
    ISBN 978-1-4548-2520-3 (alk. paper)
    1. Legal composition. 2. Law--United States--Language. I. Title. II. Title: Handbook for legal writers.
    KF250.B68 2013
    808.06'634—dc23

                                                2012050476

About Wolters Kluwer Law & Business

Wolters Kluwer Law & Business is a leading global provider of intelligent information and digital solutions for legal and business professionals in key specialty areas and respected educational resources for professors and law students. Wolters Kluwer Law & Business connects legal and business professionals as well as those in the education market with timely, specialized authoritative content and information-enabled solutions to support success through productivity, accuracy, and mobility.

Serving customers worldwide, Wolters Kluwer Law & Business products include those under the Aspen Publishers, CCH, Kluwer Law International, Loislaw, Best Case, ftwilliam.com, and MediRegs family of products.

CCH products have been a trusted resource since 1913 and are highly regarded resources for legal, securities, antitrust and trade regulation, government contracting, banking, pension, payroll, employment and labor, and healthcare reimbursement and compliance professionals.

Aspen Publishers products provide essential information to attorneys, business professionals, and law students. Written by preeminent authorities, the product line offers analytical and practical information in a range of specialty practice areas from securities law and intellectual property to mergers and acquisitions and pension/benefits. Aspen's trusted legal education resources provide professors and students with high-quality, up-to-date, and effective resources for successful instruction and study in all areas of the law.

Kluwer Law International products provide the global business community with reliable international legal information in English. Legal practitioners, corporate counsel, and business executives around the world rely on Kluwer Law journals, looseleafs, books, and electronic products for comprehensive information in many areas of international legal practice.

Loislaw is a comprehensive online legal research product providing legal content to law firm practitioners of various specializations. Loislaw provides attorneys with the ability to quickly and efficiently find the necessary legal information they need, when and where they need it, by facilitating access to primary law as well as state-specific law, records, forms, and treatises.

Best Case Solutions is the leading bankruptcy software product to the bankruptcy industry. It provides software and workflow tools to flawlessly streamline petition preparation and the electronic filing process, while timely incorporating ever-changing court requirements.

ftwilliam.com offers employee benefits professionals the highest quality plan documents (retirement, welfare, and nonqualified) and government forms (5500/PBGC, 1099 and IRS) software at highly competitive prices.

MediRegs products provide integrated health care compliance content and software solutions for professionals in healthcare, higher education, and life sciences, including professionals in accounting, law, and consulting.

Wolters Kluwer Law & Business, a division of Wolters Kluwer, is headquartered in New York. Wolters Kluwer is a market-leading global information services company focused on professionals.

In memory of Josephine LaPointe Bouchoux,
much loved by her many students and her family

A teacher affects eternity; he can never tell where his influence stops.
—*Henry Adams*

summary of contents

contents

Chapter 2. Punctuation　31

Section Two ■ Features of Effective Legal Writing and Organization   77

Chapter 4. Features of Effective Legal Writing   79

Section Three ■ Legal Documents, Legal Conventions, and Common Legal Writing Blunders 135

Chapter 6. Legal Correspondence 137

Chapter 7. Legal Memoranda   163

Chapter 8. Legal Briefs   179

Chapter 9. Pleadings and Transactional Documents   199

Section Four ■ Postwriting Steps and Document Design   229

Chapter 11. Postwriting Steps   231

Chapter 12. Document Design   243

foreword

In many professions it is sufficient to perform a task, such as the athlete who plays a game or the artist who paints a portrait. The legal profession, however, rests on communication and requires its professionals not only to know the law but also to write about it. Legal writing takes many forms. Some documents, such as internal office memoranda, are intended to explain the law to the reader. Other documents, such as court briefs, are intended to persuade the reader. No matter what the form of the document, however, it must be accurate, clearly presented, readable, and concise.

The good news is that good legal writing is simply good writing. It should not differ greatly from other forms of writing. On the other hand, there are some quirks to legal writing that deserve special attention. Legal writing is more formal than other forms of writing. For example, the use of contractions is rare, and the use of the personal pronouns *I, we,* and *our* is uncommon (because the focus of a document should be on the client's position, not on the writer's opinions).

This Handbook is designed to be a thorough guide that legal writers can use to answer not only the "big" writing questions (such as determining the elements of a court brief) but the many "small" questions that continually occur during the writing process (such as when a comma precedes the words *and* and *but*, when the word *court* should be capitalized, and when the writer should indent quotations).

The Handbook begins with the mechanics of writing: grammar, punctuation, and spelling. Errors in these technical areas will distract the reader and detract from your message. Once a writer has mastered or reviewed these basics, the writer will be ready to address the characteristics of effective legal writing, namely, the tools used to ensure writings are accurate, clear, readable, and concise. The next section of the Handbook is devoted to legal documents. The most commonly prepared documents in law practice are described: letters, memoranda, court briefs, pleadings, and transactional documents. Sample letters, a sample memorandum, and trial and appellate briefs are included. Sections on standard legal conventions and common legal blunders are included in Section Three. Finally, the Handbook concludes with a thorough treatment of editing and proofreading your work and designing it to be visually appealing. The inside front cover shows you the brief table of contents, and the inside back cover reminds you of the elements of a well-written project. Mark up your Handbook, put comments in the margins, and use sticky notes to flag frequently used sections.

Throughout the Handbook, references to helpful writing websites are given and exercises are provided to challenge your understanding and mastery of topics. Additional exercises (and their answer keys) are provided on a companion website, www.aspenlawschool.com/books/bouchoux_aspenhandbook_3e. To reduce clutter, examples are generally shown in italics rather than enclosed by quotation marks.

The Appendixes provide an overview of citation form; a guide for English as a Second Language students; a sample appellate brief; answer keys for the Challenges in the Handbook; a Glossary of Terms used in this Handbook; a Glossary of Usage, describing and defining some frequently confused words in the legal profession, such as *affect* and *effect*; and a sample case brief.

As to citation form, Appendix A shows examples of frequently used citation forms. There are two primary guides on citation form: *The Bluebook: A Uniform System of Citation* (Columbia Law Review Ass'n et al. eds., 19th ed. 2010) (*The Bluebook*), which is the oldest and still most widely used manual on citation form, and ALWD & Darby Dickerson, *ALWD Citation Manual* (4th ed., Aspen Publishers 2010) (*ALWD*, called "all wood"), created by the Association of Legal Writing Directors to provide an easy and efficient alternative to the user-unfriendly *Bluebook*. In many instances, the *ALWD* format for citations is identical to *Bluebook* format. Appendix A gives examples of some citations for both *ALWD* and *The Bluebook*, but this Handbook is not meant to be a citation guide. Additionally, although every effort has been made to refer to useful websites, those sites can change both their content and addresses without notice. References to websites are not endorsements of those sites.

This third edition of this Handbook includes several new features, including the following:

- New exercises and challenges to test mastery of topics discussed;
- Updated websites;
- Expanded information on achieving conciseness;
- Additional information on writing letters to adverse counsel;
- Expanded discussion on the use of email and texting in the workplace;
- Additional practical tips such as handling URLs that end sentences and following sentences with one space or two; and
- New sample documents.

This Handbook is designed to be used as a supplement to the texts you use in your writing classes and not as a replacement for those texts. Use the Handbook to provide additional information on the writing process and to enhance your understanding of the preparation of various legal documents. Use the Challenges and supplementary exercises to test your mastery of the subject matter. A reference tool such as this Handbook introduces you to concepts you will study in more depth in your legal writing courses and serves as a refresher of some writing basics you learned before you began your legal education. Thus, the Handbook serves as another tool in your writing arsenal and a complement to your assigned writing texts, which provide comprehensive information on legal analysis.

Finally, writing is a skill that you can master by repeated practice. If you are inexperienced at writing, keep practicing. Enjoy writing and understand that your writing not only says something about the topic you discuss but also something about you. Make sure your finished project is understood by the reader and reflects well on you.

Deborah E. Bouchoux
Fall 2012

help for writers

No matter what their level of experience, all writers need two tools: a dictionary and a style guide. Dictionaries help you determine the spelling and usage of words, and style guides provide basic rules of grammar and punctuation as well as information on usage in general. A good dictionary can be found in any bookstore. Consider using a well-known dictionary, such as *Merriam-Webster's Collegiate Dictionary*, now in its eleventh edition. As to style guides, which are also available in most bookstores and online, consider the following:

- *The Chicago Manual of Style* (16th ed. 2010). *The Chicago Manual of Style* is considered the classic guide for writers and editors; however, it includes a great deal of information about publishing, which is not particularly pertinent for legal writers.
- *The Gregg Reference Manual* (11th ed. 2011) by William A. Sabin. This excellent reference manual, published by McGraw-Hill, contains not only comprehensive information about writing basics (with numerous examples) but also information on preparing letters and tables and on editing and proofreading. Its coverage is very thorough, and it answers nearly every question imaginable about punctuation, grammar, usage, and document formatting and presentation.
- *The United States Government Printing Office Style Manual* (30th ed. 2008) (*Style Manual*) is the definitive source on writing for the federal government. The *Style Manual* is available for downloading and printing at www. gpoaccess.gov/stylemanual/index.html. The *Style Manual* is arranged in easy-to-read chapters. For example, Chapter 3 presents rules on capitalization and Chapter 8 presents rules on punctuation. The *Style Manual* is an excellent, free resource, and its use is approved by *Bluebook* Rule 8 and *ALWD* at 7, which direct readers to the *Style Manual* for certain issues not addressed by *The Bluebook* or *ALWD*.

Finally, no book on writing would be complete without an endorsement of *The Elements of Style*, by William Strunk, Jr. and E.B. White, now in its fourth edition. This "little book" has long been considered the classic and authoritative source for writers. Portions of the original *The Elements of Style* (1918) are available online at www.bartleby.com.

acknowledgments

I would like to express my sincere appreciation to the many individuals who contributed greatly to the development of this text. As always, my first thoughts and gratitude go to Susan M. Sullivan, Director of the Paralegal Program at the University of San Diego, who gave me my first teaching job and opened the door to a thoroughly gratifying career. Sue has been a valued friend as well as a much-admired colleague over the years.

A special thank you to my family: my husband, Donald, and our children Meaghan, twins Elizabeth and Patrick, and Robert, for their patience and understanding while I completed this text. A special thank you goes to Robert for his computer "tech support."

Many thanks also to the various reviewers who evaluated the manuscript on behalf of the publisher. Their comments were insightful and instructive. I have also received continuing evaluation from my students throughout my more than twenty-year career as a legal educator. I am especially indebted to the ESL students in my Advanced Legal Research and Writing class, who provided their thoughts and comments on legal writing when English is a second language.

Finally, a special thank you to the individuals at Wolters Kluwer and Aspen Publishers who generously provided guidance and support throughout the development of this Handbook, including Carol McGeehan, Publisher; Eric Holt, Executive Editorial Director; Christine Hannan, Managing Editor, Legal Education; David Herzig, Associate Publisher, College Market; and Sylvia Rebert, Project Manager for Progressive Publishing Alternatives. A special thank you goes to Rick Mixter, Director of Digital Development, who was the chief advocate for the Handbook and guided it from inception to publication.

Aspen
Handbook
for Legal
Writers

The Mechanics of Writing: Grammar, Punctuation, and Spelling

■ **Section One** of the Handbook reviews some of the common rules of grammar, punctuation, and spelling. Flaws in these technical areas, such as awkward sentence construction, incorrect punctuation, and spelling errors, distract readers from your message, make them doubt your abilities, and show carelessness on your part. The way you communicate communicates information about you. Make sure you're right not only with regard to the big issues, such as case analysis, but also with regard to the little issues, such as the mechanics of writing.

chapter 1

Grammar

StyleLinks

www.gpoaccess.gov/stylemanual/index.html
The Government Printing Office *Style Manual* is one of the most widely accepted manuals on English usage. The entire *Style Manual* is available at this site.

http://owl.english.purdue.edu/owl
Purdue University's Online Writing Lab offers excellent information on grammar and writing as well as exercises and answer keys.

http://grammar.ccc.commnet.edu/grammar
The site provides an excellent and thorough *Guide to Grammar & Writing* offered by The Capital Community College Foundation. Numerous interactive quizzes are designed to test knowledge.

www.kentlaw.edu/academics/lrw/grinker/LWTA.htm
Subtitled *The Law Student's Guide to Good Writing*, this excellent website offered by Professor Mark A. Grinker of Chicago-Kent College of Law provides explanations and examples of rules of grammar, punctuation, and good writing. Exercises and answers are provided.

http://andromeda.rutgers.edu/~jlynch/Writing/index.html
Professor Jack Lynch of Rutgers University offers an excellent guide to grammar and style.

A. Introduction

We use correct grammar to communicate clearly. Don't let the traditional rules of grammar and its incomprehensible terms (such as *pluperfect* or *subjunctive*) intimidate you. You do not need to know the names of the parts of speech to be a good writer, just as you do not need to know all the parts of an oven to be a good cook.

Professor Panagiotis Ipeirotis of New York University published a study in 2011 concluding that well-written reviews on the Internet help sell products and services, even when the reviews are negative. The quality of the review itself (its grammar, punctuation, and spelling) is what affected sales. In recognition of this effect, Zappos .com has been using Amazon's Mechanical Turk (an online crowdsourcing venue) to fix spelling and grammar errors in an effort to improve the quality of product reviews and thus increase demand for its products. Zappos.com reportedly has spent about $500,000 fixing poorly written reviews. Leaving aside the propriety of fixing users' reviews, it seems clear that the mechanics of good communication inspire confidence about a product, even when the communication itself is negative.

B. Sentence Fragments

The sentence is the cornerstone of all writing. A well-written sentence conveys information to the reader. A poorly written sentence causes confusion and ambiguity. Legal writing is more formal than many other kinds of writing, and an incomplete sentence in a legal document will be noticed immediately. Thus, although you may see sentence fragments in novels and other types of writings, they are not acceptable in legal writing.

Sentence fragments (also called *incomplete sentences*) are usually caused by the failure to include a subject and a verb in a sentence. Fragments also occur when writers assume that a *dependent clause* (one that cannot stand on its own) is a sentence by itself.

To remedy sentence fragments:

- Attach the fragment to an adjacent complete sentence (usually by correcting punctuation); or
- Make the dependent clause or fragment into a complete sentence.

Sentence Fragments	Corrections
The plaintiff pointed to the defendant. The man who was wearing the red tie.	The plaintiff pointed to the defendant, who was the man wearing the red tie.
I proposed two changes. Revising section one and omitting section four.	I proposed two changes: revising section one and omitting section four.
The plaintiff was late for the hearing. Which infuriated the judge.	The plaintiff was late for the hearing, which infuriated the judge.
	or
	The plaintiff was late for the hearing. This tardiness infuriated the judge.

C. Run-On Sentences

In many ways, a run-on sentence is the opposite of a sentence fragment. A run-on sentence combines two sentences into one. There are two causes of a run-on sentence:

- A comma joins two main or independent clauses (this type of run-on sentence is usually called a *comma splice*); or
- No punctuation joins two main clauses (this type of run-on sentence is sometimes called a *fused sentence*).

Fix these sentences by inserting the correct punctuation (usually a semicolon, if the two clauses are closely related) or by making the clauses into separate sentences. In many cases, a comma splice can be fixed by using a coordinating conjunction (the words *for, and, nor, but, or, yet,* and *so*) after the comma.

Comma Splices	Corrections
Please have the paralegal review the complaint, it must be filed today.	Please have the paralegal review the complaint; it must be filed today. *or* Please have the paralegal review the complaint. It must be filed today.
The defendant was early for the trial, his attorney was not.	The defendant was early for the trial, but his attorney was not. *or* The defendant was early for the trial. His attorney was not.

Fused Sentence	Corrections
The jurors were deadlocked they could not reach a verdict.	The jurors were deadlocked; they could not reach a verdict. *or* The jurors were deadlocked. They could not reach a verdict.

Challenge ? Sentences

Rewrite the following to correct them.

1. Tell the deponent to review the transcript, it must be reviewed by Friday.
2. His argument was too long. At least in my opinion.
3. Adam drafted the agreement. Which included a nondisclosure provision.
4. I am not attending the meeting, Susan is.
5. The corporation is insolvent, it cannot pay its debts.
6. The dividend payment was unlawful. According to Steven.

D. Subject-Verb Agreement

A verb must agree with its subject. Singular subjects correspond with singular verbs (as in *The plaintiff is testifying*) and plural subjects must correspond with plural verbs (as in *The plaintiffs are testifying*).

Most problems in subject-verb agreement occur when:

- A subject has more than one word;
- The subject is an indefinite pronoun (such as *everyone*);
- The subject is a collective noun (such as *committee*); or
- Words or phrases intervene between the subject and the verb.

1. Multiple-Word Subjects

☐ **Rule One: Singular subjects joined by *and* usually take a plural verb.**

Incorrect	Correct
The judge and the jury was unpersuaded by the witness's testimony.	The judge and jury were unpersuaded by the witness's testimony.

 Try mentally replacing multiple-word subjects with the word *they* to determine the correct verb, as in *They were unpersuaded by the witness's testimony.*

Exception to Rule One: When the parts of the subject describe a singular idea or are thought of as a unit, they are singular and take a singular verb, as in Macaroni and cheese is my favorite lunch *or* The corporation's president and secretary is Eve Stanley.

☐ **Rule Two: Singular subjects joined by *or* or *nor* take a singular verb.**

Incorrect	Correct
Neither the defendant nor his attorney were prepared.	Neither the defendant *nor* his attorney *was* prepared.

☐ **Rule Three: Plural subjects joined by *or* or *nor* take a plural verb.**

Incorrect	Correct
Either the records or the receipts is missing.	Either the records *or* the receipts *are* missing.

☐ **Rule Four: When the subject is composed of a singular word and a plural word, and they are joined by *or* or *nor*, the verb should agree with the nearer word.**

	Correct
	Neither the jurors nor the *judge has* left.

Note, however, that sentences such as these "sound" better with plural verbs; thus, try to place the plural subject nearer to the verb.

Better

Neither the judge nor the *jurors have* left.

☐ **Rule Five: When a compound subject (a subject with more than one word) is preceded by the words *each* or *every*, the verb is usually singular.**

Correct

Each plaintiff, defendant, and witness *was* present in the courtroom.

2. Indefinite Pronouns

Indefinite pronouns are pronouns that do not refer to a specific person or thing. Many of them end in *-one* or *-body.*

Indefinite pronouns can be singular or plural. Singular indefinite pronouns take singular verbs, and plural indefinite pronouns take plural verbs. Some indefinite pronouns (such as *all, any, none,* or *some*) may be singular or plural, depending on the noun to which they refer. If one of these pronouns refers to a singular noun, use a singular verb; if the pronoun refers to a plural noun, use a plural verb. Thus, both of the following are correct: *None of the documents were delivered* and *None of the document was reviewed.*

Following are some common indefinite pronouns:

Singular Indefinite Pronouns

anybody
anyone
each
either
every
everybody
everyone
neither
nobody
no one
nothing
one
somebody
someone
something

Plural Indefinite Pronouns

both
few
many
others
several

Singular or Plural Indefinite Pronouns

all
any
more
most
none
some

Correct Examples

▨ *Each* of the complaints *alleges* malpractice.
▨ *Everyone* in the courtroom *was* seated.

- *No one was* absent from the board meeting.
- *Many* of the documents *were* missing from the file.
- *Both* contracts *contain* errors.
- *Neither* of the plaintiffs *lives* in the county.

Caution: Remember that a few indefinite pronouns (all, any, more, most, none, and some) can be singular or plural depending on the word to which they refer.

Correct Examples

- *All* the board *members were* present for the meeting.
- *All* the *money is* counted.
- *Some* of the *documents were* missing.
- *Some* of the *document was* edited.

3. Collective Nouns and Company Names

Collective nouns are nouns that stand for a group of people or things, such as *committee, corporation, crowd, evidence, jury, staff,* and *team.* These collective nouns are usually singular because they refer to the group as a unit and they thus take singular verbs. The word *court* is also viewed as a collective noun (even when there is only one trial judge), and it is always treated as a singular word. Similarly, organizational names (General Electric Company or Starbucks Corporation) are usually treated as singular.

Incorrect	Correct
The jury have adjourned to deliberate.	The jury has adjourned to deliberate.
The evidence show probable cause.	The evidence shows probable cause.
The court have decided the case.	The court has decided the case.
The board of directors have passed a resolution.	The board of directors has passed a resolution.
Starbucks are holding their annual meeting today.	Starbucks is holding its annual meeting today.

If you wish to discuss the individuals that compose the unit, use the following forms:

Correct
The jurors have adjourned to deliberate.
The members of the court have decided the case.
The members of the board of directors have passed a resolution.

Note, however, that in British usage, collective nouns are usually treated as plurals, and thus it would be common to read *The team are playing at home today.*

Tips ➡ On Singular Nouns

- Always use a plural verb with the pronoun *you* even when *you* is singular, as in *You alone are prepared.* Use a singular verb after the phrase *one of*, as in *One of my laptops is missing.*
- Expressions of time and money are usually singular, as in *Three hours is enough time to edit the brief* and *One hundred thousand dollars is the settlement offer.*
- Geographic names such as *the United States* are usually treated as singular nouns, as in *The United States has pledged foreign aid.*

---

4. Intervening Words

Subject-verb agreement problems often occur when words or phrases (often prepositional phrases) intervene between a subject and its verb. These intervening expressions often confuse writers, who may be tempted to match the verb with the noun in the intervening phrase rather than with the subject of the sentence. To be correct, identify the subject of the sentence, and ignore intervening words.

Incorrect	Correct
The discrepancy between the books and the accounting records have been resolved.	The *discrepancy* between the books and the accounting records *has* been resolved.
The remainder of the goods to be distributed are in storage.	The *remainder* of the goods to be distributed *is* in storage.
One of the best experts are available.	*One* of the best experts *is* available.

Caution: Phrases or words such as together with, including, as well as, or in addition to do not change the number of the verb. If the subject is singular, select a singular verb; if the subject is plural, select a plural verb.

Correct Examples

- The *attorney*, together with the paralegals, *has* reviewed the contract.
- The *exhibits*, as well as the report, *show* a pattern of traffic congestion.

5. Inverted Sentence Order

In most sentences, the subject is placed before the verb, as in *Two copies of the contract are enclosed.* When this standard sentence structure is inverted and a verb precedes its subject, make sure they agree.

Correct Examples Enclosed *are* two *copies* of the contract.

         In the written proposals for settlement, there *is* a *suggestion* for compromise.

Caution: Be careful with sentences or phrases beginning with there is *and* there are. *These expressions signal that the sentence is inverted. In these sentences, the subject follows the verb. Be sure to use* is *for singular subjects and* are *for plural subjects.*

Correct Examples

■ There *is* an *exhibit* in the folder.
■ There *are* many *options* to consider.

Challenge ? Subject-Verb Agreement

Select the correct word.

1. Although both attorneys were delayed, neither was/were apologetic.
2. Either the printer or the editors has/have misplaced the files.
3. Neither the defendants nor the plaintiff are/is present.
4. Each of the firm's offices have/has its own ethics policies.
5. Several of the firm's offices have/has their own ethics policies.
6. Everybody was asked to silence their/his or her cell phone.
7. More than one exhibit is/are missing.
8. More than five exhibits is/are missing.
9. The committee meet/meets on Monday.
10. No one in their/his or her wildest dreams could have predicted an acquittal.
11. General Electric has/have decided to cancel its/their lease.
12. The agreement, as well as the exhibits, display/displays careful drafting.

E. Modifiers

Modifiers are words that modify other words by describing, limiting, or qualifying those other words. An adjective such as *big* is a modifier because it describes another word. Adverbs (such as *slowly*) are also modifiers. Modifiers should be placed as close as possible to the words they modify.

1. Misplaced Modifier Phrases

The term *misplaced modifier* refers to a modifier that has been located in a sentence in such a way as to cause ambiguity (and often humor). To avoid trouble with modifiers, keep phrases and words close to the words they modify.

Consider the following examples of misplaced modifiers:

- *The defendant was described as a tall man with a hat weighing 180 pounds.* (This sentence suggests that the hat weighs 180 pounds.)
- *He provided exhibits to the attorneys on CD-ROMs.* (This sentence suggests that the attorneys were on CD-ROMs.)
- *I read about the crime that was committed in today's newspaper.* (This sentence suggests that the crime was committed in the newspaper.)
- *He placed a transcript on the table that was blue.* (This sentence is confusing because it isn't clear whether the transcript is blue or whether the table is blue.)

To remedy a misplaced modifier, move the modifying phrase close to the words it refers to or modifies.

Correct

- *The defendant was described as a 180-pound, tall man with a hat.*
- *He provided exhibits on CD-ROMs to the attorneys.*
- *In today's newspaper, I read about the crime that was committed.*
- *He placed a blue transcript on the table* or *He placed a transcript on the blue table.*

Similarly, a 2007 headline in the *Washington Post* announced "Woman, 30, Is Found Shot in Home by Children," suggesting incorrectly that the children had shot her. A correctly worded headline would have read "Slain Woman Found at Home by Her Children."

2. Misplaced Prepositional Phrases

One common type of misplaced modifier is a prepositional phrase that is located in the wrong place in a sentence. Consider the following examples:

- *These guidelines provide tips for protecting your safety from our staff.* (This sentence suggests that the staff cannot be trusted with your safety.)
- *The attorney will discuss my proposal to fill the excavation pit with the corporation's officers.* (This sentence suggests that the pit will be filled with the corporation's officers.)

To remedy this error, place prepositional phrases after the words they modify.

Correct

- *These guidelines from our staff provide tips for protecting your safety.*
- *The attorney will discuss with the corporation's officers my proposal to fill the excavation pit.*

3. Limiting Modifiers

The following words, all of which are called *limiting words* because they restrict the meaning of other words, are notorious causes of ambiguity and should be placed immediately before the word or group of words you intend to limit or restrict.

almost
even
exact, exactly
hardly
just
mere, merely
nearly
only
scarcely
simply
sole, solely

Review the following sentence: *The witness identified Jack as the burglar.* Now consider the placement of the word *only* in the following versions of the sentence:

- *Only* the witness identified Jack as the burglar.
- The *only* witness identified Jack as the burglar.
- The witness *only* identified Jack as the burglar.
- The witness identified *only* Jack as the burglar.
- The witness identified Jack *only* as the burglar.
- The witness identified Jack as *only* the burglar.
- The witness identified Jack as the *only* burglar.

Note that varying the placement of the word *only* in the sentence can produce seven different meanings. For clarity, place these troublesome words immediately before the word or words they are intended to limit or describe.

4. Dangling Modifiers

A modifier is said to "dangle" when it does not logically modify anything in its sentence. Most dangling modifiers occur in phrases introducing sentences (especially in phrases beginning with an *-ing* word), and although the phrases include a verb form, they do not include a subject. This modifier isn't merely separated from the word it modifies, it is missing a subject to modify.

Dangling

- *Upon entering the conference room, an exhibit came to my attention.*
  (This sentence suggests that the exhibit entered the conference room.)
- *Waiting in the courtroom, his eyes became tired.*
  (This sentence suggests that the eyes were waiting in the courtroom.)
- *When not in use, the city stores the display in a warehouse.*
  (This sentence suggests that the city is not in use rather than that the display is not in use.)

To remedy a dangling modifier, either identify the actor in or immediately after the introductory modifier, or reword the modifying phrase so that it identifies the actor.

Revised

- *Upon entering the courtroom, I noticed an exhibit.*
  (The actor *I* is identified immediately after the introductory phrase.)
- *As he waited in the courtroom, his eyes became tired.*
  (The modifying phrase is reworded to identify the subject *he*.)
- *When the display is not in use, the city stores it in a warehouse.*
  (The subject *display* is identified in the introductory phrase.)

5. Squinting Modifiers

A squinting modifier is a modifier placed so that it is not clear whether it modifies the word before it or the one after it, as in the following sentence:

Lawyers who prepare briefs often can improve their writing skills.

The placement of the word *often* renders the sentence capable of two interpretations: Lawyers who prepare many briefs improve their writing skills or lawyers who prepare briefs can often improve their writing skills.

Fix a squinting modifier by moving it so that it clearly refers to the intended word.

Revised

- *Lawyers who often prepare briefs can improve their writing skills.*
- *Lawyers who prepare briefs can often improve their writing skills.*

Tip → For Correcting Dangling Modifiers

Most sentences that include dangling modifiers are written in the passive voice. Changing to active voice corrects the dangling modifier because an actor or subject is identified in the phrase that begins the sentence.
  Example:

- When a boy, my father changed careers (passive voice).
- When *I* was a boy, my father changed careers (active voice, actor identified in modifying phrase).

Challenge ? Modifiers

Rewrite the following.

1. Having argued the case, the threat of a mistrial was disturbing.
2. Studying the evidence, the decision was clear.
3. At the age of three, doctors diagnosed Luke with autism.
4. The suspect was found hiding behind a tree armed with a gun.
5. Carter agreed to deed his home to Beth after his death.
6. After complaining of pain, Alex was transported to the hospital in an abundance of caution.

F. Split Infinitives

An infinitive is the word *to* together with a verb, as in *to run, to plead,* and *to scream.* An infinitive is said to be "split" when a word (usually an adverb) is inserted between the word *to* and the verb, as in *to quickly run, to convincingly plead,* and *to loudly scream.*

Nearly all writing experts now recognize that there is no formal rule against splitting an infinitive, and split infinitives are commonly seen in nonlegal writing, including newspaper articles; however, legal readers tend to be conservative and may be annoyed or distracted by a split infinitive. Because many split infinitives are so easily corrected (by merely moving the adverb that causes the "split" after the infinitive), correct them when you can and avoid splitting an infinitive unless you want to place emphasis on the adverb or you need to remedy an awkward sounding phrase, as in *to boldly go where no man has gone before.*

Split Infinitive	Corrected Infinitive
The attorney asked me *to thoroughly review* the documents.	The attorney asked me *to review* the documents *thoroughly.*
The judge ordered us *to immediately produce* the documents.	The judge ordered us *to produce* the documents *immediately.*

☐ **Rule: Do not insert *not* or *never* in an infinitive because the result is awkward and incorrect.**

Split Infinitive	Corrected Infinitive
She agreed *to not examine* the witness.	She agreed *not to examine* the witness.

Because legal writing is more formal than other styles of writing and because legal readers are notorious perfectionists, err on the side of caution so readers will not be jarred by your usage. Thus, whenever possible, comply with the "old" rules of writing in legal documents unless awkwardness would result:

- Avoid splitting an infinitive;
- Avoid starting a sentence with a conjunction such as *and* or *but*; and
- Avoid ending a sentence with a preposition.

In most instances, there is a quick fix for violations of these old rules. For example, to remedy the split infinitive *to promptly investigate*, reword as *to investigate promptly.*

Ending a sentence with a preposition is something up with which I will not put.

                                        Attributed to Sir Winston Churchill

---

G. Pronouns

Pronouns are words that replace nouns. Thus, consider the sentences *John filed the complaint* and *He filed the complaint.* In the second sentence the word *he* is a pronoun because it replaces the proper noun *John.* There are many different kinds of pronouns, including personal pronouns, indefinite pronouns, and reflexive pronouns, but all pronouns must always agree with their *antecedents* (the word or phrase the pronoun refers to or replaces).

1. Personal Pronouns

Personal pronouns (*I/me, you, he/him, she/her, we/us, they/them*) change form depending on whether they function as the subject of the sentence or the object of the sentence. Most problems occur when there is more than one subject or object. For example, writers seldom have difficulty with a sentence such as *Give the document to me* (and would never write *Give the document to I*); however, when another party is added to the pronoun, as in *Give the document to John and me,* confusion often results.

☐ **Rule One: When a pronoun functions as or replaces the subject of a sentence, use *I, he, she, we,* or *they.***

Incorrect	Correct
It was me who prepared the contract.	It was I who prepared the contract.
James and her drafted the brief.	James and she drafted the brief.
Her and I will attend the meeting.	She and I will attend the meeting.
Either him or me will do the cite-checking.	Either he or I will do the cite-checking.
Us on the jury voted to convict the defendant.	We on the jury voted to convict the defendant.
It was them who informed the police.	It was they who informed the police.

☐ **Rule Two: When a pronoun functions as or replaces the object of a sentence, use *me, him, her, us,* or *them.***

Incorrect	Correct
You must give John and I directions.	You must give John and me directions.
We urge you to release Susan and he from their employment contracts.	We urge you to release Susan and him from their employment contracts.
She has provided the committee and we with the budget analysis.	She has provided the committee and us with the budget analysis.
Between you and I, the defendant is guilty.	Between you and me, the defendant is guilty.

Tip ➡ For Pronoun Use

As an aid to determining which form of pronoun to use, omit or cover up the noun and the word *and* accompanying the pronoun. This will provide a clue as to which pronoun to use.

Example: You must give Ted and me the police report.

Omit or cover up the words *Ted and* so that the sentence reads,

You must give _____ the police report.

This reading makes it clear that the correct pronoun is *me.*

It is customary to place the pronouns *I* or *me* after other pronouns or subjects. Thus, write *Deliver the records to Jack and me* rather than *Deliver the records to me and Jack.* Similarly, write *She and I attended the meeting* rather than *I and she attended the meeting.* There is nothing grammatically incorrect with the second presentations, but custom (and perhaps modesty) dictates that we refer to ourselves after we refer to others.

2. Pronoun Agreement

A pronoun must agree in number with its antecedent (the word the pronoun stands for or refers to). Singular antecedents take singular pronouns and plural antecedents take plural pronouns.

In most instances, writers instinctively choose the right pronoun based on what "sounds" right. Thus, writers seldom have difficulty with a sentence such as *The jurors brought <u>their</u> notes into the jury deliberation room.*

There are a few instances, however, that tend to cause problems for most writers: the use of indefinite pronouns, collective nouns, generic nouns, or when a prepositional phrase or several words intervene between the subject and the verb.

a. Indefinite Pronouns

☐ **Rule: Use a singular pronoun when the antecedent is a singular indefinite pronoun.**

Some antecedents are indefinite, meaning that they do not refer to any specific person or thing. The most common indefinite pronouns that take a singular form are as follows (note that many end with *-body, -one,* or *-thing*):

Singular Indefinite Pronouns

anybody, anyone, anything
each
either
every
everybody, everyone, everything
much
neither
nobody, no one, nothing
one
somebody, someone, something

When these indefinite words serve as antecedents of pronouns, select a singular pronoun.

Incorrect	Correct
Somebody forgot to file their papers.	*Somebody* forgot to file *his or her* papers.
Does everyone have their contract?	Does *everyone* have *his or her* contract?
Each fraternity member had their cap.	Each *fraternity member* had *his* cap.

Although these correct examples show proper usage, you may wish to avoid the expression *his or her* if it strikes you as wordy or stuffy. As discussed later in subsection 7, there are several ways to remedy such constructions. For example, the first example could be rewritten as *Somebody forgot to file the papers.*

☐ **Rule: Use a plural pronoun when the antecedent is a plural indefinite pronoun.**

Plural Indefinite Pronouns	Correct
both	*Several* of the defendants have called
few	*their* attorneys.
many	
several	

Remember that some indefinite pronouns (such as *all, any, none,* **or** *some*) may be singular or plural, depending on the noun to which they refer. If the pronoun refers to a singular noun, use a singular verb. If the pronoun refers to a plural noun, use a plural verb.

Correct

All of the contract *was* reviewed.
All of the contracts *were* reviewed.

b. Collective Nouns

As discussed in Section D.3, collective nouns (nouns that stand for a group of people or items) such as *committee, corporation, crowd, court,* and *jury,* are usually singular and take a singular pronoun.

Incorrect	Correct
The corporation is holding their annual meeting next week.	The corporation is holding *its* annual meeting next week.

If you wish to discuss the individuals composing the unit, for clarity use the following form:

Correct

The corporation's shareholders are holding *their* annual meeting next week.

c. Generic Nouns

A generic noun is one that could refer to either men or women, such as *athlete, attorney, defendant, juror,* or *plaintiff.* These generic nouns usually take a singular pronoun, as in *An attorney must present his or her argument* or *A juror will be compensated for his or her time on the jury.* As previously discussed, many sentences with the phrase *his or her* can be reworded to eliminate awkwardness, as in *The attorneys must present their arguments* or *Jurors will be compensated for their time on the jury.*

d. Intervening Phrases

When a phrase or word intervenes between the subject and verb of a sentence, ignore it, and match the verb to the pronoun, as in *Every one of the doctors was credible.* Remember that some indefinite pronouns (such as *all, any, most, none,* or *some*) can be singular or plural. When using these indefinite pronouns, look at the noun in the *of* phrase and match the verb to this noun.

Correct

Most of the brief was cite-checked.
Most of the briefs were cite-checked.

3. Pronoun Reference

A pronoun must relate clearly and specifically to its antecedent (the noun to which the pronoun refers).

a. Ambiguous References

A pronoun is ambiguous when it could refer to two possible antecedents. Thus, make sure that any pronoun used in a sentence refers clearly to one antecedent. This ambiguity often occurs when writers substitute pronouns for names. For example, consider the following sentence: *The document Ellen drafted for Teresa was given to her for review.* It is unclear whether *her* refers to Ellen or Teresa.

There are two ways to remedy such an ambiguity:

1. Replace the pronoun with the appropriate noun, as in *The document Ellen drafted for Teresa was given to Ellen for her review.*
2. Revise the sentence if you do not wish to repeat a noun, as in *Ellen, who drafted the document for Teresa, was later given the document for review.*

Ambiguous	Revised
Dan told Bill that he needed to draft the contract.	Dan told Bill that *Dan* needed to draft the contract.
	or
	Dan told Bill that *Bill* needed to draft the contract.

b. Implied References

Pronouns must refer to a specific stated noun in the same sentence or the previous sentence, not to a word that is implied in the sentence.

Incorrect Implied Reference	Correct Specific Reference
After the verdict was rendered, the attorney thanked *them*.	After the *jurors* rendered a verdict, the attorney thanked *them*.

c. Vague References

The pronouns *it, this, that,* and *which* are often used in a vague manner. These pronouns must refer to one specific noun.

Confusing	Revised
If you put your hand on the banister, it will get wet.	If you put your hand on the banister, *your hand* [or *the banister*] will get wet.
The expert witness always arrives on time and is well dressed. This is important.	The expert witness always arrives on time and is well dressed. *Punctuality* [or *dressing well*] is important.
Steve took out his pen and signed the will. He then put it back in his briefcase.	Steve took out his pen and signed the will. He then put *the pen* [or *the will*] back in his briefcase.

d. Indefinite Use of *It* and *They*

When using *it* or *they,* make sure that a definite noun has first been used.

Incorrect	Correct
In the case *Allen v. Burns*, it describes the doctrine of equivalents.	The case *Allen v. Burns* describes the doctrine of equivalents. It holds that . . .

4. Use of *Who* and *Whom*

Who and *whom* are used either in questions, as in *Who wrote the book?* or in subordinate clauses, as in *I am unsure who will represent the plaintiff.*

■ In questions, use *who* for a subject and *whom* for an object. Use *who* whenever *I, he, she, we,* or *they* could be substituted for *who,* and use *whom* whenever *me, him, her, us,* or *them* could be substituted for *whom.*

Correct Examples: *Who will be going to the trial?*

Explanation: In this question, *who* acts as the subject of the sentence.

Whom does the indictment name?

Explanation: In this question, the object of the sentence is *whom* and the subject is *indictment*.

■ In subordinate clauses, use *who* and *whoever* for all subjects and use *whom* and *whomever* for all objects.

Correct Examples: *Give the document to whoever needs it.*

Explanation: In this sentence, *whoever* is the subject of the subordinate clause *whoever needs it.*

It was Judge Allen whom I saw.

Explanation: In this sentence, *whom* is the object of the subordinate clause *whom I saw.*

 *Who* versus *Whom*: Remember "*m*" for *Whom*

In every use of *who* or *whom*, rephrase the question or subordinate clause and determine whether you would use *he* or *him* in its place. If *he* would be used, use *who*. If *him* would be used, use *whom*. Remember that the "m" in *him* matches up with the "m" in *whom*.

Example: Who is calling?

Test: Rewrite as *He is calling*. Replace *he* with *who*.

Example: This is the man whom I mentioned earlier.

Test: Rewrite as *I mentioned him earlier*. Replace *him* with *whom*.

---

5. Use of *That* and *Which*

That is used to introduce a restrictive clause (one that is necessary to the meaning of a sentence) and is not preceded by a comma. *Which* is nearly always used to introduce a nonrestrictive clause (a clause that is not necessary to the meaning of the sentence and that can be omitted without changing the meaning of the sentence). A *which* clause is usually preceded by a comma. Use *who* to refer to people, and use *that* or *which* to refer to groups and things.

The use of *that* or *which* depends on the writer's intent. If the writer wishes to convey essential information, *that* should be used to introduce the information; if the writer intends to define, add to, or limit information, *which* should be used to introduce the information.

Example: *The corporation that was formed in Delaware has no assets.*

Explanation: The word *that* tells us which particular corporation has no assets. There may be several corporations that have no assets, but the writer is describing which particular corporation, namely, the one formed in Delaware (rather than others formed elsewhere), has no assets. Use *that*.

Example: *The contract that was modified was admitted into evidence.*

Explanation: The word *that* tells us essential information about which particular contract was admitted into evidence (namely, the one that was modified).

Example: *The car that was damaged in the collision was my car.*

Explanation: Elimination of the *that* clause causes the sentence to lose meaning. Use *that*.

Example: *The corporation, which was formed in Delaware, has no assets.*

Explanation: The phrase *which was formed in Delaware* provides additional information about the corporation, but it is not essential to the meaning of the sentence. The *which* clause is set off by commas because it acts as a parenthetical expression; it adds a fact about the only corporation being discussed. Use *which*.

Example: *The contract, which was modified, was admitted into evidence.*

Explanation: The phrase *which was modified* tells us a nonessential fact about the only contract being discussed.

Example: *My car, which was brand new, was damaged in the collision.*

Explanation: The *which* clause adds information, but it can be dropped and the sentence will still make sense. Use *which*.

Examples: *We may wish that the argument were true, but it is not, and <u>that which</u> we cannot deny, we should not deny.*

His summation sets the standard <u>by which</u> all others should be judged.

Explanation: These two sentences are examples of the fact that the word *which* is not always preceded by a comma and *that which* is sometimes used to introduce a restrictive clause. The expressions *that which, in which, by which, of which*, and so forth are not preceded by commas.

Many writers are confused about the use of *that* and *which*, and you will likely see incorrect uses. Recognizing this confusion, many writing texts have relaxed the rules about the distinction between *that* and *which*. Nevertheless, because legal writing is so specific, try to remember to use *that* when you introduce essential information and *which* when you introduce nonessential information. See Chapter 2, Section C for additional information.

Tips ➡ That or Which?

To determine whether to start a clause with *that* or *which* consider these tips:

- If you can drop the clause and still retain the meaning of the sentence, use *which*. If you can't, use *that*.
- A clause beginning with *which* is usually set off by commas because it includes nonessential information.
- A clause beginning with *that* is not set off by commas. *That* introduces essential information; *which* seldom does.

6. Reflexive Pronouns

The reflexive pronouns are the *self* pronouns, namely, *myself, yourself, himself, herself, itself, ourselves, yourselves,* and *themselves.* Reflexive pronouns reflect back on a subject, as in *She injured herself* or *He satisfied himself that the defendant was guilty* or are used to show emphasis, as in *I myself made the decision.* Do not substitute a *self* pronoun for a personal pronoun (*I, me, he, him,* and so forth).

Incorrect	Correct
He won't give Lyndsey or myself his phone number.	He won't give Lyndsey or *me* his phone number.
The accident was witnessed by Mrs. Hendrix and himself.	The accident was witnessed by Mrs. Hendrix and *him*.
He issued a statement on behalf of his wife and him.	He issued a statement on behalf of his wife and *himself*.

Challenge ? Pronoun Use

Rewrite or select the correct pronoun.

1. Him/He and Jen argued the case.
2. Everyone is waiting for their/his and her security clearances.
3. I and Stella prepared for the meeting.
4. The judge called David to the bench, and he looked concerned.
5. To who/whom is the document directed?
6. For who/whom will you vote?
7. Who/Whom shall I say asked for Ms. Bennett?
8. You can video me and my opponent.
9. Only one in four candidates favors/favor the resolution.
10. Just between you and I/me, I think the judge ruled incorrectly.
11. Meg and myself/I will draft the interrogatories.
12. It was the committee who/that voted to approve the new hire, and its/their/it's vote was unanimous.
13. The trial presented a great opportunity for myself.

7. Gender-Linked Pronouns

Avoid using gender-linked pronouns. For example, the sentence *A nurse should always keep her thermometer handy* is objectionable because it suggests that nurses are always female. Similarly, the sentence *A judge must give his instructions to the jury* is likewise objectionable because it presupposes the judge is male.

a. Eight Techniques to Achieve Gender-Neutral Language

There are several techniques that can be used to avoid offending readers:

(1) Change singular nouns to plural nouns. Changing singular nouns to plural nouns will force the singular pronoun *he* or *she* to be changed to a neutral plural pronoun, such as *they* or *their*.

> Examples: Nurses should always keep <u>their</u> thermometers handy.
> Judges must give <u>their</u> instructions to the jury.

(2) Rewrite the sentence to avoid using any pronoun. Many sentences can be rewritten so that no pronouns are used.

> Example: A judge must give instructions to the jury.

(3) Use the noun *one*. In many instances, the pronoun *one* can be used. Note, however, that using *one* often results in a vague and stuffy sentence.

> Examples: One should always keep one's thermometer handy.
> One must give one's instructions to the jury.

(4) Use an article. Try replacing the pronoun with an article.

> Examples: A nurse should always keep <u>a</u> thermometer handy.
> A judge must give <u>the</u> instructions to the jury.

(5) Use the pronoun *who*.   Try using the pronoun *who*. For example, the sentence *If a judge does not give proper instructions to the jury, he will be reversed* can be rewritten as *A judge who does not give proper instructions to the jury will be reversed*.

(6) Use the pronoun *you*.   In some situations, the pronoun *you* can be used. Thus, rather than writing *The applicant must provide his address*, write *You must provide your address*.

(7) Use *he or she*.   In some instances, none of the techniques previously described will work smoothly. In those cases, consider using the phrase *he or she* throughout the document. The continued use of *he or she* throughout a long document, however, is often clumsy.

(8) Use *he* in transactional documents.   If you are drafting a document such as a contract, you may use *he* throughout and at the end include a statement that the use of the masculine gender is deemed to include the feminine. This technique is appropriate for transactional documents such as contracts, leases, and so forth, but it is not appropriate for letters.

b. Constructions to Avoid

Although ensuring that language is gender-neutral is an admirable goal, there are some constructions that are disfavored and should be avoided.

- Avoid *he/she, his/her,* and *s/he*
  Avoid using *he/she*. This construction creates an awkward appearance because slashes are seldom used in legal writing. Their use is noticeable and distracting to a reader. The combination *s/he* is even more noticeable and distracting and is unpronounceable.
- Avoid alternating between *he* and *she*
  Avoid alternating between the pronouns *he* and *she* in a single document, especially in a single paragraph or section. This attempt to be fair and gender-inclusive is misguided and confusing and is disruptive to the flow of a project.

Tip ⮞   Telephone Talk

When a telephone caller asks for you by name, it is grammatically correct to say, "This is he" or "This is she." Many speakers would say, "This is him" or "This is her," constructions that are grammatically incorrect but commonly used in informal speech. Try using "This is Jill" or "This is Dan."

---

c. Letters

When addressing a letter to an individual whose gender is unknown, for example, a letter to the Secretary of State of Utah, check the Internet to see if you can determine whether the individual is a man or woman. If you cannot make that determination, address the letter as *Dear Sir or Madam*. Although the word *madam* is an archaic form of address, it is correct in such a situation. When both women and men will receive the letter, consider *Dear Ladies and Gentlemen*. Similarly, when you are responding to a letter written by an individual whose name is ambiguous, such as Terry L. Lowell, do some investigative work on the Internet or call the person's office and ask how the letter should be addressed. Rest assured, you will not be the first person confused by such a name. If contacting the person is not possible or practical, you could address the letter *Dear Terry, Dear Terry Lowell,* or *Dear Colleague.*

d. Closing Thoughts on Gender-Neutral Language

Correct gender-linked pronouns to avoid offending readers *if* you can do so without creating an awkward and distracting document. For example, the use of specially crafted words such as *personholes* (rather than *manholes*) is jarring and confusing to readers. Thus, it is still acceptable (although not favored) to use *he* or *him* when changing the pronouns or rewriting the sentence would result in clumsy and distracting writing.

8. Special Pronoun Situations

a. Use of *We* and *Us*

To determine whether *we* or *us* precedes a noun, select the pronoun that would be appropriate if there were no noun in the sentence.

Correct Example:	*We attorneys will not represent the corporation.*
Test:	*We will not represent the corporation.* (You would never write *Us will not represent the corporation.*)

Correct Example: *The court refused to meet with us litigants.*

Test: *The court refused to meet with us* (not *The court refused to meet with we*).

b. Comparisons with *Than* or *As*

Comparisons using the words *than* or *as* tend to be ambiguous because writers are often inclined to use incomplete constructions. Consider the sentence *Don likes these cookies more than me.* Because the word *cookies* is used as the object of the verb, the sentence means that Don likes the cookies more than he likes me. To reduce confusion, rewrite the sentence and add clarifying language.

Confusing	Revised
Don likes these cookies more than me.	Don likes these cookies more than he likes me.
	or
	Don likes these cookies more than I do.

c. Gerunds

A gerund is a verb form that ends in *-ing,* as in *writing* or *drafting,* but that acts as a noun. A noun or pronoun that precedes a gerund should be in the possessive case (the case that indicates ownership, as in *our* book, *his* briefcase, *your* brief, and so forth).

Incorrect	Correct
The court approved of him giving the opening statement.	The court approved of *his* giving the opening statement.
I was unhappy with you addressing the jury.	I was unhappy with *your* addressing the jury.

9. Shifts in Pronouns

Maintain consistency in pronoun use in a sentence or section.

Inconsistent	Revised
All jurors must listen carefully or you may not understand the judge's instructions.	All jurors must listen carefully or they may not understand the judge's instructions.
One finds that when listening to oral argument, your mind wanders.	I find that when listening to oral argument, my mind wanders.

Challenge ? Gender-Linked and Special Pronouns

Correct the following or select the right word.

1. A surgeon should offer his patients a copy of their records.
2. A teacher always wants her students to do well.
3. I'm depending on his/him arguing the case tomorrow.
4. He resents me/my appearing at the meeting.
5. The judge asked us/we plaintiffs to attend the settlement conference.
6. I know you better than him.

H. Conjunctions

A conjunction is a word that joins together words and groups of words.

1. Coordinating Conjunctions: *For, And, Nor, But, Or, Yet, So*

Coordinating conjunctions join elements of equal grammatical status, as in the statement *The attorney and the defendant arrived late,* in which the conjunction *and* joins two nouns. The coordinating conjunctions are *for, and, nor, but, or, yet* and *so.* If you have trouble remembering these seven coordinating conjunctions, use the acronym FANBOYS to help you remember them.

Most traditional writers dislike the use of a coordinating conjunction at the beginning of a sentence, although this is becoming increasingly common, especially in newspapers and magazines. Whenever possible, avoid starting a sentence with a coordinating conjunction because it is likely to annoy and distract some readers. Moreover, it is likely to produce a sentence fragment, as in, *And also the transcript.* Thus avoid starting sentences with *and* or *but* except in very informal writing. In fact, some experts have commented that starting too many sentences with *and* or *but* sounds childish.

Disfavored	Revised
The court ruled in favor of the defendant. But the judgment was later reversed.	The court ruled in favor of the defendant, but the judgment was later reversed. *or* The court ruled in favor of the defendant, although the judgment was later reversed.

2. Correlative Conjunctions: *Both-And, Either-Or, Neither-Nor, Not Only-But Also, Whether-Or*

Correlative conjunctions are used in pairs so they work together and, like coordinating conjunctions, join elements that are of equal grammatical status. The correlative conjunctions are *both-and, either-or, neither-nor, not only-but also,* and *whether-or.*

There are three straightforward rules for ensuring correct verb selection with coordinating or correlative conjunctions:

- **If the subjects are singular words, use a singular verb.**
  (Correct Example: *Either Tom or Fred has jury duty.*)
- **If the subjects are plural words, use a plural verb.**
  (Correct Example: *Neither the plaintiffs nor the defendants were prepared for trial.*)
- **If the subject is made up of both singular and plural words, the verb must agree with the subject nearer to it.**
  (Correct Example: *Not only the plaintiff but also her attorneys have copies of the documents.*)

3. Subordinating Conjunctions

A subordinating conjunction is used to join a dependent clause (one that cannot stand by itself) to an independent clause (a main clause that can stand by itself). Some of the commonly used subordinating conjunctions are *after, although, because, before, if, once, since, unless, until, when, where,* and *while.* These conjunctions serve as smooth transitions in a sentence.

Correct Examples: Although the plaintiff testified, she did so reluctantly.

After a judgment is rendered in a case, it can then be appealed.

(Note that the phrases beginning with *although* and *after* are dependent; they cannot stand by themselves.)

Tips → Wherever Should We Place "However"?

May you start a sentence with the word *however?* The word *however* is not a coordinating conjunction; it is a conjunctive adverb and is usually used as a synonym for *nevertheless.* Many writers have been instructed against starting a sentence with *however,* although magazines and newspapers commonly do so. Strunk and White recommend against starting a sentence with *however* when you mean *nevertheless* (although it is correct to start a sentence with *however* when you mean *in whatever way,* as in *However prepared she was for the test, she was still nervous*).

It is difficult to understand the aversion to placing *however* at the beginning of a sentence when there is no such objection to starting sentences with other conjunctive adverbs such as *similarly* or *thus* or *therefore.* The safest approach may be to place *however* in the middle of a sentence, preceded by a semicolon and followed by a comma, as in the following example:

Disfavored

I attended the meeting. However, I did not make a presentation.

Revised

I attended the meeting; however, I did not make a presentation.

Correct Example: However you approach the issue, be consistent.

Challenge ? Conjunction Junction

Punctuate correctly or correct the following.

1. He likes drafting and to edit briefs.
2. Lily stayed for two hours. And then decided to leave.
3. The judge not only admonished the attorney and also sanctioned her.
4. Either Mark or Martin has/have the transcript.
5. Either she must attend the meeting or prepare for the consequences.
6. The board neither wanted to merge nor to consolidate.

The writer who neglects
punctuation, or mispunctuates, is
liable to be misunderstood . . . .
Edgar Allan Poe (1848)

chapter 2

Punctuation

StyleLinks

www.gpoaccess.gov/stylemanual/index.html
Select Chapter 8 of the Government Printing Office *Style Manual* for information and rules on punctuation.

http://owl.english.purdue.edu/handouts/grammar
Purdue University's Online Writing Lab offers excellent information on punctuation, together with exercises and answer keys.

http://grammar.ccc.commnet.edu/grammar/marks/marks.htm
This site provides a thorough review of rules relating to punctuation.

www.grammarbook.com
This site offers an overview of punctuation rules, exercises, and answer keys.

www.nationalpunctuationday.com
This site reviews punctuation marks and gives examples of correct uses of each.

A. Introduction

When you speak, you use pauses and changes in voice inflection as well as gestures to signal meaning to the listener. In writing, these signals are given through the use of punctuation. Punctuation makes writing more understandable to a reader. For example, a period instructs the reader that a complete thought or sentence is concluded. Without periods, all of a writing would be one incomprehensible sentence. Similarly, quotation marks signal to a reader that the exact words of another are being used.

Slight differences in punctuation may make great differences in meaning. For example, consider the alternate punctuation shown in the following trick sentences:

- Woman! Without her, man is nothing.
- Woman, without her man, is nothing.

- Mark said Lisa is smart.
- Mark, said Lisa, is smart.

- "Let's eat, Joe!"
- "Let's eat Joe!"

This part of Section One discusses ending punctuation (periods, question marks, and exclamation points), commas, apostrophes, colons, semicolons, quotation marks, parentheses, and the less frequently used marks in legal writing, namely, dashes, hyphens, and slashes.

There is some variation in punctuation. Given the same paragraph, two writers may punctuate slightly differently from each other. Nevertheless, the basic rules of punctuation have remained relatively unchanged since about the mid-1880s. Although the newer, more modern approach to punctuation, often called *open punctuation*, uses fewer marks than the older approach (for example, many modern writers and most newspapers no longer use the serial comma discussed later), legal writing, like business writing, tends to be somewhat formal. Therefore, just as was recommended in the section in this Handbook on grammar, when in doubt, err on the side of caution and use the more conventional approach to punctuation rather than some unusual approach.

B. End Punctuation

There are three punctuation marks used to end a sentence: a period (.), a question mark (?), and an exclamation point (!).

No iron can pierce the heart with such force as a period put just at the right place.

Isaac Babel (1932)

1. Using Periods

A period is generally used to indicate the end of a complete sentence.

Use a Period	Correct Examples
to signal the end of a declaratory sentence.	*The deposition will be held on Tuesday.*
to signal the end of an indirect question (one that reports what a speaker said but does not use the speaker's exact words).	*The judge asked whether the witness needed a recess.*
after a mild command.	*Please leave.*
after some abbreviations.	*The meeting will be held at 9:00 a.m. on Friday.*

Tips ➡ On Using Periods

- If a sentence ends with an abbreviation that includes a period, do not add another period.

  Incorrect: *The hearing is at 4:00 p.m..*

- If an abbreviation that ends with a period falls in the middle of a sentence, use normal punctuation after the period.

  Correct: *The hearing was to begin at 9:00 a.m., but the court reporter was late.*

- Acronyms (abbreviations that are pronounced as words, such as NATO and AIDS) are usually presented without periods.
- If a sentence ends with a website address or Uniform Resource Locator ("URL"), put a period after it, but make sure that the sentence-ending period is not included as part of the hyperlink to the URL. If you must break a URL at the end of a line, do not end that line with a period; if you do, readers may think it is the end of a sentence. Although it may look awkward, place the period at the beginning of the next line.

Spacing After Periods

Many writers place two spaces after a period ending a sentence, but it is becoming increasingly common to use just one space (because modern word processing programs automatically allow suitable spacing between and after letters). In fact, most writing guides now recommend using only one space after a period.

The use of two spaces after a period likely stems from the use of typewriters, which used monospace fonts (fonts in which each character takes up the same amount of space). Placing two spaces at the end of a sentence made the text easier to read. Many experts believe that the use of two spaces shows more visual separation between sentences and thoughts, especially when a sentence ends with an abbreviation. Nevertheless, the *Style Manual* recommends one space, as does *The Gregg Reference Manual*, noting that with today's desktop publishing standards, the use of proportional fonts predominates (fonts in which some letters, such as an "m," take up more space than other letters, such as an "i"), and one space is usually sufficient.

Note that many courts place limits on the length of briefs, in which "characters" rather than words are counted toward the limit. For some word processing programs, the extra space at the end of a sentence may be counted as one character. Thus, as a practical matter, you may wish to use one space rather than two. Whichever approach you use, be consistent.

2. Using Question Marks

Use a question mark after a direct question (one to which an answer is expected) but not after an indirect question.

Correct Examples

Who will be appointed as the arbitrator?

I asked, "Have all the exhibits been attached to the brief?"

He was effective, wasn't he?

The judge asked if the plaintiff was ready to proceed.

3. Using Exclamation Points

Exclamation points are used to emphasize an idea or statement. They are rarely used in legal writing except to show the exact words of a speaker. Exclamation points stand alone and are not used with any other punctuation mark except when they are part of a quotation.

Correct Examples

The witness screamed, "He hit me!"

What a disaster!

C. Commas

I was working on the proof of one of my poems all the morning and took out a comma. In the afternoon I put it back again.

Oscar Wilde

Commas (,) indicate brief pauses. They are considered the most troublesome of punctuation marks because of their many uses and because some of the rules regarding their use are discretionary and flexible whereas other rules are manda-tory. Moreover, their uses have changed. Many writers have been told to avoid over-use of commas, having been taught, "When in doubt, leave it out." In some instances, however, the comma adds clarity, and leaving it out causes a miscue, as in *We plan to meet with John and Ben and I will be in the office all day.*

Commas can be used to introduce, to separate, to enclose, and to show omissions.

1. Rules for Comma Use

There are thirteen rules to follow when using commas.

☐ **Rule One: Use a comma after the salutation of an informal letter and after the closing of any letter.**

Correct Examples

Dear Aunt Kay,

Sincerely,

☐ **Rule Two: Use a comma after the day and after the year in complete dates (month, day, and year), but not between a month and the year. Although writers often omit it, always place a comma after a full date when it appears within a sentence.**

Correct Examples

The trial will begin on Monday, September 3, 2012, and will conclude in January 2013.

☐ **Rule Three: Use a comma between a city and a state and after an address when the address is written in a sentence. Do not place a comma before a zip code.**

Correct Example

The witness resides at 2345 Cedar Street, Cleveland, Ohio 92117, and has resided there since January.

☐ **Rule Four: Use a comma to separate digits in numbers of four or more digits.**

Correct Example

The transcript is 4,312 pages.

Note, however, *Bluebook* Rule 6.2, which provides that commas should be used only in numbers containing five or more digits. Thus, according to *The Bluebook*, the sentence would read *The transcript is 4312 pages.* This style is disfavored by many writers and *ALWD*.

☐ **Rule Five: Use a comma to set off introductory material in a sentence. When the introductory phrase is short (fewer than three words), the comma may optionally be omitted.**

Correct Examples

According to the plaintiff, the accident occurred on Park Avenue.

Unfortunately, the judge ruled against us.

After the trial has ended, I will take a vacation.

First, the defendant entered Mrs. Harris's residence.

Although the witness was sick, she attended the hearing.

In June I will begin trial preparation.

☐ **Rule Six: Use commas to set off interruptive phrases or a transitional expression.**

Transitional expressions make connections between sentences or parts of sentences but are not essential to the meaning of a sentence. Transitional expressions include *additionally, clearly, for example, however,* and *therefore*. Transitional expressions that appear at the beginning of a sentence are followed by a comma.

Correct Examples

The jury, however, voted to acquit the defendant.

Research skills, for example, are critical for legal professionals.

The defendant, over the strenuous objection of his counsel, insisted on testifying.

Therefore, the motion was granted.

☐ **Rule Seven: Use a comma to separate two or more consecutive adjectives that equally describe the same word. If you could use the word "and" between the adjectives, use a comma.**

Correct Example

Allison was a fearful, anxious witness.

Note that *and* could also be used to join these two parallel adjectives, in which case no comma would be used.

☐ **Rule Eight: Use a comma to separate a phrase that shows contrast or contradiction.**

Correct Example

It was the plaintiff, not the defendant, who failed to attend the hearing.

☐ **Rule Nine: Use commas to separate items in a series of three or more items.**

Although the final comma in a series (often called the *Oxford comma* or the *serial comma*) is optional in most writing and is omitted in newspapers (to save space), in legal writing it is required. For example, consider the following two sentences:

I leave all my property in equal shares to Jim, Helen, Tim, and Eva.

I leave all my property in equal shares to Jim, Helen, Tim and Eva.

In the first example, it is clear that each of the individuals will receive one-fourth of the estate. In the second example, it is arguable that the estate will be divided into thirds, with Jim and Helen each receiving one-third and the group composed of Tim and Eva sharing one-third.

Similarly, consider a book dedication that reportedly read *To my parents, the Pope and Mother Teresa*. Without the serial comma after *the Pope*, the sentence implies that the writer's parents are the Pope and Mother Teresa.

Because the omission of the last comma in a series can cause ambiguity, always include it to show readers that each item is separate. Its use is never incorrect.

Correct Examples

Ray asserted the defenses of waiver, estoppel, and acquiescence.

The court found the defendant's conduct was willful, reckless, and egregious.

☐ **Rule Ten: Use a comma to separate two independent clauses connected by a coordinating conjunction, such as for, and, nor, but, or, yet, or so (the "FANBOYS").**

This rule is often violated. The comma is required before the coordinating conjunction if the clause that follows is independent, meaning one that has a subject and a verb and that can stand on its own. The comma may be omitted if the second clause is short, generally five words or fewer. A comma is not needed before the coordinating conjunction if the clause that follows cannot stand on its own.

Incorrect Examples

Stan finished law school, and is now looking for a job. (This sentence is a compound predicate, a sentence with one subject, *Stan*, and two verbs, *finished* and *is looking*. Do not use a comma with a compound predicate.)

The directors voted on the measure, and then refused to reconsider it. (A comma is not needed before "and" because the clause that follows the conjunction "and" cannot stand on its own.)

Correct Examples

Stan finished law school, and he is now looking for a job. (This sentence is a compound sentence, a sentence with two independent clauses, each with a subject and predicate or verb. Use a comma before the coordinating conjunction.)

The directors voted on the measure, and they then refused to reconsider it.

The plaintiff intended to amend the complaint, but the statute of limitations had expired.

The door closed and we left.

☐ **Rule Eleven: Use commas to set off appositives.**

An appositive is a phrase that explains the noun it follows.

Correct Example

William Emery, the noted attorney, consulted on the case.

☐ **Rule Twelve: Use a comma before and after quotations beginning or ending with words such as *he said, she stated*, and so forth.**

Correct Examples

She said, "I need the report by noon."

"I need the report by noon," she said.

"The decision of the lower court is reversed," stated Judge Allen, "and the case is remanded to the lower court to proceed according to this decision."

☐ **Rule Thirteen: Use commas to set off nonrestrictive phrases, namely, those including nonessential material.**

A nonrestrictive phrase is one that is not essential to the meaning of a sentence. It could be removed without impairing the meaning of a sentence. Commas are used to set off these nonessential phrases or clauses wherever they appear in a sentence. Nonrestrictive phrases are often introduced by the word *which*.

A restrictive phrase or clause identifies which of several possible things or people the clause refers to and thus limits or restricts the information previously given in a sentence. Restrictive phrases are essential to the meaning of a sentence and are not set off by commas. Restrictive phrases are often introduced by the word *that*. Generally, it is the writer's intent that determines whether a clause is essential or nonessential. See Chapter 1, Section G.5 for additional information.

Sentences with Restrictive Phrases	Sentences with Nonrestrictive Phrases
The corporation that was bankrupt merged with ABC Inc.	*The corporation, which was bankrupt, merged with ABC Inc.*
In this sentence, the information about the corporation's bankruptcy is included because it identifies which corporation merged with ABC Inc. (the bankrupt one). Thus, it is an essential or restrictive phrase and is not set off by commas.	In this sentence, the writer is expressing the main thought that the corporation has merged. The fact that it was bankrupt is incidental to the meaning of the sentence. Thus, the information is introduced by *which* and is set off by commas.
The judge who issued the decision entered the courthouse.	*The judge, who issued the decision, entered the courthouse.*
This sentence indicates which of several judges entered the courthouse (namely, the one that issued the decision).	This sentence simply notes an extra fact about the judge who entered the courthouse.
The tenants who complained were evicted.	*The tenants, who complained, were evicted.*
This sentence indicates that only some tenants were evicted. Other tenants (namely, those who did not complain) were not evicted.	In this sentence, all of the tenants were evicted.

Tip ➡ Restrictive and Nonrestrictive Phrases

To determine whether a phrase is essential/restrictive or nonessential/nonrestrictive, try to omit the phrase. If you can omit it without changing the meaning or structure of the sentence, it is nonessential and should be set off by commas.

Example: *The report, which was prepared by Neil, was 150 pages long.*
In this sentence, you can omit the phrase *which was prepared by Neil,* and the sentence will still make sense. Thus, surround this nonessential phrase with commas.

Example: *Reports that are too long are seldom read.*
In this sentence, omitting the *phrase that are too long* would change the meaning of the sentence. Thus, you need the *that* clause.

2. Comma Misuse

Do Not Use a Comma	Incorrect Examples
between a subject and its verb.	*The attorneys, drafted the brief.*
between a verb and an indirect quotation.	*The judge asked, whether the witness needed a recess.*
after the words *include, like,* or *such as.*	*The allegations include, fraud, breach of contract, and negligence.*
after a coordinating conjunction.	*The defendant agreed to go, and, the bailiff escorted her out of the room.*
before a dependent clause at the end of a sentence.	*The attorney was late, and was rebuked by the judge for her tardiness.*
before a parentheses.	*It was Jill, (the opposing attorney) who was held in contempt.*

Case Illustration: The Million Dollar Comma

A contract dispute in Canada focused on what has been termed a "million dollar comma." A contract between cable company Rogers Communication and telephone company Bell Aliant provided that the agreement "shall continue in force for a period of five years from the date it is made, and thereafter for successive five-year terms, unless and until terminated by one year prior notice."

In 2005 Rogers was informed by Bell Aliant that the contract was being canceled. Rogers contended that the contract could not be canceled for five years; Bell Aliant claimed that the second comma in the sentence allowed for termination of the contract at any time, upon one year's notice. A Canadian regulator sided with Bell Aliant, stating that "based on the rules of punctuation," the comma in question allowed for termination at any time, so long as one year's notice was given. The regulator stated that the second comma should have been omitted if the contract was intended to last for five years. This interpretation would have allowed Bell Aliant to cancel the contract, costing Rogers more than $2 million. An appellate panel later relied on the French version of the contract and found for Rogers. This case is a clear reminder to legal writers that the placement of a single comma can be critical.

Figure 2-1 Quick Reference: Comma Use

Rule: Use a Comma	Correct Example
after informal salutations and all closings in letters.	*Dear Henry,* *Best regards,*
after the day and after the year in a full date.	*The trial will begin on Tuesday, December 11, 2012, and will last one week.*
between elements of an address in a sentence.	*I live at 909 Beech Drive, Tampa, Florida 90923.*
after dates and addresses when they appear within sentences.	*July 18, 2012, was my first trial.*
in digits.	*The report was 16,190 pages.*
after introductory elements.	*In the present case, the plaintiff alleged fraud.*
to set off interruptive words and transitional expressions.	*His defense, however, was invalid.*
to separate consecutive parallel adjectives.	*Ellen was an organized, diligent worker.*
to separate contrasting elements.	*It was John Turner, not Jason Turner, who represented the plaintiff.*
between the items in a series of three or more items.	*To be patentable, an invention must be novel, useful, and nonobvious.*
before a coordinating conjunction that introduces an independent clause.	*The witness was late for the deposition, and the court imposed sanctions against her.*
to enclose appositive expressions.	*Judge Adams, the presiding judge, vacated the judgment.*
to introduce quotations.	*Judge Moreno ruled, "I hereby affirm the judgment."*
to set off nonessential information.	*The briefcase, a new one, was left in the courtroom.*

Tips →	On Restrictive and Nonrestrictive Elements

- If information is essential to the meaning of a sentence, it is restrictive, and it will not be introduced by a comma.
- If information is not essential to the meaning of a sentence, it is nonrestrictive, and it must be set off by commas.
- If information is introduced by the word *that*, it is restrictive and does not take a comma.
- If information is introduced by the word *which*, it is usually nonessential and will be set off by commas.

Challenge ❓ Punctuation

Punctuate the following sentences correctly, correct the punctuation errors, or indicate if the sentence is correct.

1. He plans to have lunch with Ben and Grace and I will be on vacation at that time.
2. Whether or not the weather will cooperate, is open to debate.
3. The only question the judge asked was when the motion would be heard?
4. "You then turned left, didn't you"?
5. I am responding to your July 10, 2012 report.
6. On Thursday, we will travel to Chicago.
7. After the judge left the courtroom there was a mass exodus.
8. Robert is a diligent conscientious worker.
9. The trial began in March and it is expected to last more than six weeks.
10. Sandra Allen the public defender was appointed defense counsel.
11. The exhibits were marked but they were not introduced into evidence.
12. The judge instructed the jury and left the courtroom.
13. The bailiff, called the court to order.
14. The witness stated I don't remember.
15. The witness stated that he didn't remember.
16. I researched the law but I was unable to find any cases on point.

D. Apostrophes

An apostrophe (') is used to show possession or ownership and to show omission of one or more letters, as in the contraction *don't*. Writers generally have little difficulty with contractions (except for *it's*), but the use of apostrophes to show possession, especially with regard to proper names, is often confusing.

1. Possessives

a. General Rules

There are three basic rules relating to using apostrophes to show ownership or possession.

☐ **Rule One: Add an apostrophe and an s ('s) to show possession for all singular nouns, even if the noun ends in s, k, x, or z.**

> **Correct Examples:** *The girl's coat* (the coat of the girl)
> *The plaintiff's evidence* (the evidence of the plaintiff)
> *Charles's friend* (the friend of Charles)
> *Anyone's argument* (the argument of anyone)
> *Xerox's marketing plan* (the marketing plan of Xerox)
> *The witness's testimony* (the testimony of the witness)
> *My boss's birthday* (the birthday of my boss)
> *Texas's election* (the election of Texas)
> *Congress's intent* (the intent of Congress)
> *The Marine Corps's motto* (the motto of the Marine Corps)

☐ **Rule Two: When a plural word ends in s, add only an apostrophe (') to show possession.**

> **Correct Examples:** *The ten shareholders' agenda* (the agenda of the ten shareholders)
> *The workers' job benefits* (the job benefits of the workers)
> *The judges' hearings* (the hearings of the judges)
> *Our bosses' offices* (the offices of our bosses)

☐ **Rule Three: When a word is plural and does not already end in s, add an apostrophe and an s ('s) to show possession.**

> **Correct Examples:** *The children's toys* (the toys of the children)
> *The mice's cages* (the cages of the mice)
> *The men's shoes* (the shoes of the men)

b. Proper Names

To form the plural of most family names or to show possession for most family names, follow the rules just given.

Correct Examples: *Ed Smith's pleadings were filed yesterday.*
                     The Smiths are giving a party next week.
                     The Smiths' house is large.

For names that end in a sounded *ch, s, sh, x,* or *z,* however, form the plural by adding *es* and then form the plural possessive by adding an apostrophe after the *es* (*es'*).

Correct Examples: *Tim Jones attended the conference.*
                     Ellen Lynch attended as well.
                     The Joneses are wealthy.
                     The Lynches bought a new car.
                     The Joneses' house is in Chicago.
                     The Lynches' new car is a Honda.

Tip ➡ *Lucas' or Lucas's?*

You have undoubtedly noticed that newspapers, magazines, and other publications generally use an apostrophe standing alone with a singular word ending in *s* to show possession, as in *Justice Thomas' opinion.* This construction likely has more to do with saving space than anything else. Moreover, many grammar books (and the *Style Manual*) permit the use of an apostrophe alone with a singular word ending in *s* when adding another *s* would make the word difficult to pronounce or look odd. Thus, you may *see Mr. Rogers' sweater or Lucas' book.* Nevertheless, Strunk and White and most conventional grammar books suggest the *'s,* as in *Mr. Rogers's sweater or Lucas's book.* This form is always correct. Moreover, it is consistent with shorter names, as in *Wes's car.* It looks odd to see *Wes' car.* Thus, use the form *Wes's car.*

---

c. Special Situations Involving Apostrophes

There are a few exceptions to the general rules given earlier.

- **Joint Possession.** To show joint possession, add an apostrophe and an *s* (*'s*) to the last word.

  Correct Examples: *Lewis and Clark's expedition began in 1804.*
                       My mother and father's house is large.
                       Dan and Liz's car was damaged.

- **Individual Possession.** Use an apostrophe and an *s* (*'s*) with each element to show possession for each.

> Correct Examples: *The plaintiff's and the defendant's opening*
> *statements were quite different from each other.*
> *Dan's and Liz's rings are gold.*

■ **Ancient Proper Names.** Form the possessive of ancient proper names that end in *es, is,* and *us* by adding only an apostrophe (').

> Correct Examples: *Jesus' teachings*
> *Moses' laws*

Note that it may be less awkward to reword such phrases, as in *the teachings of Jesus* and *the laws of Moses*.

■ **Company and Organization Names.** Generally, the apostrophe should not be used after names of countries and organizations that end in *s*.

> Correct Examples: *American Airlines bankruptcy filing*
> *The United States position on foreign policy*

Also, consider checking an organization's website to determine how to present its name. The following are all shown on the respective company's website:

Standard & Poor's ratings
Mrs. Fields cookies
McDonald's products
Ben & Jerry's ice cream
Starbucks stores

■ **Abstract Words.** Form the possessive of a few abstract words that end in an *s* or an *s* sound by adding an apostrophe (').

> Correct Examples: *For goodness' sake*
> *For conscience' sake*

■ **Compound Words.** For compound terms such as *mother-in-law*, form the possessive by adding an apostrophe and an *s* ('*s*) to the last word.

> Correct Examples: *My sister-in-law's files*
> *The attorney-at-law's billing statement*

■ **Units of Time and Measurement.** The possessive form of expressions of time and measurement is shown with an apostrophe and an *s* ('*s*).

> Correct Examples: *The tenant was given three weeks' notice to vacate.*
> *The trial will begin in two hours' time.*

■ **Silent Letters.** Generally, if a non-English word ends with a silent *s* or *x*, form its possessive by using only an apostrophe, as in *"This Chablis' taste is dry and fruity."*

Figure 2-2   Quick Reference: Using Apostrophes to Show Possession

Singular	Singular Possessive	Plural	Plural Possessive
The pleading	The pleading's caption is wrong.	The pleadings were filed today.	The pleadings' allegations were consistent.
Henry James	Henry James's novel is long.	The Jameses were both famous.	The Jameses' books are challenging to read.
The woman	The woman's contract was amended.	The women were in court.	The women's documents contained errors.

Case Illustration: We're Not in Kansas Anymore

The Justices of the U.S. Supreme Court themselves show variation in presenting possession for a singular noun ending in "s." For example, in *Kansas v. Marsh*, 548 U.S. 163, 168 (2006), Justice Thomas, writing for the majority, referred to "Kansas' death penalty statute." Justice Scalia's concurring opinion referred to "Kansas's death penalty statute," and Justice Souter's dissent reviewed "Kansas's capital sentencing structure."

2. Contractions

An apostrophe is used to show the omission of a letter or letters in a contraction. Other than in letters, contractions are rarely used in legal writing because they are viewed as informal words. In fact, some writing experts advise using contractions to reduce a stuffy tone in correspondence.

Correct Examples:	*don't*	do not
	can't	cannot
	shouldn't	should not
	who's	who is

One common error is the misuse of the contraction *it's. It's* is a contraction for *it is* (or *it has*). The apostrophe is used to indicate that the letter *i* (or letters *ha*) has been omitted. To show the possessive of *it,* meaning *belonging to it,* use *its.* Only use *it's* when you mean to write *it is* (or *it has*).

Similarly, only use *who's* when you mean *who is,* as in *Who's calling?* The word *whose* is the possessive form of *who,* as in *Whose pen is this?*

Correct Examples:	*It's a learned court that has the wisdom to reverse its decisions.*
	The corporation held its annual meeting yesterday.
	It's the first day of the trial.
	Who's the attorney for the plaintiff?

3. Numbers and Letters

There is some disagreement whether an apostrophe should be used to show the plural of a number or letter. The better practice and that of the *Style Manual* is to follow the general rules for forming plurals and to omit the apostrophe unless the result would be confusing.

Correct Examples:	*There are two Exhibit Bs.*
	The audit showed all 9s.
	All of the IOUs have been paid.
	The LSATs are difficult.
	The stock price fell in the 1990s.
	Be sure to dot your i's and cross your t's.

 **Tips → On Using Contractions**

- Most spell-checkers cannot accurately catch errors in the use of *it's* and *its.* Thus, careful proofreading is essential.
- Don't confuse contractions (such as *didn't*) with the possessive pronouns *yours, hers, his, theirs, ours, whose,* and *its.* Apostrophes are never used with these possessive pronouns.

Incorrect: *The file is her's.*

Challenge ? Apostrophes

Punctuate the following correctly or indicate if they are correct.

1. The 1970s were a turbulent decade.
2. Arkansas revenue decreased last year.
3. The four investors objections were noted.
4. Mr. Cox' briefcase was searched and all of it's contents removed.
5. The fundraiser will be held at the Willis home.
6. Ms. Willis deposition transcript was lost.
7. Whose/Who's attending the hearing?
8. The company just filed its annual report.
9. The three citizens complaints were ignored.
10. Chris calendar showed a conflict.
11. Our clients, the Foxs, have paid their retainer.
12. The Foxes check was cashed yesterday.
13. The FAQs on the website were helpful.
14. In three week's, I will be given two months severance.
15. Phil's and Monica brief was persuasive.
16. Mr. Baileys will was amended.
17. The Christmas card was signed "From The Smith's."
18. Meg and Steve's wedding was in August.

E. Colons

A colon (:) is usually used to signal that material follows. In sentences, a colon can only be used after an independent clause (one that can stand by itself).

Use a Colon	Examples
to introduce a list, especially after expressions such as *the following* or *as follows*.	*The defendant asserted the following three defenses: waiver; estoppel; and acquiescence.*
	(Note that the items in the list could also be separated by commas.)
to signal that clarifying information will follow.	*We have instituted a new policy: Goods may not be returned after ten days.*
to introduce a formal quotation (when the introduction is an independent clause).	*The court ruled against the defendant in unequivocal terms: "Liability is based upon this act of gross negligence."*
	(Note that most quotations may also be introduced by a comma.)

Use a Colon	Examples
after salutations in formal letters.	*Dear Mr. Garcia:*
	Dear Michael:
to separate hours from minutes.	*The hearing ended at 5:30 p.m.*

Tips ➡ On Using Colons

- Place one space after a colon. If the material following a colon is not a complete sentence, it should begin with a lowercase letter.
- If the material following a colon is a complete sentence, it may begin with either a capital letter or a lowercase letter. Many experts prefer to use a capital letter. Whichever approach you adopt, be consistent.

    Correct: *The report produced one finding: The defendant was an ex-convict.*

- Do not use a colon after a verb or after a preposition.

    Incorrect: *Entering the courtroom were: the judge, the marshal, and the bailiff.*

    You will find the answer in: the case, the statute, or the transcript.

- Do not use a colon after the expressions *for example, namely, including,* or *such as.*

    Incorrect: *The contract dealt with issues such as: term of employment; employment duties; and stock option grants.*

- Place colons outside closing quotation marks.

In many instances, either a semicolon or a colon may be used between independent clauses, as in the following example: *The argument was excellent; it was concise, logical, and persuasive.* Alternatively, you may treat independent clauses as complete sentences and use a period after each.

F. Semicolons

A semicolon (;) is usually used to separate items of equal status, such as two independent clauses.

Use a Semicolon	Examples
to connect two independent but closely related clauses that are not joined by a coordinating conjunction.	*That was his final summation; it was strong and forceful.* (Note that this could be correctly presented as two sentences.)
between two independent clauses joined by a transitional word or phrase such as *however, for example,* or *therefore.* Use a comma after the transitional expression.	*The defendant was not credible; therefore, the jury voted to convict her.* *The attorney argued persuasively; however, the judge overruled her.*
to separate items in a list containing commas.	*Standing trial for embezzlement were Connie Rivers of Portland, Oregon; Samuel Walter of Seattle, Washington; and Susan Stone of Boise, Idaho.*
to separate items in a list introduced by a colon.	*The elements to be proved in an action for breach of contract are as follows: the existence of a contract; the unjustified breach of that contract by one party; and damages caused by that breach.* (Note that these items can also be separated by commas.)

G. Quotation Marks

Quotation marks usually indicate the exact words of a speaker and appear in double form (" ") or single form (' '). Additional information relating to quotations of legal authorities is provided in Appendix A.

Use Double Quotation Marks	Correct Examples
to indicate the exact words of a speaker.	*Patrick Henry said, "Give me liberty or give me death."* *"The motion," said the judge, "is hereby granted."*
to explain or emphasize a word.	*The author misspelled the word "appellant" in the brief.* *The words "its" and "it's" are often confused.*

Use Single Quotation Marks	Correct Example
to enclose a quotation within a quotation (and use a thin space to separate single and double quotation marks).	*"It was the jury foreman," said Betty, "who announced, 'The defendant is guilty.' "*

Quotation marks are not used for indirect quotations. An indirect quotation summarizes a person's words but does not quote the person directly. Indirect quotations are often introduced by the words *that* or *whether*.

Incorrect	Correct Examples
Upon entering the courtroom, the judge said that "she expected silence from the spectators."	Upon entering the courtroom, the judge said that she expected silence from the spectators.
	Upon entering the courtroom, the judge said, "I expect silence from the spectators."

Capitalize the first word of a direct quotation if it is a complete sentence but not if it is a sentence fragment.

Correct Example

The judge said, "The judgment is reversed."

Challenge ? Punctuation

Correctly punctuate the following.

1. Susan was asked to: draft the brief, cite-check it, and file it.
2. The defendant stated his plea in unequivocal terms, "not guilty".
3. The officers at the meeting included the following. Ted Davis, president, Rachel Porter, treasurer, and Brian Nelson, secretary.
4. Lindsey has excelled in her job. For example: she was promoted twice last year.
5. The bailiff barked, Silence in the courtroom.
6. The attorney said that "he would move for a mistrial."
7. Were you the witness, asked Ryan?
8. File your motions, the judge stated, and do so promptly.
9. Susan asked "whether she could attend the hearing."
10. Susan asked May I attend the hearing?
11. Are you familiar with the doctrine of "res judicata?"

H. Parentheses

Parentheses ( ) are generally used to enclose interruptions or explanations. The use of parentheses in legal citations is discussed in Appendix A. Parentheses may enclose a word, a phrase, or a sentence.

Other Punctuation with Quotation Marks and the Use of Ellipses

- Periods and commas are always placed inside closing quotation marks. The British style is to place a period inside quotation marks only when it is part of the quoted material. American writers, however, should always place all periods and all commas inside closing quotation marks.
- Semicolons and colons are always placed outside closing quotation marks.
- Question marks and exclamation points are placed inside quotation marks only if they are part of the quoted material.

  Correct Example: *"She's guilty!" yelled the foreman of the jury.*

- When a quotation is introduced by a signal phrase, such as *she said* or *he wrote,* follow the signal phrase with a comma and begin the quotation with a capital letter.

  Correct Example: *The bailiff said, "All rise."*

- If a quotation is interrupted by explanatory words such as *he said* or *she stated,* do not use a capital letter to start the second part of the quotation unless it begins a new sentence or it would ordinarily begin with a capital.

  Correct Examples: *When the opening statements are complete," said the judge, "we will begin the trial."*

  "My only concern," he said, "is to proceed with caution."

  "Overruled," said the judge. "Proceed with your evidence."

- Use a thin space to separate single and double quotation marks. (See example in Section G.)
- When a quotation carries over from one paragraph to another, use double quotation marks at the beginning of each paragraph, but place the final double quotation marks at the end of the last paragraph only.
- Quotations of forty-nine or fewer words should be enclosed in quotation marks but not indented.
- Quotations of fifty or more words should be indented left and right, justified, and single-spaced. No outside quotation marks are used for these quotations, often called *block quotes.* The indentation of these longer quotes itself indicates a quotation. The citation for these block quotes appears at the left margin on the line following the block quotation.
- Indicate omissions in a quotation by an ellipsis (three periods separated by spaces and set off by a space before the first and after the last period).

  Correct Example: *"Punitive damages must be based upon . . . actual damages."*

- If the omitted matter includes the end of a sentence, add another period to the ellipsis, as in . . . .
- Do not use an ellipsis to begin a quotation; instead, use brackets, as in *"[E]very contract includes a covenant of good faith and fair dealing."*
- Use brackets [ ] to show changes in quotations, usually the addition of a word or letters.

  Correct Example: *"Punitive damages are based upon [actual] damage[s]."*

Use Parentheses	Correct Examples
to set off interruptions, explanations, or translations.	*His primary argument was* res ipsa loquitur *(a Latin phrase meaning "the thing speaks for itself").*
to direct the reader to other information.	*The plaintiff failed to allege materiality in the fraud cause of action. (Compl. ¶ 14.)*
to introduce defined terms or labels.	*The plaintiff, Southwest Avionics Industries ("SAI"), alleged fraud.*
to enclose numbers or dollar amounts.	*The settlement agreement was forty (40) pages.*

Other Punctuation with Parentheses

- Do not put any punctuation before a parenthetical item.
- If a parenthetical item falls within a sentence, do not capitalize the first word in the parenthetical item even if it is a complete sentence (unless the item begins with *I* or a proper noun).

  Correct: *The new partner (he arrived yesterday) will begin work on Monday.*

  Please return the signed contract by October 19, 2012 (Friday).

- If the parenthetical item does not fall within a sentence and is itself a separate sentence, it should begin with a capital letter and end with a period (or the appropriate punctuation), which should be placed within the parentheses.

  Correct: *Please return the signed contract by October 19, 2012. (This date is a Friday.)*

- Avoid having one set of parentheses follow another. Thus, the following use of parentheses should be avoided: *Your contract should be signed by Monday (September 3, 2012). (This date is Labor Day.)*

I. Other Punctuation Marks: Dashes, Hyphens, and Slashes

1. Using Dashes

Dashes create drama and draw a reader's attention. In general, however, they are considered too informal for legal writing, and, in most instances, other punctuation marks, such as commas, parentheses, or a colon, would be more appropriate.

There are two types of dashes. An em dash (—) is as wide as a typesetter's *m* key and is used in most instances because it produces a more defined break. An em dash usually shows interruptions and is made by inserting the correct symbol on a word processor or by using two hyphens. It is the most commonly used dash, and there are no spaces before or after it. It may replace commas or parentheses to show interruptions, although it is less formal and more dramatic. An en dash (–)is as wide as a typesetter's *n* key and is used primarily to show a range or span of time, as in *She was the substitute during the week of June 21–28* or *You must read pages 82–91 of the text.* An en dash is made by using one hyphen.

Use a Dash	Correct Examples
to indicate a break or interruption.	*The defendant—not his brother—testified.*
to reference certain legislation.	*The Sarbanes–Oxley Act was passed in 2002.*

2. Using Hyphens

Hyphens (-) are used in compound words and to show divisions between words at the end of lines. Most word processors automatically divide words appropriately at the end of lines (or move the entire word to the next line). Nevertheless, if you need to divide a word at the end of a line of text, use a dictionary to determine where to make the break and make sure you do not divide a proper noun. Additional examples regarding using a hyphen in compound words are found in Chapter 3.

Determining whether to hyphenate a word is often difficult. For example, both *co-owner* and *coordinate* are correct. Use a dictionary to help you determine when to hyphenate a word.

Use a Hyphen	Correct Examples
when two or more words act together to modify a noun.	*She is a well-known judge.* *The would-be informant testified.* *Her employment-related injury was severe.*
with the prefixes *all-, co-, ex-, quasi-* and *self-*.	*He is self-involved.* *Her ex-husband attended the hearing.*
with a prefix before a proper noun.	*The House Un-American Committee* *The pro-Israeli faction*
to prevent confusion.	*The status of the chicken coop will be reexamined by the co-op board on Tuesday.*
in certain awkward words.	*My mother-in-law was the runner-up.*
to divide compound numbers from twenty-one to ninety-nine.	*The defense called thirty-two witnesses.*
in fractions that are spelled out.	*Two-thirds approval is needed.*

3. Using Slashes

A slash (/) is a diagonal line (sometimes called a *virgule* or *solidus*) that usually shows options. Its meaning is *or* (not *and*). Thus, the sentence *The litigation class is pass/fail* means that one can pass the course or one can fail it. Many writers use a slash to mean *and* even though it is mark meant to show alternatives. For example, the sentence *Billy Joel is the singer/composer of the song* means that Billy Joel is either the singer or the composer of the song, but not both. Although it may be wordier, it may be necessary to explain the meaning of such a sentence, by saying *Billy Joel is the singer and the composer of the song*. In general, because writers might use it mean *or* or *and*, the slash mark is considered ambiguous and should be avoided in legal writing. In particular, the constructions *and/or*, *he/she*, and *his/her* should be avoided. Slashes are acceptable to indicate dates in informal writing, as in *The hearing will be held on 8/13/12*. Slashes are also used in a particular business-related abbreviation, *d/b/a* (*doing business as*), as in the following correct example: *The defendant identified in the caption was Patricia Allen d/b/a Creative Catering of Philadelphia*.

Challenge ? — Parentheses, Hyphens, and Other Marks

Correct the following.

1. I have paid all funds to take my all inclusive vacation to Mexico.
2. My uncle kept a pre Revolutionary musket.
3. I resent the fact that you resent my message to Lauren yesterday.
4. He was the chief operating officer, CEO, from 2007—2009.
5. She is a quick witted attorney whose quick wit charms others.
6. All documents are due by Monday (this is the first day of the new term of the court).
7. It was James, not his brother, who was married last year.

chapter 3

Spelling

StyleLinks

www.gpoaccess.gov/stylemanual/index.html
Select Chapter 5 of the Government Printing Office *Style Manual* for thorough information about spelling.

http://owl.english.purdue.edu/owl
Select "Spelling" for excellent information from Purdue University's Online Writing Lab.

www.businesswriting.com/tests/commonmisspelled.html
The Business Writing Center offers a test on the twenty-five most commonly misspelled words.

http://grammar.yourdictionary.com/spelling-and-word-lists/misspelled.html
This site offers a list of the 100 most frequently misspelled words.

www.spelling.hemscott.net
This site provides spelling worksheets and advice from an experienced English teacher.

www.dictionary.com
Check your spelling at this useful site, which also offers a thesaurus.

www.grammarbook.com
GrammarBook.com offers tips and hints for spelling correctly. Select "Spelling."

http://dictionary.law.com
Law.Com offers a dictionary of legal words and phrases.

A. Introduction

Because English is not a phonetic language, many people have difficulty spelling. One of the most distressing results of misspelling is the effect produced in the mind of a reader. If the aim of writing is to inform or persuade a reader and the reader is confronted with spelling errors, any value a product may have could well be overshadowed by the misspellings. Readers of legal documents, such as clients, attorneys, and judges, tend to be highly critical and perfectionistic. When confronted with spelling errors, they may react by assuming that if you cannot be trusted to spell properly, you cannot be trusted to conduct legal analysis properly. Thus, spelling errors cast doubt on more than your ability to spell by causing readers to question the correctness of your legal conclusions. At best, spelling errors make readers believe the writer is careless. At worst, they make readers question the writer's intelligence.

B. Strategies to Improve Spelling

Following are some tips and strategies to improve spelling.

1. Use a Dictionary

The only way to ensure that a word is spelled correctly is to use a dictionary. An excellent dictionary is *Merriam-Webster's Collegiate Dictionary*, now in its eleventh edition. A legal dictionary, such as *Black's Legal Dictionary*, will include words used in legal settings, such as *rescission*, as well as Latin terms and phrases commonly used in the profession. Don't be afraid to write in your dictionary. Circle or highlight troublesome words. When you look up a word such as *canceled* in the dictionary, you may notice that you are first given the spelling *canceled* and then the alternate spelling *cancelled*. Usually, the entry given first is the preferred spelling, and you should use this form of the word. Similarly, use the commonly accepted spelling of a word rather than some foreign or exotic spelling. For example, use *behavior* rather than *behaviour*, which is the British spelling of the word. The website www.dictionary.com is an excellent source. Note that some dictionaries are descriptive (meaning that they merely explain how a word is presently used), and others are prescriptive (meaning that they tell you how a word should be used and provide advice and notes on usage).

2. Develop a "Hit List" of Commonly Misspelled Words

Many writers find that they routinely misspell the same words. Write the ten or fifteen words you most commonly misspell on an index card and keep it near your computer or writing area. Write the correct spelling only. Refer to the list frequently and note the words that you misspell most often so you can spend additional time on these. The effort that you take in considering these words and writing them out will help you learn their correct spellings. Once you learn the words on your list, develop another list with a new group of troublesome words.

3. Pronounce Your Words Carefully

If you make a concerted effort to pronounce *than* differently from *then* and *effect* differently from *affect*, your spelling will improve. It will be difficult for you to remember to spell *environment* correctly if you pronounce the word as *enviro-ment*.

4. Use Misspelled Words as Passwords

Use one of your frequently misspelled words as a password (using its correct spelling) to access your email or ATM account. When you have mastered this word, change your password to another troublesome word.

5. Use Mnemonic Devices

Remember that the *principal of your school is your pal* to help you remember to spell the word *principal* (and not *principle*). Remember that the dessert treat after dinner has two *s*'s, just like a *strawberry shortcake*, whereas an arid, sandy desert has one *s*, just like the *Sahara Desert*. Remember to match up the *o* in the word *dome* with *capitol* when referring to the building itself and that all other uses of the word are spelled *capital*.

6. Don't Rely Only on Your Spell-Checker

Use a spell-checker to help you catch some spelling errors but recognize its limitations, namely, that it will not signal incorrect usage. Thus, for example, if you write *principle* when you mean to write *principal*, the spell-checker will not flag the incorrect word so long as it is spelled correctly. The spell-checker is an aid to good writing, not a replacement for careful proofreading and editing. Similarly, be careful about allowing your word processor to make auto corrections. In many cases, it will suggest the wrong word. In other cases, you may inadvertently select the wrong word.

Use the "find and replace" feature to correct common errors automatically. For example, if you routinely type *Untied States* rather than *United States*, the find and replace feature will locate each occurrence of the error and replace it with the correct spelling.

7. Proofread Carefully

Be thorough in your review of your finished project and read through the last draft for spelling errors. In many instances, a misspelled word will not look "right" to you, and you can readily locate your errors. If you find it difficult to catch your own errors, ask a colleague or friend to proofread your project for spelling errors. Proofreading and editing are discussed further in Chapter 11.

8. Learn Some Spelling Rules

Many spelling rules are easy to remember. Following are some helpful rules, although there are exceptions to nearly every rule.

☐ **Rule One: Place *i* before *e*, except after *c*, and except when it sounds like *ay*, as in *neighbor* or *weigh*. This rule should help you remember the correct spelling of *receive* or *eight*. There are, however, many exceptions to this rule; for example, *science*, *counterfeit*, *weird*, *seize*, *leisure*, and *neither* do not conform to the rule.**

☐ **Rule Two: When the endings *-ness* and *-ly* are added to a word, the spelling of the word remains the same. Thus, the words *thickness* and *finally* are spelled correctly. Note, however, the following exception: For words ending in *y*, such as *heavy*, change the *y* to *i* before a suffix, as in the word *heaviness*.**

☐ **Rule Three: Drop the final silent *e* before an ending or suffix that begins with a vowel.**

Correct Examples

revise + ing = revising
argue + able = arguable
compose + ition = composition

☐ **Rule Four: Keep the final silent *e* before an ending or suffix that begins with a consonant.**

Correct Examples

state + ment = statement
care + less = careless
hope + ful = hopeful
sincere + ly = sincerely

☐ **Rule Five: When adding a prefix to a word, the word remains the same.**

Correct Examples

un + anticipated = unanticipated
mis + spell = misspell
non + disclosure = nondisclosure

☐ **Rule Six: To determine if an ending of a word is spelled *-able* or *-ible*, follow these tips:**

- If the base of a word is itself a word, the ending *-able* is more commonly used, as in the following correct examples: *assignable, preferable, removable,* and *predictable*. Many more words end in *-able* than *-ible*.
- If the base of a word is not a word, the ending *-ible* is more commonly used, as in the following correct examples: *admissible, permissible,* and *feasible*.
- Words that end in *-ible* often have negative forms, such as *illegible* or *inedible*. Also, *-ible* is not used after vowels.

☐ **Rule Seven: Words ending in *-ant*, *-ent*, *-ance*, and *-ence* follow no predictable pattern. Thus, you will likely need a dictionary to ensure the correct spelling of the following words although many of them sound nearly identical: *defendant, dependent, resistant,* and *persistent*.**

☐ **Rule Eight: Words ending with the sound of *seed* follow three rules:**

- Almost all words ending with the sound of *seed* end in *-cede*, as in *recede, intercede,* and *precede*.
- Only one word ends in *-sede*: *supersede*.
- Only three words end in *-ceed*: *exceed, proceed,* and *succeed*.

☐ **Rule Nine: Omit hyphens with most prefixes and suffixes. Although there are some exceptions, generally omit hyphens with prefixes, as in the correctly spelled words *reexamine* and *unannotated*, and with most suffixes, as in the correctly spelled words *childish* and *troublesome*. Hyphens are discussed further in the next section.**

Special Spelling Problems: Doubling Final Consonants and Forming Plurals

Doubling Final Consonants

Generally, the only words that double their consonants before a suffix beginning with a vowel (such as -ed or -ing) is added are those that satisfy the following criteria:

- o They have only one syllable or are stressed on the last syllable;
- o They have only one vowel in the only or last syllable; and
- o They end in a single consonant.

Examples: bag⟶bagged⟶bagging⟶baggage
rob⟶robbed⟶robbing⟶robber
forgot→forgotten
begin →beginner →beginning

Forming Plurals

- Plurals are usually formed by adding an *s* to a noun, as in *plaintiffs, complaints,* and *judges.*
- If a singular word ends in a sibilant (*ch, s, ss, sh, x,* or *z*), form the plural by adding *es,* as in *taxes, bosses,* and *lunches.*
- Most words that end in a consonant followed by a *y* form the plural by changing the *y* to *i* and adding *es,* as in *baby/babies* and *proxy/proxies.*
- Most nouns that end in *f* or *fe* form plurals by changing the *f* to *v* and adding *s* or *es,* as in *life/lives* (but there are exceptions, as in *belief/beliefs*).
- Form the plural of a compound term by adding *s* to the most significant term, as in *attorneys general, mothers-in-law,* and *senators-elect.*
- When a singular noun ends in *o* preceded by a consonant, use a dictionary to verify the plural form because sometimes the plural is formed by adding an *s* and sometimes it is formed by adding *es.*

Examples: *tomato → tomatoes*   *hero ⟶ heroes*
ego ⟶ egos   *memo → memos*

C. Compound Words

A compound word is a word comprising two ideas or words, such as *able-bodied* or *courtroom.* Some compound words, such as *cyberspace,* are so new that they may not be found in dictionaries. Thus, spelling compound words correctly presents certain challenges.

There are generally three ways to spell compound words: as two separate words, as in *the attorney is well known*; as hyphenated words, as in *all-inclusive*; and as one word, as in *jetlag*. Generally, words tend to evolve from two words, to the hyphenated form, to one word. For example, the word *online* progressed from *on line*, to *on-line*, to the commonly accepted spelling *online*. Use the one-word form whenever possible. To be sure of the spelling and presentation of a compound word, use a dictionary. If the word is not listed, present it as two separate words.

At the time of the writing of this text, most dictionaries (which often lag behind popular usage) present "e-mail" with a lowercase "e" and a hyphen. It is becoming increasingly common, however, to present the word as "email," as is shown in this text and as is consistent with the evolution of words from hyphenated form to one word. Be consistent in your use.

There are few fixed rules regarding the spelling of compound words, but following are some general guidelines.

☐ **Rule One: Use a hyphen between a prefix and a proper noun or a word beginning with a capital letter.**

Correct Examples

anti-American
mid-December

☐ **Rule Two: Use a hyphen after the following prefixes:** *all-, ex-, half-, quarter-, quasi-,* **and** *self-.*

Correct Examples

all-inclusive
ex-president
quasi-contract
self-centered

☐ **Rule Three: Use a hyphen with the suffix** *-elect,* **as in** *senator-elect Anderson.*

☐ **Rule Four: Generally, omit a hyphen when a prefix ends in** *e* **or** *o* **and the base word begins with the same letter.**

Correct Examples

reexamine
coordinate
reevaluate
preexisting

There are several exceptions to this rule, most of which require the use of a hyphen to prevent words from being confused with each other.

Correct Examples

She can recover damages after she re-covers the sofa.

He bought a chicken coop, which he intends to keep in his New York City co-op.

Hal and Sue are co-owners of the building.

The witness has re-signed the will.

He will re-create the spa and the area in which to recreate.

☐ **Rule Five:** Hyphenate compounds for numbers from twenty-one to ninety-nine as in *forty-eight allegations* and *one hundred and twenty-first claim.*

☐ **Rule Six:** Hyphenate spelled-out fractions, as in *one-half* and *three-fourths.*

☐ **Rule Seven:** Use a hyphen when joining a single letter to a word, as in *X-ray* and *U-turn.*

☐ **Rule Eight:** When a compound word acts as single modifier or adjective before a noun, hyphenate the words so that it is clear they are acting as a unit. Generally, do not use a hyphen if one of the two words ends in *ly* or if the first element is a comparative or superlative.

Correct Examples

She is a well-respected judge.

We will prepare a follow-up brief.

The corporation's short-term profits are at risk.

The widely read memo is concise.

He is the best known author I have met.

☐ **Rule Nine:** When a compound adjective follows a noun, omit the hyphen. Similarly, words need not be hyphenated if they are not acting as a single modifier or adjective before a noun. Remember this example: *A high-school student attends high school.*

Correct Examples

The judge is well respected.

We will follow up with a brief.

In the short term, the corporation's profits are at risk.

Challenge ? Spelling

Select the correct word:

1. We cannot accommodate/accomodate your request.
2. The defendant has acknowldged/acknowledged liability.
3. The existence/existance of the contract is not in dispute.
4. The omission/ommision of Exhibit B was inadvertent/inadvertant.
5. I will precede/preceed her in entering the courtroom.
6. The pro-Italian/proItalian group will testify on Monday.
7. We will reestablish/re-establish contact next week.
8. The judge will ensure/insure that they do not withhold/withold evidence.
9. The brief had ten separate/seperate exhibits, which I definitely/definately felt were too many.
10. The computer program is user friendly/user-friendly.
11. The user friendly/user-friendly computer program was installed on Friday.
12. The publicly traded/publicly-traded stock of Facebook, Inc. is offered on NASDAQ.

D. Capitalization

She lived in capital letters.

Al Carmine (1985)
Eulogy for Marion Tanner, the model for Auntie Mame

StyleLinks

www.gpoaccess.gov/stylemanual/index.html
Select Chapters 3 and 4 of the Government Printing Office *Style Manual* for information about capitalization.

http://grammar.ccc.commnet.edu/grammar
Select "Capitalization" from the *Guide to Grammar & Writing* for information and quizzes on capitalization.

1. General Capitalization Rules

Follow these rules when capitalizing:

Rule: Always Capitalize	Correct Examples
the pronoun *I*.	*Lee and I recognized the defendant.*
the first word in a sentence.	*File the brief this afternoon.*
the first word of a direct quotation if it is a complete sentence but not if it is a sentence fragment.	*The judge stated, "The evidence in this case is clearly contradictory." The judge stated that the evidence was "clearly contradictory."*
the first word following a colon if what follows the colon is a complete sentence.	*The brief contained the following error: It misidentified the reference to the court record.*
names of languages and specific courses but not general fields of study.	*I studied Spanish, sociology, and French. Next year I will take Algebra II and history.*
defined terms.	*Sandra Carias ("Tenant") will rent the premises at 123 Elm Street (the "Premises"). Tenant may take occupancy of the Premises on December 1, 2012.*
headings and titles (capitalize the initial word, the word following a colon, and, per *Bluebook* R. 8, all other words except articles, conjunctions, and prepositions of four or fewer words).	*Battery: An Intentional Touching* *Insider Trading in Corporate Transactions*
proper nouns.	
▪ names of people	*Allison M. Taylor*
▪ geographical names and structures	*Lake Superior, Central Park, the Washington Monument*
▪ regions (if designating a specific locality or region)	*I love the East and the Appalachian Trail.* *Head west until you see the courthouse in northern Virginia.*
▪ days of the week, months, holidays, and historical events (but not seasons)	*Memorial Day is my favorite holiday because it signals the beginning of summer.* *The Great Depression was the most significant economic event of the twentieth century.*

Rule: Always Capitalize	Correct Examples
government departments and agencies	*Department of Labor*
	House of Representatives
	Congress (but congressional inquiry)
specific organizations	*The American Medical Association lobbied against the bill.*
titles (when used with the person's name and for important public figures)	*He saw Representative Wilson on television.*
	The clerk is a staunch supporter of Vice President Biden and the President.
	The declaration was submitted by Professor Barnes.
	Ohio's Judge Andrews was the first federal judge appointed by Congress last fall.
	The Secretary will state the policy of the EPA.
titles such as "president" when they substitute for a person's name	*The President will address the nation today about his presidential veto.*
names of schools and businesses	*Walt Whitman High School*
	General Mills Co. files periodic reports with the Securities and Exchange Commission.
family titles that stand alone or are used with a name.	*I asked Uncle Jim if Mother would like to attend her cousin's wedding.*

Capital Ideas

Correct	Correct
Senator Schumer	The senator testified today in Congress.
The South of France	a southern flair
Nike Corp.	the company or the corporation
Chief Financial Officer Smith	Smith, the chief financial officer
I asked Dad.	I asked my dad.
London Bridge	the famous bridge
Ash Street	the street near my home
New York City	the city of San Diego
Democratic Party	a political party
Judge Lopez	Jan Lopez, a federal judge
The Department of Commerce	a federal agency
Battle of Bull Run	a famous battle
Fourth of July	fifth of July
Coach Saunders	the team coach
Doctor Alvarez	the admitting doctor
Congress	a congressional committee
Christianity	a religion
Governor McNenly	Ted McNenly, the governor
Georgetown University	an eastern school
The Federal Bureau of Investigation	The Bureau reported its results.
Director Mueller	The Director of the FBI

Tips ➡ For Using Capital Letters

- Avoid using all capital letters in a communication (unless they are used in shorter headings). Text in all capital letters is difficult to read.
- Using all capital letters in email is viewed as shouting.
- Reproduce personal and company names exactly as the person or company does, including any punctuation.
- Capitalize *federal* only when it is the name of an agency as in *the Federal Reserve Board* or when the word it modifies is capitalized. Do not capitalize *federal* when it is used as an adjective, as in *Fay Carson is a federal judge, Bob works for the federal government,* or *The Federal Constitution requires a vote for federal appropriations.*
- Although there is some disagreement about how to present words associated with the Internet, most dictionaries capitalize *Internet* and *World Wide Web* but not *website.* The word *email* is usually not capitalized and is often presented with a hyphen (e-mail), although this text uses the more modern approach and presents it as one word, without a hyphen, as in *email.*
- Generally, trademarks are presented in all capital letters, as in STARBUCKS or COKE.

2. Capitalization in Legal Documents

Following are some of the more common *Bluebook* and *ALWD* rules for capitalization in legal documents, such as court briefs and legal memoranda. See Appendix A for additional information on citation form.

Rules for Practitioners — Capitalize	Examples
Act (when referring to a specific act).	*The Sarbanes–Oxley Act was passed in 2002.*
Circuit (when using the word with a name or a number).	*The Ninth Circuit held otherwise and this court agrees.*
Code (only when referring to a specific code).	*the 1954 Code, the Code of Federal Regulations*
	State codes are far from uniform.
Constitution.	
▓ when referring to the U.S. Constitution	*the U.S. Constitution*
▓ when referring to parts of the Constitution in text	*the Supremacy Clause, the First Amendment*
Court.	
▓ when naming any court in full	*the Court of Appeals for the Sixth Circuit; the Iowa Supreme Court*
▓ when referring to the United States Supreme Court	*the Court's opinion in* Brown v. Board of Education
▓ when referring to the court in a document submitted to that court	*This Court is respectfully urged to grant this Motion to Dismiss.*
Federal.	
▓ when the word it modifies is capitalized	*the Federal Drug Administration*
	the federal budget
Judge or Justice.	
▓ when referring to a specific individual	*Judge Brown was the first federal judge appointed this year.*
▓ when referring to any Justice of the United States Supreme Court	*The dissent of the Justices was lengthy.*
Party designations (Plaintiff, Defendant, and so forth) when referring to the parties in the matter that is the subject of the document.	*Although the Defendant has moved to change venue in this case . . . .*
	In that 1989 case, the plaintiff alleged negligence.

Rules for Practitioners—Capitalize State or Commonwealth.	Examples
▪ when it is part of the full title of a state	*the State of Hawaii*
	the Commonwealth of Virginia
▪ when used as an adjective	*the State Inspector General*
▪ when the state is a party to litigation	*The State has requested the death penalty in this case.*
titles of court documents (for documents filed in that action but not when used in a generic manner).	*In his Second Amended Complaint, the Plaintiff alleged fraud. This is inconsistent with Plaintiff's responses to the interrogatories prepared by him earlier this month.*

 ## Tip On Capitalization

Both *The Bluebook* (Rule 8) and *ALWD* (Rule 3.5) endorse the use of the U.S. Government Printing Office *Style Manual* for capitalization rules not covered by their rules.

E. Abbreviations

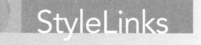 ### StyleLinks

www.gpoaccess.gov/stylemanual/index.html
See Chapter 9 of the *Style Manual* for information on the standard abbreviations recommended for use in government documents.

http://grammar.ccc.commnet.edu/grammar
Select "Abbreviations" for information about and examples of abbreviations.

1. General Principles

An abbreviation is a shortened form of a word (such as *Corp.* for *Corporation*) or a symbol used in place of a word (such as using & for *and*). The following discussion relates to using abbreviations in textual matter, such as correspondence and legal memoranda. Using abbreviations in legal citations (for example, 123 A.L.R.3d 439) is discussed in Appendix A.

Generally, because legal writing is more formal than other types of writing, abbreviations are not commonly used, except when the abbreviation is extremely well known, such as using *a.m.* when indicating time or using *Dr.* for *Doctor*. To determine the correct abbreviation for a word, consult a dictionary or consult some of the online sources identified earlier. In particular, the U.S. Government Printing Office *Style Manual* is a well-respected authority.

Never start a sentence with a number, an abbreviation, or a symbol. Sentences start with complete words. The only exceptions to this rule are for commonly known and accepted abbreviations (such as *Mr.* for *Mister*), acronyms, and years, as in *2012 was a record year for corporate profits*. This construction can look odd, so consider revising, as in *Corporate profits hit a record high in 2012*.

- **Periods in Abbreviations.** Most, but not all, abbreviations end with periods. Abbreviations composed of all capital letters and acronyms, such as *NAACP* or *AIDS*, do not generally include periods. *Bluebook* Rule 6.1 states that when an entity is commonly referred to in spoken language by its initials rather than by its full name (for example, *CIA* and *SEC*), such abbreviations may be used without periods in text and in case names. *ALWD* Rule 12.2 is similar.

- **Titles.** Use abbreviations for titles before and after proper names. If an abbreviation is used with a person's name, the name stands alone and is not accompanied by another abbreviation, such as *Ms.* or *Mr.*

Before Proper Name	After Proper Name
Dr. Eve Blake	Eve Blake, M.D. (not Ms. Eve Blake, M.D.)
Mr. Luis Santiago	Luis Santiago, Esq. (not Mr. Luis Santiago, Esq.)
Sen. Graham	

- **Acronyms.** Use abbreviations (all capital letters and no periods) for most acronyms (an abbreviation that spells out a pronounceable word, such as *MADD* or *RICO*). In legal writing, it is customary to spell out a word or organization name in full the first time it is given, immediately indicate its abbreviation in parentheses, usually in quotation marks, and then use the abbreviation consistently thereafter.

Correct Example:	The National Organization for Women ("NOW") has chapters in all fifty states. The headquarters of NOW is in Washington, D.C.

■ **United States.** Abbreviate *United States* as U.S. only when it is used as an adjective.

Correct Example: *The current U.S. policy provides an interesting overview of the trade position of the United States.*

■ **Days, Months, and Addresses.** Do not abbreviate parts of addresses or names of months and days when they are written in sentences. Such abbreviations are acceptable in tables and charts but disrupt the flow of a narrative presentation.

Correct Example: *The witness resided at 290 Forest Grove Drive, Dallas, Texas 90124 until Tuesday.*

Incorrect Example: *The witness resided at 290 Forest Grove Dr., Dallas, TX 90124 until Tues.*

Note that *Bluebook* Table T.12 and *ALWD* Appendix 3 provide abbreviations for months of the year when they are used in citations.

■ **Company Names.** Follow a company's or organization's preference for presentation of its name. Review the company's letterhead, its website, or official filings, and reproduce the name as shown. Thus, a review of the reports filed by Microsoft with the SEC shows the correct presentation of its name as *Microsoft Corporation*. It would thus be inappropriate to refer to the company as *Microsoft Corp*. Use the punctuation the company uses, as in *Land O'Lakes, Inc.*

■ **A.M. and P.M.** Use *a.m.* and *p.m.* only with specific numerals.

Correct Example: *The trial is scheduled for 9:30 a.m.*

Incorrect Example: *The trial is scheduled for 9:30 in the a.m.*

Note, however, that *Bluebook* Rule 18.2.2 shows AM rather than a.m.

■ **Numerals.** Although most authorities, including the *Style Manual*, provide that words should be used for the numerals one through nine, and that figures are used for numerals 10 and greater, *Bluebook* Rule 6.2(a) is quite different and requires legal writers to spell out the numerals zero to ninety-nine in text and in footnotes. *ALWD* Rule 4.2 is similar. *The Bluebook* also provides that commas are used in numerals only when the numeral has five or more digits. This *Bluebook* rule is contrary to most style manuals and is ignored by most practitioners.

Style Manual **Example:**   *The transcript was 4,230 pages.*

Bluebook **Example:**   *The transcript was 4230 pages.*

ALWD **Example:**   *The transcript was 4,230 pages.*

- **Money.** According to *Bluebook* Rule 6.2(d), the dollar symbol ($) and figures should be used whenever numerals or figures are used, and the words should be spelled out whenever numerals are spelled out. There is no space after the dollar symbol.

Bluebook **Examples:**   *The filing fee is Twenty-Five Dollars.*
                             The filing fee is $350.

Note, however, that to ensure there are no errors in monetary amounts, most practitioners prefer to spell out any amount in words, and then show the figures in parentheses, as follows: *The judgment was entered for Forty Thousand and Twenty-One Dollars ($40,021).* Because small numbers and words are easier to work with than large ones, spell out the words *million, billion,* and so forth, rather than using zeroes as in *The jury awarded $14 million to the plaintiff* (not *$14,000,000*).

- **Percentages.** According to *Bluebook* Rule 6.2(d), the percent symbol (%) and figures should be used whenever numerals or figures are used, and the word *percent* should be spelled out whenever numerals are spelled out. There is no space before the percent symbol.

Bluebook **Examples:**   *The interest rate was four percent.*
                             Profits increased 126% this year.

- **Ampersand.** The word *ampersand* is a corruption of the phrase *and per se and,* and it is the name for the symbol (&) used in place of the word *and.* Do not use an ampersand symbol in writing. Use the symbol only when a company does in its presentation of its name and only in the names of cases in case citations according to citation rules (discussed in Appendix A).
- **Symbol for** At. The symbol @ should be used only in email addresses, not in the normal flow of text.

Challenge   ❓   Capitalization and Abbreviations

Correct the following:
1. She has alleged a violation of her Constitutional/constitutional rights.
2. Our federal/Federal constitution/Constitution guarantees us freedom of speech.
3. This winter/Winter was harsh in the East/east.
4. To change the law, Congress/congress will need to pass a congressional/Congressional amendment.
5. In this action, the Defendant/defendant filed his second amended answer/Second Amended Answer.
6. In the case *Roe v. Wade*, the Defendant/defendant was the attorney general/Attorney General of the state/State of Texas.
7. Generally, state Codes/codes address residency requirements for divorce.
8. Five/5 years ago, the defendant was acquitted.
9. The witness is in her seventies/'70s.
10. U.S./United States law requires strict adherence to statutory/statuary formalities.
11. The meeting will begin at 10:00 a.m..

2. Legal Abbreviations

Although abbreviations in citations are more fully discussed in Appendix A, following are some of the more common *Bluebook* and *ALWD* rules.

- ■ *Bluebook:* Spell out the numerals zero to ninety-nine in text and in footnotes (as in *The complaint named eighty defendants, sixteen of which were corporations*). *ALWD:* ALWD notes that in the legal field, the convention is to spell out zero to ninety-nine and use numerals for higher numbers.
- ■ *Bluebook:* Use commas in numerals only when the numeral has five or more digits (as in *4012* and *50,145*). *ALWD:* Insert a comma between the third and fourth digits (as in *4,012*).
- ■ *Bluebook:* Spell out the words *section* and *paragraph* in text except when referring to a provision in the U.S. Code or a federal regulation. *ALWD:* Either use the symbols or spell out the words. The section symbol (§) and paragraph symbol (¶) are always followed by a space under both *Bluebook* and *ALWD* rules.

Bluebook **Example:**   *The provisions of 18 U.S.C. § 101 (2006) control, but section 52 of California's Penal Code provides additional guidelines that are useful in interpreting § 101.*

Tips ➡ On Using Numbers

- Spell out a number that begins a sentence.
- Spell out numbers up to 100, as in *sixty-four exhibits* (*Bluebook* and *ALWD* rule).
- A numeral's plural is formed by adding an *s*, as in *1990s*.
- Use numerals if you are referring to a section of a document, as in *The employer's duties are described in Paragraph 5.*
- Spell out indefinite expressions, as in *He is in his twenties.*
- Use numerals for statute references, as in *Title 17 of the United States Code* and *Chapter 11 bankruptcy petitions.*
- If one item in a series should be expressed as a numeral, use numerals for all of the items, as in *The documents were 18, 89, and 104 pages, respectively.*
- When presenting ordinals in legal citations, such as 1st, 2d, 3d, or 4th, set them "on line" as shown here. Do not use a superscript, as in 1st.

Tips ➡ For Using Abbreviations

- When in doubt, spell it out.
- Never start a sentence with an abbreviation, a numeral, or a symbol. Thus, write *One hundred days after the incident, you must file your claim.* Note, however, that most style manuals allow one to start a sentence with a well-known or commonly used abbreviation such as *Mr.* or *Mrs.* and with an acronym, as in *SEC Rules require periodic filing.*
- If a sentence ends with an abbreviation that includes a period, do not add another one.

    Incorrect: *The meeting will begin at 9:30 a.m..*

- Be consistent in the use of abbreviations. Once you have selected an abbreviation form, use it consistently throughout your project.
- Follow a company's preference for abbreviations in its name.
- Follow an individual's preference for the treatment of abbreviations such as *Jr.* and *Sr.*

sectiontwo

Features of Effective Legal Writing and Organization

■ All well-written legal documents share the following features: They are accurate, clear, readable, concise, and well organized. Section Two provides a variety of strategies to ensure your writing meets these goals so that you communicate effectively to your reader, whether that reader is a client, colleague, adversary, or judge.

chapter 4

Features of Effective Legal Writing

StyleLinks

www.plainlanguage.gov
This website, offered by a group of federal employees, The Plain Language Information and Action Network, provides excellent information on plain writing as well as its major guidance document *Federal Plain Language Guidelines*.

www.sec.gov/pdf/handbook.pdf
The Securities and Exchange Commission (SEC) offers its excellent publication, *Plain English Handbook*, with numerous examples and tips for producing understandable documents.

http://law.lclark.edu/programs/legal_analysis_and_writing/resources.php
Lewis & Clark Law School offers links to numerous websites that provide useful and practical information on legal writing.

A. Introduction

The cornerstone of the legal profession is communication—communication with a client, colleague, adverse party, or judge. In most cases the communication will be in written form. Even in those instances in which you communicate orally, you will often follow up with a written letter, email, or memo to a file. Thus, effective legal writing is critical to success in the legal profession.

B. The Plain English Movement

One of the recurring criticisms of legal writing is that it is incomprehensible to the average reader because of its use of jargon, redundancies, and archaic words and phrases. The use of words and phrases such as *aforesaid* and *notwithstanding anything in the foregoing to the contrary* confuses and angers readers.

The increased activism of consumers frustrated with the inability to understand their insurance policies, mortgage documents, or car loan agreements led to the requirement in many states that certain documents be written in "plain English." In 1998 President Clinton signed a presidential memo requiring all federal agencies to use plain language for most of their written communications. The plain language initiative rests on three principles:

- Writing should be reader-oriented;
- Writing should use natural expressions, using commonly known and used words; and
- Documents should be visually appealing.

In 2010 Congress passed the Plain Writing Act of 2010 (5 U.S.C. § 103 (Supp. 2010)), which requires executive agencies to use "plain language," defined as "language that is clear, concise, well-organized, and follows other best practices appropriate to the subject or field and intended audience." Plain language must be used in various documents, particularly those the public uses to obtain any government services or benefits or in filing taxes. The law, however, does not apply to the actual regulations of agencies, which continue to be difficult to read.

Many government agencies follow the *Federal Plain Language Guidelines* located at www.plainlanguage.gov. It is clear that improved communications helps the public. For example, when the Department of Veterans Affairs redrafted a standard form to make it clearer, telephone calls to the Department about the form decreased from 1,200 to 200 each year. According to the *Federal Plain Language Guidelines*, the first rule of plain language is to write for your audience.

A number of state agencies have also adopted plain language techniques. For example, the Judicial Council of California revised its civil and criminal jury instructions in plain language so they would adequately communicate the law to jurors. These instructions have received a number of awards for their clarity.

Writing in plain English so your reader understands you is not an easy task. Many legal concepts are complex and translating them into plain English is difficult. Similarly, some use of "legalese," such as Latin phrases, may be unavoidable in certain instances. Nevertheless, well-written documents share the following features:

- They are accurate in every respect, including the "small" items, such as dates, addresses, and dollar amounts;
- They comply with American English rules of grammar, punctuation, and spelling;
- They use definite, concrete, and familiar language;
- They are organized in a manner that enhances comprehension;
- They avoid using double negatives;
- They omit surplus information and redundancy; and
- They enhance readability through attractive design and layout.

Highly respected and renowned financier Warren E. Buffett explains that when writing Berkshire Hathaway's annual report, he pretends he's talking to his sisters. Although highly intelligent, they are not accounting or financial experts. Mr. Buffett believes that he will be successful if they understand his writing. Similarly, U.S. Supreme Court Justice Stephen Breyer has said that he tries to write his legal opinions so that they are understandable to high school students. Thus, legal writing need not be showy or pretentious. It need only be understood.

C. Accuracy

The difference between the right word and the almost right word is the difference between lightning and the lightning bug.

Attributed to Mark Twain

1. Introduction

The most important characteristic of legal writing is accuracy. Clients will rely on the information and opinions given to them by legal professionals. Judges, supervisors, administrators, and others must know the information provided to them is correct. Thus, being right is fundamental to effective legal writing. No amount of skillfully presented material can overcome a faulty statement.

Be accurate with regard not only to the "big" issues, such as legal conclusions and arguments, but also as to the "small" elements of a writing, such as names, dates, and dollar amounts. An error in the client's name or address will attract more attention than anything else in a document. Just as spelling errors cast doubt on your ability, accuracy errors also have a disproportionately negative effect on the reader. The legal profession has become more adversarial in recent years and even clients (sometimes, especially clients) are quick to point out an error. Thus, because your audience is highly critical, you must be as accurate and precise as possible. Generally, other than inattention to detail, there are three causes for a lack of precision in legal writing: picking the wrong word, using a vague word, and selecting a word that has an unwanted connotation.

One notorious cause of imprecise writing is an overreliance on forms. Drafting a lease requires more than merely locating another lease in your office and then changing the names and addresses. When you use a form originally drafted for another client, proofread carefully to ensure that you do not import unsuitable language. Use the "find and replace" feature in your word processor to ensure the first client's name has been replaced with the second and that any references that might pertain only to the first client (such as the pronouns *he* or *him*) have been replaced with words and phrases appropriate for the second client.

2. Word Choice

The selection of an improper word will result in inaccuracy in your writing. Similarly, the use of qualifying language or words can cause unintended meanings. For example, no employee would be comforted by reading, "There are no immediate plans to downsize your department." Although the writer may have intended to reassure the reader that his or her job was secure, the use of the qualifier *immediate* implies that there are plans to downsize; they simply are not immediate.

For accuracy, select the most descriptive and specific word possible. Descriptive words lend strength and vitality to your writing. Moreover, the selection of an incorrect word can be fatal in legal writing. An instruction to a defendant that a judgment *may* be paid will produce a far different result than an instruction that a judgment *must* be paid.

A number of words commonly used in legal writing cause trouble. Although many words and word pairs are discussed in the Glossary of Usage in Appendix F of this Handbook, a quick review of some words commonly confused or misused in legal writing follows:

- **And/or:** A number of courts have been called on to interpret the meaning of this expression. Although this expression is short, it is often unclear because the reader is not sure whether the writer means "and" or "or" or both. For precision, instead of writing *the boys and/or the girls*, write *the boys or girls, or both*.
- **Argue:** Courts do not argue cases; lawyers do. Do not write *the court argued . . . .* Similarly, courts do not *contend, believe,* or *feel*. Conversely, courts *rule, decide, hold, state, conclude,* and so forth.
- **Compose/comprise.** *Compose* means *to make up*, as in *The brief is composed of three sections. Comprise* means *to include, contain,* or *consist of*, as in *The house comprises three wings.* Do not use the word *of* after the word *comprise.* It is as incorrect to write *The lawsuit is comprised of three counts* as it is to write *The lawsuit is included of three counts.* To use the word *comprise* properly, remember to place the "whole" item first and the "parts" item second, as in *A deck of cards comprises fifty-two cards* or *A zoo comprises many animals*.

- **Convince/persuade.** Use *convince* when you refer to changing someone's opinion, as in *I convinced her that John was an unreliable witness.* Use *persuade* when you refer to getting someone to take action, as in *I persuaded her to dismiss her case.* Generally, *persuade* is used with the word *to*.
- **Court:** The word *court* is singular, as in *the court has affirmed.* You may refer to a court by the name of its chief justice. Thus, when discussing *Brown v. Board of Education*, you may write *the Warren Court held that . . . .* A few legal writers object to references to a court by the name of a case and would thus frown upon *the Brown Court held that . . .* although such use is common in practice and frequently seen in court opinions themselves. In fact, the U.S. Supreme Court's Guide for Counsel in Cases to be argued before the Court specifically instructs attorneys, "[d]o not refer to an opinion of the Court by saying: 'In Justice Ginsburg's opinion.' You should say: 'In the Court's opinion, written by Justice Ginsburg.'" Sup. Ct. Guide for Couns. 11 (2011).
- **Dicta:** *Dicta* is plural and refers to extraneous remarks made by a judge, as in *Justice Sanders has continually noted in dicta that . . . .* *Dictum* is singular and refers to a single remark or observation.
- **Fact, contention:** A *fact* is something that has occurred or can be verified. A *contention* is an allegation that something has occurred.
- **Find, hold:** When a court makes a *finding*, it has decided certain facts. When a court makes a pronouncement about a legal issue, it issues a *holding*.
- **Guilty, liable:** In a criminal case, a defendant is found *guilty*. In a civil case, a defendant is found *liable* for damages.
- **I, my, we, our, us:** Personal pronouns (*I, my, we, our, us*) are used only in legal correspondence. They are not used in documents submitted to courts or in legal memoranda. Thus, write *Petitioner will show*, not *We will show*.
- **Judgment:** In legal writing and in most American writings, spell as *judgment*. In Great Britain, the word is spelled *judgement*.
- **Memoranda, memorandum:** *Memoranda* is plural and refers to several documents, whereas a *memorandum* is singular and refers to one document.
- **Motion:** A motion is an application made to a court requesting that the court issue an order in a pending case, such as a motion for change of venue. A lawyer *makes a motion* or *moves for summary judgment*.
- **Oral, verbal:** *Oral* means something spoken, as in *The plaintiff's oral testimony at trial was consistent with her earlier deposition testimony.* *Verbal* means a communication in words and could refer to a written or a spoken communication. Be precise.
- **Overrule, reverse:** A court *overrules* prior decisions in its jurisdiction. For example, in 2012 a court could overrule a precedent from a 1960 case. A court *reverses* the very case before it. Thus, if a defendant is found guilty by the trial court and appeals the decision, and the appellate court agrees with the defendant's reasoning, it will *reverse* the improper decision from the court below.

■ **Prescribe, proscribe:** *Prescribe* means to order, as in *The doctor prescribed medication. Proscribe* means to prohibit, as in *Iowa law proscribes falsification of documents.*

■ **Proved, proven:** Use *proven* as an adjective, as in *a proven fact. Proved* is the past participle of the word *prove*, as in *She has proved her case.* The legal maxim *Innocent until proven guilty* is an exception to the rule that *proven* is used as an adjective.

Case Illustration: The Meaning of the Word *Between*

Case:	*Lefeavre v. Pennington*, 230 S.W.2d 46 (Ark. 1950)
Facts:	The Arkansas Supreme Court was called upon to interpret a will that read "The Bal. to be divided equally between all of our nephews and nieces on my wife's side and my niece, Nathalee Pennington . . . ." There were twenty-two nieces and nephews on the wife's side, and they contended that the property should be distributed equally among all of the beneficiaries so that each would receive one twenty-third.
Holding:	The court divided the property into two equal shares, stating that the use of the word *between* showed that the testator intended to divide the property in two equal shares; had the testator intended otherwise, the word *among* would have been used.

3. Vague Words

To ensure accuracy in your writing, use concrete and descriptive words. Avoid vague and abstract words such as *matter, development, situation,* and *problem,* which provide little, if any, information to a reader. Thus, sentences beginning *Regarding this matter* or *Regarding the former issue* offer no guidance to the reader as to what *this matter* or *issue* might be. A better approach is to write *Regarding your lease.*

Similarly, avoid using words such as *above* or *herein.* For example, if in paragraph 12 of an agreement you use the words *as described above,* the reader does not know where in the previous eleven paragraphs the information was discussed. State, *as described in paragraph 4(b).*

Abstract words such as *justice* or *fairness* may be confusing because they mean different things to different people. Thus, be careful in the use of such words and consider selecting concrete nouns in their place.

Sometimes vagueness is caused by a lack of specificity. Will a reader understand a statement that *the plaintiff was injured* or that *the temperature in the employee lounge is too cold?* Why not write *the plaintiff suffered a broken leg* or *the temperature in the employee lounge is 65 degrees Fahrenheit?* Write *in 2012* rather than *recently.*

The words *it* and *this* are often used in an indefinite manner. Consider the following:

The court ruled the defendant should be granted probation. This enables the defendant to participate in a work release program.

The word *this* could refer either to the court's ruling or to the defendant's probation. When using *it* or *this*, you should repeat the word that *it* or *this* refers to, as in the following:

The court ruled the defendant should be granted probation. Probation will enable the defendant to participate in a work release program.

▶ **Tip: Use the "find and replace" feature on your word processor to locate sentences beginning with *It is*, *There is*, or *There are*. Sentences beginning with these words tend to be vague, ambiguous, and wordy.**

Vague Examples	Revised Examples
There is copyright infringement when a copyrighted work is reproduced without the owner's permission.	*Copyright infringement occurs when a copyrighted work is reproduced without the owner's permission.*
It says in the case that the legislation is not retroactive.	*The case states that the legislation is not retroactive.*
The former cause of action was dismissed.	*The negligence cause of action was dismissed.*
There are many convicts who have appealed.	*Many convicts have appealed.*

Some Vague Words

- aspect
- concept
- element
- factor
- incident
- matter
- operation
- process
- resource
- syndrome
- system
- utility
- variable

4. Intentional Vagueness

In some instances, you may wish to be intentionally vague. For example, in ordering the desegregation of public schools, the U.S. Supreme Court stated that the task should proceed *with all deliberate speed. Brown v. Bd. of Educ.*, 349 U.S. 294, 301 (1955) (emphasis added). Many experts believe the selection of this expression was itself deliberate, reflecting the Court's reluctance to impose strict time limits for such a complex task.

Similarly, many legal agreements use a variety of terms that are intentionally vague. For example, settlement agreements routinely require the parties to act in *good faith* or to *meet and confer* in the event of a dispute. Custody agreements often allow for *reasonable visitation*. In such cases, the drafters have usually artfully selected these vague phrases so that the parties can resolve their disputes, with full knowledge that a court may later be called on to determine what is *reasonable* or whether actions were in *good faith*.

In sum, if there is vagueness in your writing, make sure it is intentional.

5. Word Connotation

Many words have more than one meaning. When you select a word, consider its connotation, or suggested meaning. There is a great difference, for example, in referring to an item as *cheap* rather than *affordable*. The word *cheap* connotes shoddy or low quality whereas *affordable* conveys either a neutral or desirable meaning. Consider the effect of telling someone that he or she is *stubborn* rather than *firm* or *blunt* rather than *candid*.

Certain words carry hostile or negative undertones and will immediately make a reader defensive or angry. For example, consider the following: *The judge who decided the sexual harassment case was young.* Although the statement may be true, the subtle message it conveys is that the judge was so young and inexperienced that the decision was likely incorrect. Use a dictionary and a thesaurus to ensure that you have selected the appropriate word.

Avoid the words *clearly* and *obviously*, which carry a hostile tone.

Consider the following word pairs and note that using a word on the left may unintentionally convey the meaning on the right.

Word	Possible Connotation
old, elderly	feeble, infirm, incompetent
proud	vain
venerable, established	old, outmoded
late (with a payment)	delinquent
long, lasting	endless
neat, organized	obsessive, compulsive
enthusiastic	hyperactive, manic
cautious	timid
simple	unintelligent
delay	hinder, obstruct
debate	argue

6. Special Word Problems: Made-Up Words, Slang and Colloquial Expressions, and Offensive Language

When writers begin to write as they would speak, there are usually three problems with the words they select: The words may be made-up, slang or colloquial expressions, or offensive.

a. Made-Up Words and Phrases

If the aim of writing is to communicate, how can a reader understand words that don't exist? Although you may have heard of, used, and even written some made-up or coined words such as *dialogued, Borked,* or *liaising,* these "words" are not generally found in most dictionaries because they are not yet recognized words in English. Similarly, the use of the suffix *-wise* has created a host of coined words, such as *taxwise* and *revenuewise.* Our conversation and writing are often influenced by business and technology terms. Thus, a number of terms, such as *cutting edge, synergy,* and *empower* are overused. Do not write *We need to* <u>interface</u> *to resolve the litigation* when you mean *meet.* Do not use *impact* as a verb. Write *His credit history will affect his ability to obtain a loan* (not *His credit history will* <u>impact</u> *his ability to obtain a loan*). Although English is an evolving language, do not use a word before it has evolved into an entry in a standard dictionary.

Words and Expressions to Avoid	Substitutions
an *impactful* exhibit	a dramatic exhibit
incentivize the employees	encourage or motivate the employees
We *efforted* the project.	We worked on the project.
We were *tasked* with finding a solution.	We were asked (or requested) to find a solution.
Gift your clients with this pen.	Give your clients this pen.
We should meet and *strategize* a solution.	We should meet to find a solution.
John is Carol's *mentee.*	Carol is John's mentor.
We should *dialogue* about the case.	We should discuss the case.
We should *concretize* our plans.	We should finalize our plans.
I find the budget decrease *concerning.*	I find the budget decrease alarming [or *disturbing*].

Made-Up and Overused Words and Phrases: Conference Room Bingo

One game circulating on the Internet (see www.jokeindex.com) demonstrates the pervasiveness of made-up or overused business expressions and challenges attendees to note how often the following words or phrases are spoken in a meeting. The game of "conference room bingo" is won when all of the listed words have been used in the meeting.

- synergy
- bottom line
- revisit
- bandwidth
- out of the loop
- proactive
- think outside the box
- hardball
- touch base

- game plan
- leverage
- fast track
- mindset
- win-win
- empower
- benchmark
- best practice

b. Slang and Colloquial Expressions

Slang is informal language, often used by a particular group. Although slang may be dramatic and forceful when spoken, it is too flippant for any formal writing (unless reporting the exact words of a speaker). Colloquial language is common everyday language, and it is inappropriate for legal writing. Generally, avoid any words marked as *inf* (for *informal*) or *coll* (for *colloquial*) in a dictionary.

Slang or Colloquial	Revised
The plaintiff was ripped off.	The plaintiff was defrauded.
The premises had heavy-duty defects.	The premises had significant defects.
The plaintiff got used to the pain.	The plaintiff became accustomed to the pain.
The parties began to get along.	The parties began to cooperate.
The doctor did not measure up to the standard of care.	The doctor did not satisfy the standard of care. (or The doctor breached the standard of care.)
The plaintiff is entitled to get the documents.	The plaintiff is entitled to obtain the documents. (or The plaintiff is entitled to the documents.)
The case stepped up to each reviewing court.	The case was appealed to each reviewing court.

Somewhat similar to slang and colloquial expressions are *idioms*, phrases the meaning of which cannot be understood from the ordinary meaning of the words, as in the use of the phrase *give in* to mean *surrender* or *yield*. Many legal idioms are confusing because of the prepositions used with them. For example, are you *enjoined from* taking action or are you *enjoined to* take action? Both are correct. Once you have some experience in reading cases and legal materials, you will have a better understanding of legal idioms. Some common idioms used in legal writing are listed on page 91 of this chapter.

c. Offensive Language

Language can be offensive because it is sexist or biased or suggests stereotypes. Avoid references to personal characteristics, such as sex, race, or disability. Offensive language distracts from the message and focuses attention on the writer. It is sometimes so jarring that any underlying message is lost entirely. The use of gender-linked pronouns is also discussed in Chapter 1. Following are some examples of sexist words and expressions and suggested replacements.

Sexist Language	Revised
A judge should issue his decision promptly.	Judges should issue their decisions promptly.
	A judge should issue a decision promptly.
Mr. Carr and Barbara Carr attended.	Mr. and Mrs. Carr attended.
businessman	business executives, managers
chairman	chairperson, chair, head, presiding officer
congressman	congressperson, congressional representative
draftsman	drafter
foreman	foreperson, supervisor
layman	layperson
male nurse	nurse
man-hours	worker hours, work hours, labor
man and wife	man and woman, husband and wife
mankind	humanity, people
newsman	reporter
woman lawyer, woman judge	lawyer, judge
workman	worker (especially in reference to workers' compensation)

Use common sense and sensitivity when describing people and try to use the term that the group prefers. For example, since the 1992 Rehabilitation Act Amendments, the use of the word *handicapped* has been largely replaced by the word *disabled*. Use *hearing impaired* rather than *deaf*. Use *mentally ill* rather than *insane* (unless the word *insane* is used in its strict legal sense, as defined by a case or statute), and use *mentally impaired* rather than *retarded*.

Avoid outmoded and pejorative expressions such as *Chinese fire drill*, *Indian giver*, *Mexican standoff*, or *Protestant work ethic*. The racial designation used to describe African Americans has changed from *colored*, to *Negro*, to the current uses of *black* and *African American*. At present, there are significant disputes regarding the use of the words *Hispanic* and *Latino* with some individuals strongly preferring one term and others preferring the other. A similar dispute exists regarding the terms *American Indian* and *Native American*. Consider using the Internet and viewing the websites of organizations such as the NAACP or the National Congress of American Indians for guidance. Consider using a specific term such as *Seminole* rather than *Indian*, or *Japanese* rather than *Asian*.

Consider whether it is necessary to describe a person in terms of race, religion, or sex at all. In many instances, a description of a person is simply not relevant. For example, writing that *Justice Sotomayor is a well-respected female jurist* implies that Justice Sotomayor is well respected even though she is a woman. Write instead that *Justice Sotomayor is a well-respected jurist*.

In sum, be sensitive when describing people, selecting neutral language whenever possible, but don't be so politically correct that you describe a short witness as someone who is *vertically challenged*.

Challenge ? Word Choice

Select the correct word or rewrite to improve meaning.

1. Senior government officials and their wives will attend the conference next week.
2. Writing for the majority, Chief Justice Roberts felt the statute should be invalidated.
3. We have not yet had a chance to conversate about the document production.
4. The issue will need to be addressed at Monday's meeting.
5. The exhibit binder is comprised of three sections.
6. Making payments on a mortgage helps equitize ownership interests in real estate.
7. The human resources department has been tasked with locating workmen with the right competencies.
8. There are some documents that are missing.
9. Nick is currently officing out of his house.
10. Kate is known as a pushy advocate.

D. Clarity

> Words, like glass, obscure when they do not aid vision.
>
> Joseph Joubert, *Pensees* (1842)

The second feature of effective legal writing is clarity, namely, ensuring that your project is easily understood by the reader. Your writing style should be invisible. It is bad writing that is noticeable. Because legal writings are read not for pleasure, but for function, readers expect you to make your point clearly and quickly.

The three primary legal writing flaws that obscure clarity are elegant variation, the overuse of negatives, and improper word order.

Common Idioms in Legal Writing

Following are some common idioms or expressions seen in legal writing with the correct preposition given.

- Abide by a ruling; abide in a house
- Abstain from taking action
- Accede to demands
- According to the case; in accord with the case
- Acquiesce in a reorganization plan
- Agree on a resolution; agree to the demands; agree with a person
- Angry with the witness (not angry *at*); angry about the verdict
- Appeal to a court (not appeal *at* a court); appeal by the plaintiff
- Compare with the previous case; compare to a summer's day (metaphorical use)
- Comply with the demands (not comply *to*)
- Concur with the defendant's interpretation; concur in the majority opinion
- Damages of $50,000; damages for negligence; damages in the libel case; damages from the defendant
- Defrauded into buying the house; defrauded by the defendant's action
- Demand on the debtor; demand for money
- Depart from a previous ruling
- Different from (not different *than*)
- Disclaimer of a warranty; disclaimer by the seller; disclaimer in the contract
- Discovery of documents; discovery by the plaintiff; discovery under the Federal Rules of Civil Procedure
- Dissent in this case; dissent from the majority opinion
- Enjoined from taking further action (meaning *prohibited*); enjoined to take further action (meaning *compelled*)
- Estopped from taking action; estopped by one's behavior
- Inadmissible into (or *as*) evidence; inadmissible for the purpose of impeachment
- Insured against loss; insurance on the property; insurance for the business

(continued)

Common Idioms in Legal Writing

- Intervene between the parties; intervene in a dispute or case
- Irrelevant to the case
- Judgment of the court; judgment for the plaintiff; judgment against the defendant; judgment in the case
- Lawyer for the plaintiff; lawyer with (or *at* or *of*) the firm
- Opposed to the proposal
- Party to (or *in*) a lawsuit
- Plead not guilty to the charge of murder; plead for mercy; plead in response to the complaint; pleaded not guilty yesterday (preferred to *pled* not guilty yesterday)
- Proxy for Ellen; proxy to vote on Ellen's behalf
- Ratification of a contract; ratification by a party
- Related to the issue
- Released from a debt; released into custody; released by the court
- Relevant to the issue
- Remand to a lower court; remand by (or *from*) a higher court; remanded for further proceedings
- Stipulation by the plaintiff; stipulation of facts

1. Elegant Variation or the Slender Yellow Fruit Syndrome

Elegant variation refers to the practice of substituting one term for another in a document to avoid repetition of a term. Writers are often reluctant to repeat a term, believing that repetition of a term is boring or unsophisticated. Unfortunately, selecting alternate terms creates the impression that something entirely different is intended. Consider the following sentence:

> *Four of the defendant's witnesses were women, whereas all of the plaintiff's witnesses were ladies.*

In an attempt not to repeat the word *women,* the writer conveys something entirely different about the two groups of witnesses.

In her excellent book *Woe Is I,* author Patricia T. O'Conner notes that editors frequently call this practice the Slender Yellow Fruit Syndrome: "It is best explained by example: *Freddie was offered an apple and a banana, and he chose the slender yellow fruit.*"

Elegant variation is deadly in legal writing. For example, if you are reading a document that continually refers to the owner of property as the *landlord* and then suddenly refers to the *lessor,* you would be correct to assume that the newly introduced *lessor* is not the same individual as the previously described *landlord.*

Be cautious about varying words and terms used in legal writings. Although you may believe that selecting alternative terms shows your extensive vocabulary and lends interest to the document, you unintentionally may be creating the impression that there is a reason that different terms have been selected and that there is a legal distinction to be drawn based on this variation.

In particular, once you have given a label to an individual, use the term consistently. For example, assume that the introduction to a document refers to *the buyer, Patrick L. Moore ("Moore")*. You have now created a defined term. Every later reference to the individual must be to *Moore*. Referring to the individual as *buyer* or *Mr. Moore* is inappropriate. Use the "find and replace" feature of your word processor to ensure terms are used consistently.

Illustration: No Elegant Variation

Note the repetition in Sir Winston Churchill's speech about Dunkirk, delivered in 1940. There is little, if any, elegant variation. Rather, each repetition of the word *fight* makes for a stronger and more forceful statement.

> [W]e shall not flag or fail. We shall go on to the end. We shall fight in France, we shall fight on the seas and oceans, we shall fight with growing confidence and growing strength in the air, we shall defend our Island, whatever the cost may be, we shall fight on the beaches, we shall fight on the landing grounds. We shall fight in the fields and in the streets, we shall fight in the hills; we shall never surrender.

Challenge ? Elegant Variation

Rewrite the following statements.

1. The congressman from Texas introduced legislation last week that would change the tax code. The politician's proposed law would increase taxes on dividends. Moreover, the statesman's proposal relating to distributions would decrease the tax rate for corporations.
2. Under the terms of the contract, the defendant was obligated to deliver the goods to the plaintiff. The agreement also provided that the materials should be insured. Finally, the parties' understanding was that the items should be delivered within ten days.
3. Benefits for senior citizens will increase in July. The elderly will see an increase of five percent in their monthly payments. Aged citizens need not take any action to receive the increase.
4. Many students learn better by listening than reading. These pupils report improved comprehension. Learners likewise report less eyestrain when they hear rather than read material.
5. The attorneys filed the petition for a writ of certiorari. The lawyers then filed the well-researched brief with the court. Their diligence was rewarded when the court ruled for the advocates' client.

2. Negatives

The overuse of negatives is often confusing to readers. Although statutes are often set forth in negative fashion by describing what is prohibited, using more than two negative words in a sentence usually forces the reader to stop and think through what has been said. The phrase *not unlikely* must be translated to *probable*. The phrase *not unimportant* must be converted to *important*. In fact, these are examples of *litotes*, expressions that make an assertion by denying their opposite, as in *not unmindful*. Legal writing is prone to the use of these expressions, although their use in other contexts might be ludicrous, as in a reference to a "not unblack dog" as George Orwell noted.

Consider the following statement from a recent U.S. Supreme Court decision: "But given the fact that the District Court found that the 32 months required by TRPA to formulate the 1984 Regional Plan was not unreasonable, we could not possibly conclude that every delay of over one year is constitutionally unacceptable." *Tahoe-Sierra Pres. Council v. Tahoe Reg'l Planning Agency*, 535 U.S. 302, 341-43 (2002).

A reader would likely need to read the statement several times to make sense of it. Anytime the reader is interrupted from reading the project, your message is weakened. As a writer, your task is to ensure that a reader proceeds smoothly through the document without needing to stop and puzzle over phrases. For example, the statement *No individual shall be prohibited from refusing to submit to a breathalyzer examination* is confusing. It requires a reader to consider three negative words: *no*, *prohibited*, and *refusing*.

In drafting projects, keep in mind that there are many more negative words than the obvious ones *no*, *none*, or *never*. Many words function in a negative fashion, such as *deny, except, limit, preclude, refuse, void*, and so forth. Although it is impossible to purge your writing of all negative terms, you should carefully scrutinize your writing to ensure that you have not used too many negative words that obscure your meaning.

The other disadvantages of using negative words are that they are not as forceful as affirmative expressions and they are generally wordier than affirmative expressions. For example, it is more effective and shorter to say *the plaintiff was late for her deposition* than *the plaintiff failed to timely appear for her deposition*. To give strength and vitality to your writing, and to enhance clarity, use affirmative and positive terms.

Challenge   ?   Negative Expressions

Rewrite the following negative expressions.

1. Individuals other than the claimant may not receive these funds.
2. I do not find it implausible that there is no trademark infringement in this case.
3. He has failed to comply with the ban against smoking.
4. The judge did not accept the argument that the two amendments were not the same.
5. I am not able to determine if the proposal is not unlike others that the plaintiff has refused to accept.

Substitutions for Negative Expressions

Consider replacing negative phrases or compounds with a single word that means the same thing.

Negative Compound	Single Word
not able	unable
not accept	reject
not certain	uncertain
not unlike	similar
does not have	lacks
does not include	excludes, omits
not often	rarely, infrequently
not . . . unless	only if
not . . . except	only if
not . . . until	only when
did not recall	forgot
did not comply with	violated

Primary Source: From *Plain English Handbook*, www.sec.gov.

Case Illustrations: Tied Up in Nots

Consider the following clunkers from court opinions:

- "This principle is so well established that no parent should expect that a termination of amounts designated spousal support but in fact needed to augment an insufficient child support award insures against an upward modification of child support after the spousal support ends." *In re Marriage of Catalano*, 251 Cal. Rptr. 370, 375 (Ct. App. 1988).
- "In an appropriate case, there is no reason why courts, on a motion to dismiss, could not identify a response as not 'clearly unreasonable' as a matter of law." *Davis v. Monroe Cnty. Bd. of Educ.*, 526 U.S. 629, 649 (1999).

Backward ran the sentences until reeled the mind.

Wolcott Gibbs (about the style of *Time* magazine)

3. Word Order

The most common sentence structure in the English language is the placement of the subject first, the verb second, and the object third. Thus, the sentence *The defendant attacked the victim* is phrased in this standard way. Although the thought can certainly be expressed in another way (such as *The victim was attacked by the defendant*), readers typically anticipate that sentences will follow the expected pattern of subject, verb, and object. Place your main thought or message at the beginning of your sentence.

Although you may not want to structure every sentence in a project in the same fashion, excessive variation from the expected sentence structure may cause confusion and lack of clarity. Just as you should avoid exotic spellings of words because they draw attention to your writing rather than your message, avoid unusual sentence structure.

Vary from the anticipated sentence structure of subject, verb, and object when you want to draw attention to a thought. Thus, if you have a point you want to emphasize, vary the way it is structured. This technique will create interest. For example, consider the following two sentences:

> Ordinary Structure: *My first trial was the most memorable event of my career.*
>
> Inverted Structure: *The most memorable event of my career was my first trial.*

Note how the second example builds interest and creates drama.

Keep this technique in mind if you need to "bury" a weak portion of an argument. Phrase it in the manner commonly anticipated by readers because this will draw the least amount of attention to it.

One of the other benefits of using "normal" sentence structure is that you will automatically phrase your thoughts in the active voice. When you vary from the anticipated order in sentences, the result is often conversion to the passive voice, which creates a weaker (and often longer) sentence.

Case Illustrations: The Risks of Poor Writing

Courts are becoming increasingly impatient with poorly written briefs. In one recent case, *In re King*, No. 05-56485-C, 2006 U.S. Bankr. WL 581256 (Bankr. W.D. Tex. Feb. 21, 2006), the court noted that it could determine neither the substance of the defendant's legal argument nor the relief requested by the defendant. The court therefore denied the defendant's motion "for being incomprehensible." Thus, poor writing can result in an adverse ruling for a client. Similarly, in *United States v. Devine*, 787 F.2d 1086, 1089 (7th Cir. 1986), the court affirmed a defendant's conviction for a variety of reasons, including the poor quality of the defendant's brief, noting that "the brief was desultory in nature; in general a poorly written product with numerous typographical errors. It was obviously never edited by a caring professional. As a panel of judges already overburdened with cases and paper, we find it insulting to have to dutifully comb through a brief which even its author found little reason to give such attention. We condemn this type of shoddy professionalism."

E. Readability

Because the subject matter discussed in legal writing is often complex, and frequently boring, you need to make your project as readable as possible. Clients will be unfamiliar with legal topics. Judges and other legal professionals will be too busy to struggle through a complex and pompous document. Remember that the more complicated a topic is, the greater the need is for readability. One way to check for readability is to have a layperson read your document to see if he or she understands it.

Readability Tests

Several readability formulas can be used to determine the readability of a project. One of the best known tests is the Flesch Reading Ease Formula, which determines readability by using a calculation based on the average sentence length and average number of syllables in words. Reading tests, however, tend to rely on surface or technical characteristics and cannot test coherence; average sentence length and average syllables per word are indirect predictors of the readability and comprehensibility of a writing. Some government agencies, including the Department of Defense, require that certain documents meet the Flesch-Kinkaid Grade Level scale (which identifies the grade level of a writing), and some states also require that certain documents be written at a defined Flesch-Kincaid Grade Level (often, ninth grade).

Microsoft Word users can evaluate their projects against the Flesch Reading Ease scale and against the Flesch-Kinkaid Grade Level scale. To activate this feature, follow these steps:

- Go to the "Tools" menu and select "Options."
- Select "Spelling and Grammar."
- Check "Show readability statistics" and then select "OK."

To run the test on a document you write, select "Tools" and then "Spelling and Grammar." A dialog box will disclose the readability scores, giving the percentage of passive sentences and the grade level of your document, such as *11.6*.

To enhance readability:

1. Prefer the Active Voice

StyleLinks

http://grammar.ccc.commnet.edu/grammar/passive.htm
Select "Passive and Active Voices" for excellent information and examples for using active voice. A quiz is provided as well.

http://owl.english.purdue.edu/owl/resource/539/1
This site offers a thorough explanation of the difference between active and passive voice.

The quickest fix for plodding documents is the use of the active voice. The active voice focuses attention on the subject of the sentence that performs or causes certain action. The active voice is consistent with standard English sentence structure of subject, verb, and object and is more forceful than the passive voice, which makes the subject of the sentence the recipient of the action.

The passive voice focuses attention on the object of the action by placing it first and relegating the subject or actor of the sentence to an inferior position.

Passive Voice	Active Voice
A meeting was held by the corporation.	The corporation held a meeting.
An argument for acquittal was made by the defendant's attorney.	The defendant's attorney argued for acquittal.
Testimony was given by the doctor that the patient consented to the operation.	The doctor testified that the patient consented to the operation.
The policy was announced by the committee.	The committee announced the policy.

Note that in these passive constructions the person or the thing doing the action is introduced with the word *by*. This is a tip that you have shifted into the passive voice. Similarly, sentences in which no actor is named are passive, such as *The judge was informed that the juror was sick.* You can readily spot sentences in the passive voice because they will always combine some form of the verb *to be* (*am, are, been, is, was, were,* and so forth) with a verb in the past tense (as in *was announced*).

The active voice is stronger and more forceful than the passive voice. For example, consider the well-known NIKE Inc. slogan JUST DO IT®. What would be the effect of the slogan if it were phrased, DOING IT SHOULD BE DONE BY YOU? Similarly, what if Rev. Martin Luther King, Jr. had said, "A dream was had by me" rather than the powerful "I have a dream"?

Additionally, readers comprehend a sentence in the active voice more quickly because it follows the way they normally process information. They do not have to search through the sentence looking for the actor or subject. Finally, another advantage of using the active voice is that it usually produces shorter sentences.

There are situations, however, in which the passive voice may be preferable. Generally, use passive voice when the thing being acted on is more important than the actor, when the actor is either unknown or obvious, or when you wish to deflect attention from the actor. For example, assume your law firm represents a defendant accused of fraud. Instead of stating *The defendant deposited checks in his bank account,* you could write *Checks were deposited in the defendant's bank account.* This use of the passive voice shifts the focus away from the defendant. The reader is informed of what occurred but not who did it. In fact, some experts refer to this approach as using *weasel words* because there is no indication as to who is responsible for an act. The classic illustration of a weasel statement is seen in the recent statement of a politician accused of wrongdoing who stated, *Mistakes were made* rather than *I made a mistake*. What better way to deflect responsibility than to have a sentence with no one in it?

▶ **Tip: Most word processors have a feature that will flag the use of passive voice. This feature is a useful guide but can be distracting.**

Challenge (?) Word Order and Active Voice

Rewrite the following:

1. The judge scheduled a settlement conference on Friday.
2. Responding to the interrogatories was a task given to Beth.
3. Asking difficult questions is part of the job of an attorney.
4. Oral argument was scheduled by the clerk of the court.
5. Changes to the tax code are likely to be met with vigorous opposition.
6. The directors were informed that corporate revenues had declined.
7. An increase in executive compensation was approved by the shareholders.
8. A dividend was declared by the corporation.
9. A proposal to the buyer to make a counter offer was issued by the seller.

2. Use Lists

Another way to enhance readability is to use lists when discussing complex matters. Lists not only enable readers to comprehend information quickly, they also create visual drama and interest because they are usually numbered or bulleted and set apart from the rest of the text. Lists (sometimes called *tabulation*) are especially helpful for setting forth the elements of a cause of action, components of a definition, and so forth.

Lists can be structured in several ways, but to increase interest:

■ Set the list off from the rest of your narrative by spaces above and below the list;
■ Indent your list;
■ Identify the items in your list with numbers, letters, or "bullets" (which can be formulated automatically by word processors); and
■ Punctuate correctly by putting a semicolon after each item except the last item and include *or* or *and* before the last item.

Most lists are introduced by a phrase such as *the following* and a colon. Each component in the list must fit grammatically with the words in front of the colon.

Not all lists need to be indented. If the list is short, perhaps a series of three or four words, you may separate each item from the next by a comma, and include the list as part of your narrative text. You may also insert parenthetical numbers or letters before each item.

Correct Example: *The employee is required to perform the following duties: (1) supervise department meetings, (2) audit the company's financial records, and (3) attend monthly executive sessions.*

The grammatical structure of all the items in any list must be identical or parallel. Thus, if the first word in a list is a gerund (a verb form ending in *-ing* such as *preparing*), all of the following items must also begin with a gerund. Similarly, the items in the list must be either all complete sentences or all phrases. This type of consistency is called *parallel structure*. Note that each item in the preceding bulleted list begins with a verb in the present tense (*set, indent, identify,* and *punctuate*).

Incorrect	Correct
The elements of a cause of action for breach of contract are as follows:	*The elements of a cause of action for breach of contract are as follows:*
▪ *an agreement;*	▪ *an agreement;*
▪ *a breach of that agreement by one party; and*	▪ *a breach of that agreement by one party; and*
▪ *the act of the breaching party must have caused damage.*	▪ *damage caused by the act of the breaching party.*

Parallel structure is discussed further next.

3. Use Parallel Structure

I came, I saw, I conquered.

Words attributed to Julius Caesar by Plutarch

StyleLinks

http://owl.english.purdue.edu/owl/resource/623/1
Purdue University's Online Writing Lab offers excellent information on parallel form.

http://grammar.ccc.commnet.edu/grammar/parallelism.htm
This *Guide to Grammar & Writing* provides instruction on using parallel structure as well as quizzes to test your knowledge.

a. Introduction

Consider the following revision of Caesar's words: *I came, then I was seeing, after which I engaged in conquering.* The original statement (*I came, I saw, I conquered*) is a striking example of parallelism or parallel structure, matching grammatical structures through the use of the same pronoun followed by simple verbs in the past tense. Parallelism requires ensuring that ideas or elements in a sentence are presented in similar or parallel form, so that adjectives are paralleled by adjectives, nouns by nouns, gerunds by gerunds, and so forth. Thus, the sentence *The attorney alleged fraud and negligence* is parallel because it uses a noun and then another noun. The sentence *The defendant's conduct was reckless, willful, and malicious* is parallel because all words describing the defendant's conduct are adjectives.

Nonparallel	Parallel
The speakers were exhausted, drained, and needed food.	*The speakers were exhausted, drained, and hungry.*
The board of directors will invest the money to provide shareholders with income, protection of their assets, and achieving tax benefits.	*The board of directors will invest the money <u>to provide</u> shareholders with income, <u>to protect</u> their assets, and <u>to achieve</u> tax benefits.*

Not only is parallel structure a grammatical requirement, it also is an opportunity to achieve balance and effect in writing. Consider the following two quotations, each of which uses parallel structure to deliver a compelling message.

> *[A]sk not what your country can do for you—ask what you can do for your country.*
>> *President John F. Kennedy (1961)*

> *We will not tire, we will not falter, and we will not fail.*
>> *President George W. Bush (2001)*

There are four particular situations that require you to ensure parallel structure: when using coordinating conjunctions, when using correlative conjunctions, when making comparisons, and when using lists and headings.

b. Coordinating Conjunctions

The coordinating conjunctions *for, and, nor, but, or, yet,* and *so* (the "FANBOYS") always indicate a need for parallelism. Phrases linked by any of these words must be parallel in structure.

Nonparallel	Parallel
The system is capable of retrieving records, processing data, and communication with the server.	The system is capable of retrieving records, processing data, and communicating with the server.
Ted loves reading, writing, and research.	Ted loves to read, write, and research.
	or
	Ted loves reading, writing, and researching.

c. Correlative Conjunctions

Correlative conjunctions (pairs of words that connect elements such as *either-or*, *neither-nor*, and *not only-but also*) require elements in parallel form. The grammatical structure following the second part of the correlative conjunction (for example, the word *or* when using *either-or*) should mimic the structure following the first part. Make sure that any element you repeat is placed after the first part of the correlative conjunction (for example, after *either* when using *either-or*).

Nonparallel	Parallel
I will act <u>as either</u> a mediator <u>or as</u> an arbitrator.	I will act <u>either as</u> a mediator <u>or as</u> an arbitrator.
Jackie expects <u>not only to be</u> offered the job <u>but also she expects</u> to be well paid.	Jackie expects <u>not only to be</u> offered the job <u>but also to be</u> well paid.

d. Comparisons

Use correct parallel structure when making comparisons using the words *than* or *as*.

Nonparallel	Parallel
The exhibits in the first trial were more effective than the second trial.	The exhibits in the first trial were more effective than the exhibits in the second trial.
It is more important to write the brief than arguing it.	It is more important to write the brief than to argue it.
My appellate brief is shorter than her.	My appellate brief is shorter than hers.

e. Lists and Headings

When making lists, using headings, or placing items in a series, make sure the structure is parallel. Presentation must be parallel or consistent as well so that if the first heading in a document or item in a list is a complete sentence, later ones should also be full sentences. Similarly, if the first heading or item is a clause, later ones should also be clauses. Faulty parallel structure is often seen in résumés when applicants describe their job experience.

Nonparallel	Parallel
My experience includes:	*My experience includes:*
▩ *drafting documents;*	▩ *drafting documents;*
▩ *assisting in trial preparation; and*	▩ *assisting in trial preparation; and*
▩ *preparation of pleadings.*	▩ *preparing pleadings.*

Tips ➡ On Using Parallel Structure

● It is not significant what grammatical structure you use for a series, list, or group of headings as long as the use is consistent:

Examples: *prepare, assist, write*

prepared, assisted, wrote

preparing, assisting, writing

● When you introduce items or elements with an article (*a, an, the*), a preposition (such as *to*), or a pronoun (*his, her*), the introductory word may either appear before the first item only or be repeated before each item.

Nonparallel	Parallel
She wanted to hike, swim, and to run.	*She wanted <u>to</u> hike, swim, and run.*
	or
	She wanted <u>to</u> hike, <u>to</u> swim, and <u>to</u> run.

● To check for parallel structure:

○ Examine words that appear on either side of the words *and* and *or*; Put words and phrases in columns to make sure they match in their structure;

○ Read aloud and listen to the rhythm and sounds of elements to ensure they sound the same; and

○ Consider introducing each element with the same word, such as *by*, as in

You can increase profits <u>by</u> cutting costs, <u>by</u> consolidating operations, or <u>by</u> reducing overhead.

If you like, once you determine the list is parallel, you may remove the introductory word (in this example, *by*) from all but the first word in the list.

Challenge   ❓   Parallel Structure

Correct the following:

1. The directors set three goals for the year: increasing revenue, acquiring another company, and a decreased reliance on foreign energy sources.
2. I found her to be charming, witty, and I also thought she was affectionate.
3. The treasurer's duties are to maintain payroll records, prepare the yearly report, and to attend all board meetings.
4. Either you should begin to prepare for trial or conduct settlement negotiations.
5. Samuel's approach to drafting the agreement was better than her.
6. The office has room for a new conference table but not storage.
7. I objected that the question was hearsay and also on the grounds of irrelevancy.

4. Avoid Nominalizations

StyleLinks

http://jerz.setonhill.edu/writing/grammar-and-syntax/nominalization
This site provides a brief overview of nominalizations as well as examples of and remedies for nominalizations.

A nominalization occurs when you take a verb or adjective and turn it into a noun. Although a nominalization itself is technically correct, overuse of nominalizations drains your writing of forcefulness and makes it read as if written by a bureaucrat.

Nominalizations	Examples with Verbs
The defendant made an <u>argument</u>.	The defendant argued.
The court issued a <u>decision</u> in the case.	The court decided the case.
The judge provided an <u>explanation</u> of the order.	The judge explained the order.
We will give <u>consideration</u> to our options.	We will consider our options.

As you can see, nominalizations not only take strong verbs and convert them into dull nouns, they also tend to add wordiness to sentences. Although not all nominalizations can be avoided, their repeated use will render your writing unimaginative.

▶ **Tip: To avoid nominalizations, use the active voice and watch for words that end in *-ion*, *-ent*, and *-ant*.**

5. Avoid Legalese

The language of the law must not be foreign to the ears of those who are to obey it.

Learned Hand, *The Spirit of Liberty* (1959)

StyleLinks

www.law.ucla.edu/volokh/legalese.htm
This site, called *Eschew, Evade, and/or Eradicate Legalese*, by Professor Eugene Volokh of UCLA, provides a thorough list of archaic and stuffy legal terms together with suggested replacements.

www.kentlaw.edu/academics/lrw/grinker/LwtaLegalese.htm
Professor Grinker of Chicago-Kent College of Law offers examples of legalese and exercises to test your ability to eliminate legalese from your writing.

a. Introduction

Jargon is the specialized language of a profession. The type of jargon used in the legal profession is called *legalese*. Legalese displays the following features:

- Archaic words, such as *opine* and *beseech*;
- Redundancies, such as *unless and until*;
- Legal terms of art and Latin expressions, such as *collateral estoppel* and *ab initio*.

The use of legalese frustrates readers and produces incomprehensible writing. Some critics have suggested that there are two reasons legalese is used: to enhance the prestige of the writer and to keep the reader in the dark. In other instances, legalese or inflated language is used by newcomers to the profession in the mistaken belief that they need to write "like lawyers." As a number of experts have noted, however, good legal writing is simply good writing.

Confine your use of Latin to those phrases and words that are readily understood. If possible, use the English translation for the term, such as replacing *ex contractu* with *from the contract*. In other instances, Latin phrases are used as signals of well-known concepts or as terms of art, as in phrases such as *res judicata, habeas corpus*, and so forth. These terms will pose no problems for legal readers. If you are unsure whether the reader will understand a term, provide a brief definition, as in *The review board will examine the issues de novo (afresh) when it meets on Tuesday.*

Consistent with the trend toward plain English, try to avoid using legal jargon. Often archaic or jargon-filled phrases can be omitted entirely or replaced with more familiar terms.

Jargon	Revised
THIS AGREEMENT is made and entered into this fourth day of May 2013, by and between ABC Inc. (hereinafter referred to as "Landlord") and Susan Adams (hereinafter referred to as "Tenant") regarding the premises and covenants hereinafter set forth.	This Lease is entered into May 4, 2013, between ABC Inc. ("Landlord") and Susan Adams ("Tenant") regarding the following facts.

The omission or replacement of archaic words and phrases with familiar ones not only enhances readability but also produces a more concise writing.

You may not be able to omit all of the legalese you would like, particularly when drafting wills, deeds, contracts, and other legal documents that have more rigid structures. These documents are often drafted in accord with standard forms and long-standing conventions. Nevertheless, you can easily omit most legalese from correspondence with clients, internal office memos, and documents filed with courts. For example, the phrases *enclosed please find* or *enclosed herewith is* are often used in letters that enclose other documents. Although there is nothing grammatically wrong with these expressions, they are examples of legalese. If something is enclosed, won't the reader find it? Simply use the phrase *enclosed is* followed by a description of the item enclosed.

If you are using unfamiliar legal terms or Latin phrases, be sure to give a brief but unobtrusive definition for your reader. A client will be completely bewildered by a letter informing him or her that *the doctrine of laches precludes your claim.* Rewrite as follows:

> The doctrine of laches (an unreasonable and prejudicial delay) precludes your claim.

Although the insertion of a definition or explanatory phrase produces a longer document, the effect of enhanced readability is well worth the extra words.

Even if a document is prepared for another legal professional who will likely be familiar with the Latin phrase or legal term, add the definition because it often serves as a smooth transition for any reader. Readers experienced with the terms will not be offended by your inclusion of an explanation and will readily skip over it. Other less experienced readers, such as a law clerk or a client receiving a copy of the writing, will be greatly assisted by the "translation" you provide.

b. Indirect Writing

One form of legalese is indirect writing. In some cases, legal professionals are reluctant to give bad news and adopt a broad, vague manner of writing. Although legal writing should not be blunt, it must be accurate, and the use of indirect language or euphemisms obscures meaning. Be direct without being insensitive or engaging in doublespeak. In the world of doublespeak, employees are never fired, they are *dehired, laid off, rightsized,* or *downsized.* There is no failure, only *incomplete success.* There are no tax increases, only *revenue enhancements.* There are no salespersons sending you spam, there are *relationship managers* delivering their *direct marketing messages.* Be wary of such indirection in others' writing, and do not use it in your own.

c. Pretentious Writing

Persons who reside and dwell in silicone-based habitats should cease and desist from hurling compact mineral material.

In other words, people who live in glass houses shouldn't throw stones. Legalese often takes the form of showy or pretentious writing meant to impress the reader. This style of elaborate writing annoys readers. Adopt a writing style that focuses on the reader's comprehension rather than one aimed at showing off your vocabulary or knowledge.

Pretentious	Revised
Until such time as we promulgate the revised Employee Handbook pursuant to the decision of the company, the currently existing manual relating to and setting forth employee policies should continue to be utilized.	Use the current Employee Handbook until the revised handbook is issued.

Consider the following pretentious statement by a district court: "A dismissal is appropriate where the complaint is a labyrinthian prolixity of unrelated and vituperative charges that defie[s] comprehension and the amended complaint fails to cure prolixity and incomprehensibility." *Thomson v. Olson,* 866 F. Supp. 1267, 1270 (D.N.D. 1994). Strive to make sure your reading is understood.

 Curing Legalese

Consider the following suggestions to cure legalese.

Instead of This	Substitute
ab initio	from the beginning
albeit	although
antecedent to	before
apprise	inform
arguendo	for the sake of argument
assent	agree
bona fide effort	a good faith effort
case at bar	this case
case of first impression	novel question
commence	start; begin
concerning the matter of	about
contiguous to	next to
conveyance	transfer
elucidate	explain
endeavor	try
et al.	and others (persons)
evidences (as in the document *evidences*)	shows
execute (as in *execute* the will)	sign
firstly, secondly	first, second
forthwith	now; immediately
hence	thus
herein	here; in this document
implement	carry out
in reference to; in regard to	regarding; about
instant case	this case
inter alia	among other things
in the event that	if
I opine that	it is my opinion; I believe
prefatory to	before
pray	ask, demand, request
remainder; residue	rest
said (as in *said* document)	omit *said* or use *this*
subsequent to	after
terminate	end
to wit	namely
viz.	namely; that is to say

Tip → Some Archaic Word Forms

Note that almost any word with *-forth (henceforth, forthwith)*, *-in (therein, wherein)*, *-at (thereat, whereat)*, *-upon (whereupon)*, *-as (whereas)*, *-by (thereby, whereby)*, *-here (herein, hereinafter)* and other similar prefixes and suffixes qualifies as legalese and should be avoided. In most instances, replacement with a modern word is easy. Thus, *thereafter* becomes *from then on*, *hereinabove* becomes *above*, and so forth.

Challenge ?   Nominalizations and Legalese

Rewrite the following:

1. The brief gives an analysis of the business judgment doctrine and offers an explanation of it.
2. The committee issued a report that offered a suggestion to produce an increase in sales.
3. We will conduct an investigation into the allegation that the defendant issued a denial of any fraud.
4. Enclosed herewith is the most recent addendum to the contract, which is dated the fourteenth of August. We would appreciate your reviewing and executing the same in the spaces designated for such and transmitting it to us.
5. We are writing this letter to remind you to maintain all pertinent corporate documents so that the company does not face an assertion of spoliation in the instant case at bar.
6. At all times herein mentioned, Plaintiff was a resident of Texas and was possessed of three patents.
7. We intend to provide a full and complete disclosure of all materials that were the subject of our earlier discussion.
8. We opine that the new trust document eliminates and reduces prolix provisions.

6. Keep Subjects and Verbs Close Together

To make sense of any sentence, a reader needs a subject and a verb. Thus, readers tend to look for these first when reading. Legal writing is known for creating huge gaps between the subject of a sentence and its verb. When too many words intervene between the subject and the verb, readers no longer remember what the sentence is about by the time they locate the verb. They are then forced to backtrack and hunt for the subject. Moreover, when subjects and verbs are placed far apart there is a greater chance that they will not agree in number.

Although you need not immediately follow every subject in every sentence with a verb, avoid large gaps between these two parts of a sentence. Statutes are especially notorious for separating subjects and verbs by long word strings.

There are two ways to remedy a large gap between a subject and a verb:

- Take the words that intervene between the subject and verb and make them into their own sentence; or
- Rewrite the sentence, moving the intervening words either to the beginning or to the end of the sentence.

Before	After
The partnership, an entity organized and existing under Missouri law and formed after the passage of the Missouri General Partnership Act, is composed of Adams, Baker, and Carr.	*The partnership is composed of Adams, Baker, and Carr. It is an entity organized and existing under Missouri law and was formed after the passage of the Missouri General Partnership Act.*

Challenge   Keeping Subjects and Verbs Close

Rewrite the following:

1. The tenant, who had previously complained about the leaky roof and the lack of security at the premises, began to withhold rent in January.
2. The contract's provision that proposed arbitration rather than litigation in the event of disputes, and under which the prevailing party would be entitled to attorneys' fees, was valid because it was freely agreed to by the parties.
3. Holders of Common A and Common B stock will be entitled to receive on each payment date, to the extent funds are available therefor, a distribution.

7. Use Forceful Words

Because legal writing is formal, writers often tend to adopt an emotionless, pallid tone in their writing. Although your writing should not read like a romance novel, the use of vivid and forceful words not only will keep your readers interested but also will aid in converting them to your viewpoint.

Emphasis cannot be obtained by merely underlining or italicizing words or phrases or by adding a modifier such as *very* or *hardly*. You need to select a word forceful enough to carry the meaning you desire. Avoiding nominalizations (see Section E.4 of this chapter) will produce stronger verbs. Use a thesaurus or dictionary to help you select words that are vivid and strong.

Weak	Forceful
The defendant said he knew where the witness was located.	The defendant boasted that he knew where the witness was secreted.
Mr. Fowell misrepresented the condition of the premises.	Mr. Fowell lied about the condition of the premises.
very sad	sorrowful
not allowed	forbidden, prohibited
disagree with	contradict
acknowledge guilt	confess
could not believe	was incredulous
withdraw a statement	recant
made a material misrepresentation of fact	lied

Conversely, do not take a concrete word, which is strong in and of itself, and dilute it, such as by converting *improbable* to *somewhat unlikely* or *rapid* to *very fast*. Note that some words stand on their own and cannot be limited, such as *unique*, which means the only one of its kind. Something cannot be *quite unique* or *rather unique*.

8. Repeat Strong Words and Phrases

Although you want to avoid redundancy in legal writing, there are certain strategies in which repetition can add emphasis to your writing. The repetition of a key word or phrase creates interest and adds drama to writing. Review Sir Winston Churchill's speech about Dunkirk in Section D.1 of this chapter for an especially compelling example of the effective use of repetition. Consider also the following statement:

> The defendant misled the plaintiff. He misled her by promising the premises were quiet. He misled her by promising the premises were habitable. He misled her by promising the premises were safe.

Each repetition of the words *misled* and *promising* builds on the previous reference. When you use this technique, be sure to structure the sentence so you end with the strongest element, as in the following example:

> She was a diligent worker. She was a loyal friend. She was a loving mother.

9. Vary the Length of Sentences

Short sentences are easier to understand than long, complex sentences. Nevertheless, you do not want a project filled with sentences of approximately the same length. Such a writing would be tedious to read.

Just as you may occasionally want to vary the pattern of your sentences from the standard sentence order (subject-verb-object) to add interest, vary the length of your sentences to enhance readability. For example, a short sentence such as *He agreed* is concise and powerful. Generally, sentences that exceed three lines are too long for most readers. On the other hand, you do not want a writing filled only with short sentences. Such a project would have a choppy and abrupt tone and would read like a telegram.

Choppy Sentences	Revised
The landlord sent her the rent statement. She refused to pay. He sued her for the back rent. A jury trial was held. The jury ruled for the tenant.	*The landlord sent her the rent statement. She refused to pay and was sued by the landlord for the back rent. A jury trial was held, and the jury ruled for the tenant.*

10. Use Effective Transitions

StyleLinks

http://writingcenter.unc.edu/handouts/transitions
The Writing Center of the University of North Carolina offers excellent information on the use of transitional expressions.

http://owl.english.purdue.edu/owl/resource/574/02
The Online Writing Lab at Purdue University offers a useful list of common transitional words and expressions.

To move smoothly from one sentence, paragraph, or idea to another, use a transition word or phrase. Without transitions, sentences and paragraphs would be isolated and would lack links to each other. Transitions connect what you have said with what will follow and lend cohesiveness to your document.

Transitions can appear within or between sentences, between paragraphs, and between sections of a document. Transitions within sentences tend to be single words, such as *however* and *although*. Transitions between paragraphs show the logical relationship of one paragraph to another. These transitions may be words, phrases, or sentences. For example, a paragraph that begins with the phrase *In contrast* tells the reader that the paragraph to follow is different from the preceding paragraph. Make sure that each paragraph is logically tied to the one before it and the one after it. Transitions also help readers anticipate information. Thus, the sentence *There are two tests to determine insolvency* sets the stage for analysis and discussion of the two tests.

Most writers tend to rely on the same transition words. Two of the favorites are *however* and *therefore*. If you find yourself continually introducing sentences and paragraphs with the same words, examine your project and try to find other transitions to lend variety and interest to your writing.

If readers or instructors note that your writing seems abrupt or choppy or if they question how your ideas or sections are related, these are signals that you may need to work on your transitions.

See Figure 4-1 for some effective transitions.

11. Avoid Shifts in Tense

The basic tense of a verb can be past, present, or future, as in *I wrote the brief, I write the brief*, and *I will write the brief*. One of the most jarring faults in legal writing is an improper shift in tense. When a discussion begins in one tense and abruptly shifts without reason to another, readers are confused. Generally, the verb form in the first phrase or sentence establishes the tense for the rest of the phrase or sentences in a paragraph. The tenses of verbs should shift only when they reflect actual changes in time as in *After I write the brief I will file it with the court.*

Figure 4-1   Common Transition Words and Phrases

To Introduce	To Show Contrast	To Show Similarity	To Restate
in general initially primarily to	although but by comparison conversely however in contrast nevertheless on the contrary on the other hand yet	equally important in the same way just as likewise similarly	in other words more simply put to clarify

To Emphasize	To Show Additions	To Show Examples	To Show Sequence
certainly definitely indeed in fact undeniably	additionally again also besides furthermore in addition moreover	for example for instance in fact namely specifically that is to illustrate	first, second, third, etc. following this next previously subsequently then

To Summarize	To Show Conclusions
finally in brief in conclusion in summary to conclude to summarize	accordingly as a result because consequently inasmuch as therefore thus

Challenge ❓ Transition Words

Rewrite the following to make them smoother.

1. Shareholders are not usually liable for corporate obligations. Failing to respect that the corporation is a separate entity may lead to shareholder liability. Two acts are commonly seen. They may justify imposing liability on shareholders for corporate obligations. They are commingling of personal and corporate funds or failing to observe corporate formalities.

2. Patent law was significantly reformed in 2011. The America Invents Act changed patent law. No longer will a patent be awarded to the first to invent. The United States will award a patent to the first to file a patent application. This should reduce disputes over inventorship. It harmonizes U.S. law with that of most foreign countries.

Incorrect Tense Shift:	*The court <u>held</u> that corporate promoters are liable unless they are expressly released from lease obligations. The court also <u>analyzes</u> the personal liability of promoters as joint venturers.*
Consistent Tense:	*The court <u>held</u> that corporate promoters are liable unless they are expressly released from lease obligations. The court also <u>analyzed</u> the personal liability of promoters as joint venturers.*
Correct Tense Shift:	*The promoter <u>has argued</u> that he should be released from the lease agreement. Plaintiff <u>will show</u> that this argument is not supported by Ohio law.*

There are three basic rules for using tense in legal writing:

☐ **Rule One: Use the past tense to describe events that occurred in the past.**

When discussing events that occurred in the past, use the past tense. Shift from this only when facts are developing or may occur in the future.

Correct Example:	A corporation *issued* a type of stock that *had* the right to vote but no right to dividends. The owners of the stock *brought* a class action and *alleged* that the stock *deprived* them of an economic interest of ownership and *was* therefore invalid.

☐ **Rule Two: Use the past tense to describe what a court did in a case.**

When discussing published case law, discuss the facts of the case, its procedural background, and the court's reasoning in the past tense.

Correct Example:	In *Stroh v. Blackhawk Holding Co.*, 272 N.E.2d 1 (Ill. 1971), the lower court held that the class of stock was valid. The case *was appealed* to the Illinois Supreme Court, which *affirmed* the lower court's decision. The court *analyzed* the Illinois statutes and the articles of incorporation and *concluded* that both *allowed* the corporation to deny dividend rights so long as voting rights *were* not limited or denied.

☐ **Rule Three: Use the present tense when discussing current legal rules and principles, whether they are found in statutes, cases, or other legal authorities.**

Correct Example:	Illinois statutes and the articles of incorporation *allow* stock to be divided into classes with various preferences so long as voting rights *are* not prohibited.

Challenge ❓ Shifts in Verb Tense

Rewrite the following:

1. The company's trade secret protection program called for using encryption technology and also employed iris scanners.
2. The board of directors formed a nominating committee to assist in finding candidates and an audit committee whose responsibilities included oversight of financial reporting.
3. The court held that the extension of the period of duration of copyright protection was valid. The court further notes that under the Constitution, Congress has the power to regulate copyright law.
4. The plaintiff alleged fraud, which arises out of an omission of a material fact.

F. Conciseness

Vigorous writing is concise.

William Strunk Jr., *The Elements of Style* (1918)

StyleLinks

http://owl.english.purdue.edu/handouts/general/gl_concise.html
Purdue University's Online Writing Lab offers excellent information and exercises on writing concisely.

http://grammar.ccc.commnet.edu/grammar/concise.htm
This *Guide to Grammar & Writing* provides a thorough review of methods to achieve conciseness in writing as well as a variety of quizzes.

www.bartleby.com
Select "Strunk's Elements of Style" Section III.13 for tips on omitting needless words.

1. Introduction

The length of a project does not necessarily indicate its quality. Some of the most compelling and well-known writings are the briefest. For example, the Gettysburg Address has 286 words; yet, just one federal statute relating to Medicare has more than 700 words.

Although almost all writers agree in principle that conciseness (being brief but meaningful) is an admirable goal in legal writing, conciseness is not easily accomplished. Many of us have difficulty abandoning our own words. Moreover, the topics discussed in legal documents are often complex, requiring thoughtful analysis. Finally, over-review of a document causes increased length. Each professional who works on a project will feel a need to improve a writing, generally by adding to it, changing *now* to *at the present time* and *if* to *in the event that*. Documents also grow in length because of the ease of word processing, which allows legal writers to take a previously drafted document and continually tinker with it, adding extra words and sections with a click of a keystroke.

Although judges complain about lawyers' inability to write succinctly, some writing experts suggest that judges themselves contribute to the mass of legal publication by writing longer opinions, with more footnotes, and more separate opinions.

Some of the writing strategies previously discussed will help achieve conciseness. Recall that using active voice and eliminating nominalizations will produce a more concise project.

Be merciless. Your reader's time is at a premium, and you cannot afford to frustrate the reader with redundancy and long-winded phrases. Additionally, more and more courts are imposing page limits and word count limits for submissions. Documents that exceed the stated requirements are rejected. Thus, failure to be brief may be legal malpractice.

2. Omit Needless Words

There are numerous phrases in English that we use simply by habit. Many of these can be eliminated or reduced to a more concise word or phrase. Careful writing and revising will help you eliminate extra words. Ask yourself if you absolutely need a phrase and whether there is an effective substitute for it. Many commonly used possessive phrases can be replaced by single words with no loss of meaning. For example, use apostrophes rather than prepositions for some expressions, as in *plaintiff's allegations* rather than *allegations of the plaintiff*. In particular, avoid constructions that include more than one preposition, such as *in regard to*. Use *regarding*. See Figure 4-2 for examples of wordy phrases.

Figure 4-2   Some Wordy Phrases

Long-Winded Phrases	Substitutions
after the conclusion of	after
all of	all
any and all	any *or* all
as a result of	consequently, therefore
as to whether	whether
at such time as	when
at the present time	now
despite the fact that	although
due to the fact that	because
during the time that	during, when
for the purpose of	for, to
in accordance with	by, under
in addition to	additionally, moreover
in connection with	about, regarding
in order to	to
in regard to	regarding, concerning
in the event that	if
it is often the case that	often, frequently
prior to	before
pursuant to	under, according
subsequent to	after
whether or not	whether
with reference to *or* with regard to	regarding, concerning
with the exception of	except

The word *the* is often needed and cannot be omitted. For example, write *The trademark owner licensed the mark to the company* rather than *Trademark owner licensed the mark to company*. Eliminating *the* results in a choppy, telegram-like tone.

▶ Tip: Watch for phrases including both *the* and *of*, as in *the amount of* or *the case of*. In many instances, the entire phrase can be deleted.

Empty Words	Revision
The plaintiff was awarded damages in the amount of $50,000.	*The plaintiff was awarded damages of $50,000.*

▶ Tip: To reduce sentence length, consider using citations by themselves rather than in introductory phrases, such as *the court held in* . . . .

Wordy	Revision
The California Supreme Court held in Allen v. Carr, 909 P.2d 14, 16 (Cal. 1990), that landlords must give written notice to tenants before evicting them.	*Landlords must give written notice to tenants before evicting them. Allen v. Carr, 909 P.2d 14, 16 (Cal. 1990).*

3. Avoid "Throat-Clearing" Introductions

"Throat-clearing" refers to introductions that are mere preludes for the main topic to follow. Writers often feel compelled to warm up readers by preparing them for the main idea rather than simply presenting the idea.

Throat-Clearing Phrases	Substitutions
In this regard it is important to recall that Smith v. Jones was overruled.	*Smith v. Jones was overruled.*
The first issue to be considered is . . .	*First*
We intend to show that the statute does not apply.	*The statute does not apply.*
It is interesting to note that the contract was amended.	*The contract was amended.*
The fact of the matter is that the employee resigned.	*The employee resigned.*

Other overused introductory words are *clearly* and *obviously*. Writers often add *clearly* before introducing a conclusion, believing that this word will lend persuasive force. To paraphrase a famous jurist, adding the word *clearly* to a sentence won't make it clear; and if the sentence is clear, you don't need the word *clearly*.

The word *obviously* should be avoided for the same reason as *clearly*. Moreover, *obviously* carries a hostile meaning. By introducing a sentence or topic with *obviously* you signal to readers that you believe they lack the capacity to understand the meaning of the sentence on their own.

4. Avoid Redundancy

A common criticism of legal writing is that those in the legal profession are enamored of redundancy. They cannot merely say *null*. They must say *null and void and of no legal force or effect*. Is all this needed? If something is null, isn't it void? If it is void, can it have legal effect?

The reason legal writing is so prone to word doubling (and tripling) lies in the history of our language. English has its roots in Latin and French as well as in the language of the Celts and the Anglo-Saxons. Often word pairings were used to ensure that readers would understand phrases regardless of their background or station in life. Thus, the French word *peace* joined with the Latin word *quiet*. These redundant doublings have persisted long after any need for them. Their use today is often the result of habit rather than necessity.

If you find yourself using these "stock" redundancies, stop and ask whether one word is sufficient. Make sure that each word in a writing performs a function.

Some word pairs are more than redundant; they are unintentionally silly. Consider the following:

basic fundamentals
close proximity
cooperate together
current status
final result
past history
personal opinion
previous experience
small in size
vitally necessary

Common Legal Redundancies

acknowledge and agree	give, devise, and bequeath
alter, change, or modify	grant and convey
buy or purchase	keep and maintain
cease and desist	made and entered into
consented and agreed	null and void and of no legal effect
covenant, warrant, and represent	order and direct
due and owing	own or possess
each and every	refuse and fail
false and untrue	release, remise, and discharge
force or effect	right, title, and interest
free and clear	terms and conditions
full and complete	true and correct
	unless and until

Challenge ？ Conciseness

Select a more concise word or phrase for the following.

- previous to
- half of
- period of time
- collaborate together
- adversely impact
- afford an opportunity
- as prescribed by
- temporary reprieve
- preliminary to

Rewrite the following to make them more concise:

1. The will has been entirely and completely revised, altered, and modified.
2. The motion, which was recently filed, was granted.
3. The defendant arrived at the trial by means of automobile.
4. The board of directors has appointed and named Ellen Edwards as treasurer.
5. Anthony served as chair for a period of two years.
6. Once the pleadings are filed, we will proceed forward with discovery.
7. It is incumbent upon the employees to act in accordance with company rules and policies.
8. The defendant's defenses are few in number and arise from the same identical fact pattern.

5. Avoid Repetition

Once you have stated your contention or communicated the information you need to communicate, stop. Many writers believe they should make every point three times by telling the reader what the project will say, saying it, and then reminding the reader of what was said.

There is no place in legal writing for such needless repetition. The only exception to the rule of avoiding repeating your argument is that in a long document, readers often appreciate a separate conclusion, which briefly and concisely summarizes the analysis.

Tips → To Achieve Conciseness

- Use active voice.

  Passive: *The case was decided by the jury.*

  Revised: *The jury decided the case.*

- Change nominalization to verbs.

  Nominalization: *The attorney made an objection to the question.*

  Revised: *The attorney objected to the question.*

- Change unneeded *that*, *which*, and *who* clauses into phrases.

  Wordy: *The brief, which was recently filed . . .*

  Revised: *The recently filed brief . . .*

  Wordy: *The attorney who is representing the plaintiff . . .*

  Revised: *The plaintiff's attorney . . .*

- Watch sentences beginning with *It is*, *There is*, or *There are*. These introductory phrases can often be eliminated.

  Wordy: *It is the judge who issues the order.*

  Revised: *The judge issues the order.*

  Wordy: *There are three elements that must be proved.*

  Revised: *Three elements must be proved.*

- Combine sentences. You can often combine sentences without losing any meaning.

  Wordy: *As reported by the committee, the company's sales are improving. The report was released three weeks ago.*

  Revised: *As reported by the committee three weeks ago, the company's sales are improving.*

- Sometimes the word *that* is necessary. Let clarity guide you. For example, *He knew her testimony was scheduled* is as clear as *He knew that her testimony was scheduled*. On the other hand, consider the sentence *The judge stated on Friday the case would be dismissed*. A *that* is needed for clarity, as in *The judge stated that on Friday the case would be dismissed* or *The judge stated on Friday that the case would be dismissed*.

chapter 5

Organization and the Writing Process

StyleLinks

http://writingcenter.tamu.edu/c/composing-process/brainstorming-prewriting
Texas A & M University offers a variety of handouts on getting started,
freewriting, and the writing process.

www.writing.ku.edu/students/guides.shtml
The University of Kansas offers several writing guides with information on
prewriting steps and outlines.

http://owl.english.purdue.edu/owl/section/1/1
Purdue University's Online Writing Lab offers strategies on coping with writing
anxiety, tips for starting writing, and tips for developing outlines.

http://grammar.ccc.commnet.edu/grammar
Select "Freewriting," "Outlining," or "Clustering" for information and examples
of writing outlines and organizational techniques.

www.alanmacfarlane.com/savage/typewriter.pdf
Author Alan MacFarlane provides an essay on writing methods with thoughts on
writing in longhand, typing, and freewriting.

A. Introduction

A writing project must be well organized so that its reader can quickly find the information needed. Readers who are bombarded with a jumble of thoughts and impressions will often abandon a project. Thus, every writing project needs a coherent structure. There are a number of outlining techniques you can use to achieve internal organization.

Once you have decided on a basic plan for the entire project, you can then focus on its major sections, the beginning, middle, and end, and then consider where to place information that should be emphasized and information that should be minimized.

Finally, some methods of writing are faster and more efficient than others, and some techniques writers engage in during the writing process, such as micro-editing, are often time wasters.

B. Order and Internal Organization

1. Outlines

Just as you would never begin a car trip to a far-off destination without a road map, you should never begin a writing project without some idea of how to approach it. A project that is poorly organized not only fails to inform or persuade the reader, it may so frustrate the reader that it will not be read.

The best system for organizing any writing project is to use an outline. Although the most complete outline includes full sentences or topics divided into headings and subheadings, an outline need not be so formal. The looseleaf notebook containing the notes you took while researching or the index cards containing notes of your research results are working outlines. By shuffling the index cards or the pages in your notebook, you are outlining, that is, organizing your approach to your writing. Some word processing programs include software for outlining and taking notes. Take your laptop to the library so your note taking is speedy.

It is not the format of the outline that is important; the mere existence of any type of outline forces you to consider and organize the structure of your writing. The outline should disclose the basic sections of your project and the order in which they will be addressed.

Following are some common methods of outlining that do not involve a formal outline (one with Roman numbers, formal headings, and so forth). Preparing an outline will not only help you achieve order in your writing but also serve as an effective prewriting technique to break writer's block.

a. Brainstorming and Freewriting

If the notes taken during research are not helpful in preparing an outline, simply jot down on paper in list form all the words and phrases you can think of that relate to your project. Keep writing and listing the entries; do not worry about organizing these entries yet. This outlining technique is usually called *brainstorming*, and it is similar to word association. After you have finished listing every topic you can think of, carefully examine the list and then group related items together. After you have settled on these rough groupings, decide the order in which the groups should be discussed, and then assign a label or title to each group. Writers often discover that their list provides ideas for the structure of the project. Keep your list handy as you write your first draft; you may discover other ideas that should be included in the project.

Somewhat similar to brainstorming is *freewriting*, a technique that is usually used to break writer's block. Freewriting involves setting a timer and writing or typing nonstop as fast as you can for ten to fifteen minutes. Do not worry about spelling, grammar, or usage. Just write sentence after sentence about your project without stopping. This nonstop writing will prevent you from editing your thoughts and rejecting ideas. Print and examine your freewriting sample to see if you gain any insight about how to organize your project. You may well find that this very rough first draft gives you some ideas for organizing your project.

b. Clustering and Tree Diagrams

Clustering is a visual method of outlining that enables writers to see the relationships among parts of a project. Place a circle or "nucleus" in the middle of a blank page of paper. Place the key word or topic of your project (for example, *statute of limitations*) in the nucleus. Now write a related topic or issue nearby. Encircle it and draw a line back to your nucleus. Continue by either branching out from the nucleus or the new circle. Trust your instincts to select new words and topics and continue linking new ideas to older ones. The final product should look like a spider web. Another similar visual approach is to use a "tree diagram" with the most important idea placed at the left margin and ideas and details becoming more specific as the branches extend outward to the right. Cluster and tree diagram outlines are nonlinear approaches to outlining and are visual methods that are attractive to many writers. In many instances, writers can tell by quickly glancing at their cluster or tree that certain sections and ideas are underdeveloped and need additional analysis.

c. Story Telling

Talk to a friend or colleague about your project. Pretend you are being interviewed. Start at the beginning by saying, "I am preparing a motion for change of venue. The facts of the case are . . . . " As you "tell the story" of your project, some organizational patterns should emerge. Don't censor yourself, and allow yourself to ramble a bit. Keep a notepad nearby, and write down ideas as you are speaking. Your notes are then a preliminary outline. Consider challenging yourself to tell the story of your project in three to five sentences. Because most of us are more comfortable talking than writing, talking it out is a good strategy for many projects.

d. Percolating

Try to allow some "down time" before you begin writing so that ideas percolate and bubble up to the surface. Nearly all writers have experienced an "aha!" moment while showering or driving that gives them a great idea for a project. Keep your writing or iPhone notepad handy so you can capture these ideas.

e. Reverse Outlining

One organizing technique recommended by many experts is reverse outlining, which involves creating an outline of what you have already written (rather than creating an outline before you write). A reverse outline allows you to review your organization and your content. To reverse outline, take your first draft and in the margin next to each paragraph (or on a separate sheet of paper) make notes about the main point of each paragraph. Use only a word or brief phrase. Then examine your list of topics, which is now an outline of your project. For example, your reverse outline for one section of a project may look like the following:

Paragraph 1:   Introduction to Business Judgment Rule

Paragraph 2:   Purpose of Business Judgment Rule

Paragraph 3:   Discussion of Facts of Case

Paragraph 4:   Examples of Directors' Breaches of Duty, Reliance on Experts, Defenses

Paragraph 5:   History and Purpose of Business Judgment Rule

Paragraph 6:   Application of Business Judgment Rule

Paragraph 7:   Conclusion

Review your outline and note any repetitious paragraphs or paragraphs that are out of sequence. For example, in the outline just shown, the information in Paragraph 5 should likely be omitted or combined with the information in either Paragraph 1 or 2. Similarly, Paragraph 4 seems to have too many topics, suggesting that this paragraph should be broken up into at least two or possibly three paragraphs. If you have trouble summing up a paragraph in a single word or brief phrase, this is likely a signal that the paragraph contains too many unrelated ideas. In contrast, if you have difficulty finding any word or phrase to summarize your paragraph, this is likely a signal that your paragraph has no unifying theme or point. Perhaps the entire paragraph can be omitted. Consider whether each paragraph leads logically into the next and whether your paragraphs are in the right order.

After you revise and edit your reverse outline, return to your project and ask yourself the following critical question: Does each paragraph support the main thrust of my argument? In other words, does each paragraph support my thesis statement? (See Section 3.b later in the chapter and Chapters 7 and 8 for discussion of thesis statements.) Make sure you have proved what you have promised the reader.

2. The Paper Chase: Using the Legal Authorities

In many instances, by the time you are ready to write, you have reams of paper. You have photocopies or printouts of pertinent statutes, cases, law review articles, and other legal authorities. Using these materials in a planned fashion will bring coherence to your project. You might use colored sticky notes and assign a color to each section of your project. For example, if you intend to discuss elements of a contract first and breach of the contract second, flag all the cases, statutes, and other documents that deal with elements of a contract with a yellow sticky note and all the documents that discuss breach of contract with an orange sticky note, and so forth. Colored marker pens can be used the same way to highlight favorable and unfavorable authorities.

This is similar to the U.S. Supreme Court rules requiring different types of briefs to have different color covers (for example, light blue for briefs on the merits for petitioners and light red for briefs in response to these). The briefs are then instantly recognizable to the Justices. If you use colored sticky notes or flags, as you begin writing you will have an instant visual outline, making it easy for you to group related arguments together. Consider using sticky notes or flags that convey conventional messages: green for authorities that support your position, red for authorities that are contrary to your position, and yellow for authorities that you haven't yet decided to include. Similarly, within each authority you can use different colored highlighters to mark sections that correspond with parts of your argument. Don't censor yourself: Record your impressions and rank the authorities by marking documents and cases with grades of A, B, C, D, and F to indicate their level of helpfulness. When taking notes, indicate whether the material is a quotation or is paraphrased (by using a "Q" or "P") and indicate the complete citation(s). This investment of time will pay off later when you write your document.

Tip ➡ Understand Your Topic

It will be nearly impossible for you to write a coherent project if you do not understand the material. Although it is neither possible nor necessary to become an expert in every area of law that you will write about, you must have some rudimentary understanding of your subject matter before you can explain it or persuade another that your position is correct. Thus, you may need to invest a bit of time in "getting your feet wet" in a topic. Use a legal encyclopedia, such as Am. Jur. 2d, and read a bit about your topic. Before you begin writing your project in earnest, write a short summary for yourself of the major points you will cover. If you find yourself struggling to write or to explain your position, this is likely a sign that you need to go "back to the books" to learn a bit more about the topic itself.

3. An Overview of Most Writing Projects

Although letters to clients differ vastly from documents submitted to courts, and although each particular type of legal writing is discussed in Section Three of this text, there are some elements and strategies common to all legal documents.

a. Introductory Section

All documents start with some form of introductory section. The beginning section of any project is important because it sets the tone for the project. This section also sets the stage for the information to follow. Almost all documents begin with a review of the facts on which the document is based. Discuss past facts in the past tense unless they are still developing. Most introductions formulate the central issue that the project will analyze. Present general information and define any terms that will appear later in the document. Because readers are impatient to get to the bottom line, consider putting the most important information first. The SEC's *Plain English Handbook* notes that it is hard for readers to understand details unless they have first been given the big picture and compares an introductory section to working on a jigsaw puzzle: It is nearly impossible to put together a jigsaw puzzle without first seeing a picture of the completed puzzle. Thus, individual pieces of information are more helpful to readers if the readers understand how the pieces fit into the overall project. It is possible that the introductory section will be dictated by the nature of the document. For example, most opinion letters start with a recitation of the facts on which they are based. Many court documents begin with a preliminary or threshold issue the court must resolve before other issues can be addressed. In any event, remember that there should be no information introduced in this section that is not later analyzed and discussed.

b. Middle Sections and Paragraphs

(1) Some General Thoughts. Use paragraphs to break up a discussion into units that are easy to read. Group related information together to identify and eliminate repetitious information. Readers will expect that each of your paragraphs relates to one distinct idea and will also expect that the first sentence of your paragraph will indicate what will follow. This signaling type of sentence is usually called the topic sentence. The sentences that follow should be logically connected to each other. In a sense, each paragraph is a mini-project because most paragraphs will begin with a topic sentence, explore and analyze the idea introduced by the topic sentence, and then wrap up. You can see that such an approach is a mirror image of any project, with its beginning, middle, and end. Readers should be able to read the topic sentence in each paragraph and understand the thrust of the paragraph. Some readers may read only the first sentence of each paragraph. Your project should be written such that these first sentences, read alone, carry the reader through the project.

Each section of your project should include a thesis statement, an assertive sentence or two that provides a framework for the discussion to follow and states the main point you are making. All sentences that follow elaborate the point you made in your thesis statement and flow from it. Review each paragraph to ensure that every sentence in the paragraph falls under the umbrella of your thesis statement. (See Chapter 7 and Chapter 8 for more information on drafting thesis statements.)

(2) Paragraph Length. Avoid paragraphs that are too long. How long is too long? Most readers have difficulty with paragraphs that cover more than half a page. Not only does the mind crave a break from a long discussion, so does the eye. Remember the visual effect of your writing and create a document that is pleasing to the eye. If your project contains several paragraphs that are more than half a page, find a place to break the information into shorter paragraphs. Although most writers have been taught that every paragraph needs at least three sentences, don't adopt such a rigid and formulaic approach to your writing. Let the subject matter guide you. Too many short paragraphs will look choppy and incomplete, but on occasion you may want to use a one- or two-sentence paragraph for emphasis and visual effect.

(3) Moving Between Ideas. To move smoothly from one sentence, paragraph, or idea to another, use a transition word, phrase, or sentence. Without transitions, ideas would appear unconnected, and there would be a telegram-like appearance and sound to the writing. Transitions connect what you have said with what will follow and lead readers logically from one idea to the next. Review the material on transition words and expressions in Section E.10 of Chapter 4 and use some variety in your transitional expressions. Word patterns such as *first, second,* and so forth also serve to link ideas. Review each paragraph of your project. In the margin of your draft, summarize in a word or key phrase the topic of the paragraph. Then review only these words or phrases to ensure that the development of your argument or project is logical and that each paragraph leads smoothly into the next. Do not end a paragraph with a mere restatement of your topic sentence. For example, if your paragraph begins *Sexual harassment in the workplace is prohibited under 42 U.S.C. § 2000e (2006),* the last sentence should not read *Therefore, as stated earlier, such sexual harassment is prohibited under 42 U.S.C. § 2000e (2006).* A better conclusion would read *Therefore, because Defendant's conduct was unwelcome to the Plaintiff and created a hostile work environment, 42 U.S.C. § 2000(e) has been violated.*

c. Conclusions

Some documents, such as court briefs, call for formal conclusions, whereas others, such as letters, end with traditional "call me if you have any questions" sentences. If your document includes a formal conclusion, review it for two possible defects: Make sure that it does not introduce any information or idea that has not been previously discussed, and make sure that it doesn't simply repeat the central issue you formulated in the introduction. Leave the reader with a strong impression.

Tip → Don't Begin at the Beginning

If you have difficulty writing your introductory paragraphs in a project, save them until the end. On many occasions, you will not have a clear idea what your project will say until you have finished writing it. At that time you may be better able to write an effective thesis statement or introductory section.

4. Using Position and Voice for Emphasis

In nearly every persuasive writing project (for example, briefs submitted to a court), there are stronger points and then points writers wish they did not have to mention. Use the location or placement of the information as well as voice to draw your reader's attention to the more compelling parts of your argument and to minimize the effect of "negative" or weak sections of your project. There are four strategies to follow:

a. Start and End Strong

The most prominent parts of a writing are its beginning and its ending. Readers tend to begin projects with enthusiasm, lose interest in the middle, and then become more attentive again when the end is in sight. Therefore, put your strongest arguments and information at the beginning and ending of your projects, your paragraphs, and your sentences.

b. Bury Negative Information

Address negative or weak spots in the middle of your project, in the middle of your paragraphs, and in the middle of your sentences. These locations attract the least attention and may even be overlooked. Be very careful when including these unfavorable portions of your writing because a careless spelling error or typo will immediately draw your reader's attention. Remember that the persuasive writing style used in briefs differs from the objective style used in legal memoranda. As is discussed in Chapter 7, in such objective projects, the writer must disclose possible weaknesses in the case. Consequently, in these writings, you will not bury negative information but will give it as much emphasis as positive information.

c. Use Passive Voice

Because active voice is much stronger and more forceful than passive voice, consider using passive voice in discussing information you wish to minimize. Review the following two sentences:

Active Voice:	*The defendant intentionally sold a house with known defects to the plaintiff.*
Passive Voice:	*The house was sold to the plaintiff.*

You can readily see that the plaintiff would prefer the first version, whereas the defendant would prefer the second. By using the passive voice you deflect attention away from the actor (the defendant) and onto the object of the action (the sale of the house). Note how the use of the passive voice in the second sentence eliminates any reference whatsoever to the defendant.

d. Avoid Forceful Language

The techniques described in Section E of Chapter 4 for making writing vivid, such as selecting descriptive and concrete words and avoiding nominalizations, should not be used when discussing negative information. Although providing detail is helpful in describing favorable facts and issues, consider discussing unfavorable facts and issues in a more general fashion.

5. Avoid Micro-Editing During the Drafting Stage

No matter what kind of document you draft, consider the following strategy: Avoid micro-editing during the writing process. Agonizing over the choice of each word and continually rephrasing sentences may be a waste of time and energy if you later decide to omit a section. Do not interpret this suggestion to mean that no revisions should be done during the writing process. It is both helpful and necessary to revise throughout the writing process. Do not, however, write your initial draft expecting that it will be the same as the final version. Insert reminders to yourself in the draft, such as "work on this" or "revise," to remind you that further work needs to be done in a certain section. When writing, if you cannot decide between two ways of expressing an idea, include them both and decide later which version to keep.

6. What to Do with Extra Material

If your first draft includes information you cannot find a place for, do not delete it. Create a new folder called "Notes and Extras" and drop the miscellaneous information into it. At the end of your project, print and review all of these notes to determine if they should be re-inserted into your project.

C. Methods of Writing

There are three primary methods used for the actual writing process: writing by hand, dictating, and writing on a word processor. Each offers some advantages.

1. Writing by Hand

Many writers are comfortable writing in longhand. As you would expect, writing in longhand is the most time-consuming method of writing. Despite this, projects written in longhand often need less revising than projects dictated or composed on a word processor. Some experts believe that the neurological process that directs thought, through fingers, is highly sophisticated and that those who write in long-hand learn to express their thoughts clearly and completely. Some writers use a combination of techniques and write delicate or complex sections in longhand so they can test for tone and accuracy and then compose other parts of the project on a word processor.

2. Dictating

Using a dictation machine is a very speedy method of writing. It can take some time, however, to shed self-consciousness when you dictate. Consider using a mini-outline when you first begin to dictate and follow it as you dictate. With time and practice, you will acquire skill at dictating together with a certain mental discipline enabling you rapidly and effectively to organize your thoughts. This skill in orally expressing complex thoughts may translate into ease and confidence in public speaking as well. Enhanced competence in oral presentation is one of the hidden benefits of dictating.

If you dictate, you will need to insert punctuation and paragraphing so the transcriber knows how to prepare the document. Similarly, you will need to spell certain words.

The popularity of dictating in law practice has waned significantly in recent years as writers have become more familiar with composing using a word processor. Nevertheless, dictating remains an effective and efficient way to draft for some writers.

3. Using a Word Processor

The most popular method of writing is composing using a word processor. Although this method is very speedy and allows considerable flexibility in changing the placement of sections, writers tend to spend excessive time revising as they go along. Do not engage in this micro-editing at the first draft stage. Every time you stop to correct minor errors that you or your spell checker can catch at a later stage is a disruption and a time waster. Your project need not be perfect with the first draft. Your initial draft should focus on including the major issues and arguments that need to be addressed. Allow your first draft to flow smoothly, and then devote effort to revision later.

If you use a word processor, consider the following:

- Save your versions frequently. Save every five to ten minutes. Most computers have functions that allow you to select how frequently the document will be saved.
- To ensure that you don't lose important information, back up your versions on disks, frequently print paper copies of the document in case the disk is corrupted, and email your document to your personal email account or to a friend for safekeeping. Use a cloud computing service such as Dropbox or iCloud to store your data.
- Use the features of your word processor to help you. Consider using the "track changes" feature to show changes between drafts. With a single keystroke, you can then accept (or reject) all changes. This feature, called *redlining*, is used when legal professionals negotiate the form and content of a document because it allows each to see at a glance the changes made by the other.
- Recognize that viewing the project one screen at a time allows you to see only a "slice" of the document. Thus, headings and other items may become inconsistent. You will need to review a hard copy of your project to check for consistency in the presentation of such items.

Tips ➡ For Getting Started

A writer keeps surprising himself . . . he doesn't know what he is saying until he sees it on the page.

Thomas Williams

For some writers, getting started is the most difficult part of a project. Consider the following strategies to break writer's block:

- **Write Something.** Write anything. Just get started. Don't assume you have to start with the beginning. Begin with the part of the project with which you are most comfortable, whether it is the statement of facts, the part of the project that is the strongest, or the conclusion. The mere act of writing any section of the project will jar a writer's block. Try freewriting, as discussed in Section B.1 of this chapter.

(continued)

Tips ➡ For Getting Started

- **Start with the Easiest Task.** If the project has several elements, start with the easiest portion, even if it is merely photocopying the exhibits, checking citation form, or preparing the table of authorities. At least you will have made some progress.
- **Tell a Story.** Just as story telling is a good organization technique, it is a good technique for getting started. Speak about the project to a friend or colleague (or close your office door and pretend to do so). This may suggest ideas on how to begin writing.
- **Set Small Goals.** Tell yourself that the statement of facts must be completed by noon. Challenge yourself to complete a certain task within one hour. Make sure the goals are reasonable, however, so that you don't set yourself up for disappointment.
- **Bargain with Yourself.** Consider making a bargain with yourself that you will work for only ten minutes on the project. Work as hard as you can, and at the end of ten minutes, give yourself permission to quit. You may well find that you've created some momentum, and you may decide to work a bit longer, making a bigger dent in your project.
- **Go Public.** Announce a "drop dead" date to a supervisor by saying, "This will be on your desk by Tuesday." You will now be committed to a deadline.
- **Keep Going.** If you draw a blank, just keep going. Move to another section and come back to the difficult spot later. If you think of two alternative ways of phrasing things, write them both, and remove one later. Mark these sections with sticky notes if writing in longhand and with "xx" or some other signal if you are word processing. You can use the "find and replace" feature to locate these troublesome passages later. Don't worry about getting it perfect; just get it done.
- **Minimize Disruptions.** Work in a place conducive to working. Put your calls on hold, close your office door, move to the library, and avoid email. If you are disrupted, leave a sticky note on your computer screen to remind yourself what you wanted to next address, or type a quick line into the draft about what you expect to do next.
- **Avoid Self-Censoring.** One of the biggest stumbling blocks to writing is that writers become so self-conscious they cannot go forward. Don't worry at this stage that something will sound awkward, unsophisticated, or silly. Understand that your first draft is just that—the first of many drafts. Allow this understanding to free you to write quickly. Don't worry about spelling, grammar, and formatting at this point. You can clean up all these problems during the revision process.

sectionthree

Legal Documents, Legal Conventions, and Common Legal Writing Blunders

■ **Section Three** of the Handbook describes the most commonly prepared documents in law practice: letters, memoranda, court briefs, pleadings, and transactional documents. Several tips and strategies for preparing these very different documents are given and sample documents are provided. This section also discusses some of the standard customs and practices seen in legal writing and some of the common faults made by beginning legal writers.

chapter 6

Legal Correspondence

StyleLinks

www.writing-business-letters.com
This site provides information on writing formal business letters with checklists
and links to numerous other resources.

http://libguides.law.ucla.edu
UCLA's School of Law offers helpful guides to legal writing. Select "Legal
Writing."

www.michbar.org/journal/pdf/pdf4article449.pdf
Wayne Schiess, writing for the *Michigan Bar Journal*, offers advice on writing
client letters.

A. The Elements of a Letter

1. Introduction

Although you will write different types of letters, there are certain "basics" that are common to all legal correspondence. The elements of legal correspondence are similar to those of general business letters. Many law firms have practice guides and templates specifying the format for all firm letters. Following are the standard components of legal correspondence.

a. Letterhead

Law firms, government offices and agencies, and corporations all use special stationery, called *letterhead*, that identifies the office by name, address, telephone and facsimile numbers, website address, and other relevant information. The information is usually at the top of the page but it is sometimes located at the bottom or along the left side of the page. Law firms with a few attorneys list all attorneys on the letterhead; law firms with several attorneys usually issue personalized letterhead to each attorney with his or her own name and email address. Use letterhead for all correspondence associated with your firm or company. Letterhead is used only for the first page of a letter. The remaining pages match the color and quality of the letterhead page but are not imprinted with the letterhead information. When drafting a letter, be sure to remember how much space the letterhead will take up in the final version.

b. Date

Every item of correspondence must include a date, written out in full by month, day, and year (for example, *August 6, 2012*). Do not use abbreviations or numbers, as in *7/23/12*. The date is usually centered two or three lines below the letterhead, although it is occasionally placed at the left margin. Because the dates in legal matters are critical, be sure the date given is the date the letter is actually mailed or sent, rather than the date of an earlier draft.

c. Special Notations

If your correspondence will be sent to the recipient by any means other than first class mail, indicate such as follows: *Hand Delivered*, or *Registered Mail*, or *By Email*. This notation should be placed at the left margin two lines below the date and two lines above the inside address. Similarly, any other special notations (often called *legends*), such as *Attorney-Client Communication—Privileged and Confidential*, should appear above the inside address.

d. Inside Address

The name and address of the recipient should appear two lines below the date or any special notations. Always follow the addressee's or organization's preferences for spelling, capitalization, and punctuation. Review the company's letterhead, written materials, or website to ensure accuracy. Include titles, if appropriate, such as Hillary Young, M.D., Jose Moreno, Esq., or Mr. Gary F. Kimball, Executive Vice President. For female recipients, use *Ms.* unless directed otherwise. The form *Mrs. William Trainor* is acceptable only in social letters. Use *Ms. Madelyn G. Trainor* in business and legal letters. See Figure 6-1 for sample inside addresses.

e. Reference or Subject Notation

The reference notation indicates the subject matter of the correspondence. The notation may refer to the title of a case, the topic to be discussed in the letter, or a file or claim number. The reference notation gives the reader an immediate snapshot of what is to be discussed and also helps you later if you need to locate a letter you previously wrote. The reference notation (abbreviated as *Re:*) is usually placed two lines below the inside address. It is placed either at the left margin or indented five spaces. As a courtesy to your reader, include his or her file or reference number if you know it, following your own reference notation.

Some sample reference notations follow:

Re: *Cochran v. Templeton Auto, Inc.*
       San Diego Superior Court Case No. 12-1324

Re: Estate of Phillips
       Our File: TM-1205
       Your File: 90126-CMM

Re: Remedies for Copyright Infringement

f. Salutation

The salutation, or greeting, is usually placed two lines below the reference notation. Unless you are well acquainted with the addressee, err on the side of formality and address the letter to Mr. Morales or Ms. Vance (rather than *Dear Mike* or *Dear Jill*). Again, unless you have been directed otherwise, address letters to females as *Ms.*

Figure 6-1   Sample Inside Addresses

Ms. Donna A. Higgins
2728 Belle Haven Drive
Alexandria, VA 22089

Janet R. Reynolds, Esq.
Allen, Calderson & Bell, L.L.P.
1776 K Street, N.W.
Washington, D.C. 20006-1819

Mr. Allen T. Navarro
Executive Vice President
Falcon Enterprises, Inc.
1893 Bowen Street
Chicago, IL 18890-1467

Director of Human Resources
Whitney Management, Inc.
2900 Arlington Avenue
Irving, TX 75248-3189

Letters to an unknown recipient should be directed to *Dear Sir or Madam.* If you know a title, you may use that, as in *Dear Commissioner.* Some letters to unknown individuals are addressed *Dear Colleague.* Salutations in business and legal letters are usually followed by a colon (although it is becoming more common to see commas used, perhaps as a sign of increased informality). See Section G of Chapter 1 for additional information on addressing individuals. Although the use of the word *Dear* in a salutation may seem overly familiar, omitting it makes a letter seem abrupt. Once you have written the salutation, do not refer to the reader by name again in the letter. Thus, do not write, *You, Mrs. Dailey, should consider the following . . . .*

In one particularly odd construction, some letters are typed "Dear Mr. Brown" and then the author will use a pen to strike through this salutation and handwrite "Bill." Avoid this contrived way to show friendliness.

g. Body

The body of the letter begins two lines below the salutation. The body is the most critical part of your correspondence because it conveys your message. The first sentence and paragraph should set the stage for the rest of your letter by indicating the purpose of the letter. Use descriptive headings in a letter only if it is so long or complex that the reader will need signals as to the sections of the letter being discussed.

Business letters and legal correspondence are usually single-spaced and then double-spaced between paragraphs. Although the second and subsequent pages of a letter will not be on letterhead, they will contain a "header" as follows:

Mr. Allen T. Navarro
Page Two
August 6, 2012

h. Closing and Signature Block

Most letters close with statements such as the following:

- Please do not hesitate to call me if you have any questions.
- Thank you in advance for your cooperation and courtesy.
- If you have any questions or comments you may reach me at the number given above.
- I look forward to meeting you next Tuesday, January 15, 2013.

The complimentary closing is usually *Sincerely, Very truly yours, Best regards,* or something similar, followed by a comma. *Very truly yours* is generally regarded as more formal and is probably used less frequently than *Sincerely.* Don't agonize over the choice of the closing because most readers don't pay a great deal of attention to this portion of a letter. If the letter is addressed to a judge, representative, or senator, you typically would use the complimentary closing *Respectfully.* Capitalize the first letter in the complimentary closing and place it two lines below the last line in the body of the letter. The closing is usually centered (although it is placed at the left margin in a block-style letter, as discussed later).

Avoid informal or unusual closings such as *Affectionately*, or *Successfully yours*. Do not merge your complimentary closing with the last line of your letter. These merged closings were fashionable hundreds of years ago but have a stilted and archaic look. An example of a merged closing is as follows:

> *Thanking you for your attention, I remain,*
> *Yours very truly,*
> Samantha Bianco

If your name is not on the letterhead, type your title underneath your typed name so that the reader will know your position in the firm. Allow four blank lines between the complimentary close and your typed name, aligned, for your handwritten signature. This section of the letter is called the signature block. Some writers prefer to use blue ink for their signatures, so readers can easily tell the document is an original rather than a copy.

i. Reference Initials, Enclosures, and Copies

Most letters indicate the author and typist by a reference as follows: *GAK/jal*, which would indicate that the author was Gregory A. Kelly and the typist or word processor was Judith A. Lane. Using the form *gak:jal* is also common. These reference initials are placed at the left margin on the second line below the writer's name and title. If you prepared or typed your own letter, omit this section.

If you are enclosing something in a letter, indicate this with the word *Enclosure* or its abbreviation *Encl.* (or *Enclosures* or *Encls.* for more than one enclosure), placed at the left margin one line below the reference initials. Some writers list or identify the items enclosed. Avoid archaic expressions such as *enclosed herewith please find*. A simple *enclosed is* is sufficient. Other writers prefer to use the term *Attachments* when documents are physically attached to the letter or to correspondence sent by email.

Copies of the letter you write may be sent to others. For example, the client will routinely be provided with copies of letters sent about the client's case because this is a way of keeping the client informed of the progress of a case. To indicate the recipients of copies, use *cc:* followed by the names of those who will be receiving copies (in alphabetical order), placed at the left margin one line below the enclosure notation. Although *cc:* originally stood for *carbon copies*, which have universally been replaced by photocopies or print-outs, the signal *cc:* remains in use and likely now stands for *courtesy copies*.

There may be instances in which you do not want the reader of your letter to know who will receive a copy of it. In such cases, simply sign your letter, mail it, and then mark the copies that will go to the unidentified individual (assume Mark Grayson) and that will be placed in the file *bcc: Mark Grayson*. This is a reference to *blind carbon copy*.

See Figure 6-2 for elements of letters.

Figure 6-2   Quick Reference: Elements of Letters

- **Letterhead:** The sender's name, address, and other pertinent information, usually centered
- **Date:** Centered two or three lines below letterhead with no abbreviations
- **Special Notations:** Indications of method of sending, privileges claimed, and so forth, at left margin, two lines below date
- **Inside Address:** Recipient's name and address, at left margin, two lines below special notations
- **Reference Notation:** Reference to case name, topic of letter, and so forth, at left margin, or indented five spaces, two lines below inside address (usually shown as "Re:")
- **Salutation:** Opening greeting, addressing all individuals as *Mr.* or *Ms.* unless directed otherwise and followed by a colon, placed two lines below reference notation
- **Body of Letter:** Begins two lines below salutation, single-spaced, with double-spacing between paragraphs, which may be indented five spaces or not indented
- **Complimentary Closing:** A closing phrase or word such as *Sincerely,* usually centered, appearing two lines below last line of body of letter
- **Signature Block:** Writer's name and title, aligned with complimentary close, four lines below complimentary close
- **Final Notations:** References to writer's and typist's initials, enclosures, and indications of those who will receive copies of letter, all appearing at left margin, beginning two lines below signature block, each appearing one line below the other

2. Format Considerations

The presentation and "look and feel" of a letter have an effect on its readability. Following are some items to consider when formatting a letter.

a. Size of Paper and Spacing

Letters are written on standard 8½" x 11" paper and are usually single-spaced and then double-spaced between component parts (for example, between the date and inside address, between the inside address and reference notation, between the reference notation and salutation, and between the body and the complimentary close) and between paragraphs.

b. Arrangement and Indenting

Some letters show no indentations for paragraphs because new paragraphs are clearly indicated by the double-spacing between paragraphs. This style is referred to as "full block form" or "left justified." In full block form, all elements of the letter, including the date and complimentary closing, begin at the left margin, and paragraphs are not indented. This is the style commonly provided as a template by most word processing programs.

The more traditional approach is to indent five spaces for new paragraphs even though they are set apart from each other by double-spacing. This style is called "modified block form." Here the date, complimentary closing, and signature block are all centered.

c. Margins and Justification

When the right-hand margin is even and every line ends at the right at the same point (as in this text), this is referred to as "right justification" or "full justification." Such letters present a very crisp appearance. One drawback, however, is that to ensure each line stops at the same spot, the computer will automatically readjust spacing, sometimes cramping some words, expanding others, and leaving "rivers" of white space running vertically through the body of the text. Reading studies show that fully justified documents are more difficult to read because the added spaces eliminate distinctive word spatial characteristics, which are needed to aid comprehension and ease of reading. Continuing improvements in word processing programs are eliminating these spacing problems. Nevertheless, some writers prefer the traditional "ragged edge" at the right margin, believing it makes the letter look less like a computer-generated form letter and more personalized. Most word processing programs now offer letter templates for business letters in which spacing and common closings are already included, allowing you to "fill in the blanks" of the form. Spacing is preset as well.

d. Widows and Orphans

Never allow a page to begin with the last line of a paragraph (called a "widow") or to end with a heading or a single line of a paragraph on the bottom of a page (called an "orphan"). Keep at least two lines of text together. Lonely lines present an unprofessional appearance. Many word processing programs have built-in features to eliminate widows and orphans.

e. Font and Typeface

Use 12-point type size for readability and use a standard typeface, such as Times New Roman or Courier. The Rules of the Supreme Court mandate type size of 12-point. Sup. Ct. R. 33. Fonts and typefaces are discussed further in Chapter 12.

B. The Audience and Tone for Legal Correspondence

I didn't have time to write a short letter, so I wrote a long one instead.
Usually attributed to Blaise Pascal

Unlike other legal writings, such as wills, pleadings, and court briefs, there is no rigid list of elements that must be included in a letter. Though all letters should, of course, contain the basics (date, salutation, body, and closing), you will be able to exercise creativity in letter writing based on the goal you seek to achieve in your letter. The tone you adopt and the order in which you elect to discuss items are at your discretion. To beginning legal writers this flexibility can be intimidating. Without a rigid format to follow, some writers become paralyzed.

Letters can be extremely effective tools. The first letter sent to a client or adversary often establishes the basis for a relationship. If your letter to adverse counsel is hostile and arrogant, you will be responded to in kind, and this will mark the tone of future communications. You never merely write; you write *to* someone. Thus, you need to do some planning and thinking before you write.

There are two critical questions to address before you begin a letter:

- Who will be reading this letter?
- What is the purpose of this letter?

The answer to the first question will set the tone for your letter, and the answer to the second question will tell you what type of letter you should write. Finally, letters to opposing counsel must be carefully drafted.

1. Who Will Be Reading This Letter?

The tone or style of your letter must be tailored to the reader. If the letter is directed to a layperson or a person inexperienced with litigation or the topic of the letter, you will need to explain the information you present in the most clear and complete fashion possible. If the letter is directed to another legal professional, you will know that your discussion of some matters need not be as detailed or elementary as for the lay reader.

If you find your letter is becoming stuffy and legalistic in style, there are three techniques you can use to warm up the tone and improve readability:

- **Use Personal Pronouns.** Using personal pronouns, especially *you*, does much to warm up a letter. Thus, rather than writing *Patentees have the right to sue for infringement of a patent*, write *As the holder of a patent, you have the right to sue for infringement*. A danger in addressing readers, however, is that it often causes a pronoun shift, as in the following: *When one alleges the alter ego doctrine, you generally try to prove a lack of corporate formalities*. In correspondence, check for pronoun shifts.

- **Use Contractions.** Although contractions are not commonly used in legal or business writing, their use in letters is more common because they tend to make letters more personal. For example, rather than writing *Patentees cannot obtain monetary damages more than six years after infringement*, write *You can't obtain money damages if infringement occurred more than six years ago.*
- **Use Headings.** Although headings are not commonly used in correspondence, you should include them in long or complex letters if they will aid comprehension. Headings provide visual relief and information cues for the reader in lengthy letters. Simple headings such as *Damages* and *Fraud* are sufficient.

2. What Is the Purpose of This Letter?

Before you begin writing any letter, focus on the central purpose of the letter. Try to distill this to one or two sentences. For example, some purposes may be as follows:

- A client needs to know a deposition has been scheduled for next month.
- A debtor needs to understand that failure to repay a debt will result in litigation.
- A client needs advice as to whether a trademark has been abandoned.

These examples represent three basic types of legal correspondence: *general correspondence* or *informative letters, demand letters,* and *opinion letters.* Once you determine what type of letter you will be writing, the appropriate style will follow naturally.

3. Special Audience: Letters to Opposing Counsel

One particular type of letter deserves special attention: letters to opposing counsel. Those new to the legal profession often fail to understand that they will likely work with the same attorneys numerous times over the course of their careers. Starting such a long-term relationship off on the wrong foot will cause a host of problems over the years and will certainly work a disservice to the client because any incivility you create will cause the other attorney to doubt your word and to demand everything in writing, causing expense to the client. Thus, remember the following when corresponding with adverse counsel:

- **Be generous.** Give your adversary the benefit of the doubt—at least the first time. If there is some dispute, be cordial, and state *Perhaps I miscommunicated . . .* rather than *It is clear that you misunderstood me.*
- **Be courteous.** Rather than writing a letter merely to confirm an extension or favor granted to you, use the opportunity to thank the party for the extension or favor. Thus, instead of writing, *I am confirming the extension . . .* write, *Thank you for granting the extension.* Avoid writing letters when you're angry

(or write the letter when you're angry, but don't send it). It costs nothing to be civil, courteous, and polite.

- **Apologize.** Apologize when you need to do so (and do so promptly). Don't make excuses or blame others by stating, *I apologize but you should have informed me* . . . . This is not an apology; it is an attack. Similarly, a statement such as *I am sorry if you feel* . . . is not an apology; it is a conditional statement. Write, *I am sorry that I* . . . or *I am sorry for any inconvenience this may have caused you.* Accept responsibility for your mistakes.

- **Grant a favor.** If you are asked for an extension of time or to continue a hearing, do so. You will need a favor someday, and you need to build up goodwill so you can ask for an extension if you are ill or have an important personal matter.

- **Watch your tone.** Read and reread your letter to ensure that your tone is businesslike and not accusatory or provocative. Your job is to shepherd the case through for the client in the most efficient and cost-effective way possible—not to create an emotional "win" for yourself. When in doubt, ask a colleague to review your letter for its tone.

A Cautionary Tale: The Perils of Incivility

Nearly every practicing attorney has either heard of or seen a situation in which the attorneys in a case became increasingly adversarial and hostile, sending numerous confrontational and accusatory letters, each of which becomes progressively more uncivil in tone. Eventually, someone makes a motion in the case, and all of the negative correspondence is attached to the motion, becoming a permanent part of the court record. The judge then chastises the parties from the bench, pointing out their incivility for everyone in the courtroom to hear, embarrassing everyone. Before you write a letter with an unfriendly tone, ask yourself, *Would I want this to be part of the court record?*

C. Types of Letters

1. General Correspondence

General correspondence letters may include letters requesting information or responding to requests for information, cover letters that accompany documents, confirmation letters that confirm some agreement or arrangement reached with another, or status or report letters providing a report to a client or insurance company on the progress of a matter. Except for status letters, these letters are often brief and may be only one or two paragraphs in length.

Follow these guidelines in preparing general correspondence:

- Include the standard components of letters described previously.
- Comply with the elements of good legal writing, such as precision, clarity, and so forth. Watch the details: If you misspell the client's name or misstate a dollar figure or a date, this will attract more attention than the substance of the letter.
- When in doubt, send a confirming letter. Confirming letters keep the file complete and help establish the progress of a case. Always send a letter to adverse counsel to confirm dates, amounts, or any other matter, such as an extension of time to respond to interrogatories. Use the confirmation letter as an opportunity to say "thank you" for any favor granted. Send a copy to the client.
- If you would like to demonstrate trust in your adversary or wish to decrease the formality and amount of correspondence in a case, you may send an email confirming a date or thanking the recipient. Comply with rules of grammar, spelling, and so forth, and print a copy for your files so that if a dispute later arises, you will be able to show your understanding of the agreement.

The Royal We

Should letters be written in the *I/me* form or the *we/our* form? Should the author say *It is my* opinion or *It is our* opinion? It depends. Consider the following:

- If the letter is from a sole practitioner, it should always be written in the *I* form.
- If the letter is written on behalf of the entire firm or a company, the *we* form is usually used.
- Most law firms take the approach that legal opinion letters provide the opinion of the firm, not the individual writer, and therefore all of their opinion letters are written in the *we* form. The letter is then signed by a partner or member on behalf of the firm itself.
- Follow your firm or office practice.

☐ **Warning: Letters providing legal opinions or giving legal advice can only be signed by properly licensed attorneys.**

2. Demand Letters

Demand letters set forth a client's demands. The most common type of demand letter is a collection letter, which outlines the basis for a debt due to a client and demands that it be paid. Other demand letters, however, demand action rather than money, for example, a demand that a landlord repair a leaky roof or that a company cease using a trademark. Your tone should be firm and businesslike, not strident.

Consider the strategy underlying the demand letter. In some instances, sending a demand letter is a statutory requirement. For example, in some states, litigation may not be instituted in certain cases unless a notice of the claim is first sent to the potential defendant. The demand letter satisfies these requirements.

To eliminate any disputes as to whether and when the letter was received, send the letter by some verifiable type of delivery, such as registered mail.

The only portion of the letter that will differ from a general correspondence letter is the content of the body of the letter.

a. Elements of Demand Letters

Include the following elements in any demand letter:

- **Introduction.** The letter should begin with an identification of your firm or company and your role, such as *We represent Ms. June Matthews regarding her automobile accident of April 8, 2013.*
- **Recitation of Facts.** Include the facts underlying the client's claim. Because your aim is to motivate the reader to take some action, phrase the factual statement as persuasively as possible.
- **Demand.** State the client's demand as clearly as possible. If this is a collection letter, specify the exact amount due. If you are demanding that the recipient take some action, such as replacing an appliance, say so. If there are several components to your demand, you may wish to set them forth in a bulleted list.
- **Consequences of Noncompliance.** Tell the reader the consequences of not complying with the demand letter. These consequences may include litigation, stopping work on a project, eviction, or some other adverse action. Although most readers will be offended by heavy-handed threats, there is nothing wrong in plainly stating what will occur if the client's demands are not met.
- **Date of Compliance.** State clearly the deadline for compliance. Do not say *You must pay the sum of $10,000 immediately.* Specify an express date, such as *by close of business on May 15, 2013*, so the reader will know exactly when compliance is expected.

b. Some Common Pitfalls in Demand Letters

Demand letters fail to meet their objectives for a variety of reasons. Following are some of the more common failings in demand letters.

(1) Factual Pitfalls. Be sure you have all the relevant facts. If a client informs you that a debtor has breached a written contract, review the contract itself, rather than accepting the client's oral summary of it. A mistake in reciting the facts will result in an immediate response by the recipient pointing out the error, and any momentum you may have had, along with your credibility, will be lost. Consider sending a draft of the demand letter to the client for review and approval before sending the letter to the intended recipient.

(2) Legal Pitfalls. You cannot send a letter demanding money for breach of contract if enforcement of the contract and threatening litigation are barred by the statute of limitations or some other law. You must conduct some minimum amount of research to ensure that the client's claim is valid and enforceable.

☐ **Ethics Warnings**
- ○ **It is a violation of ethics codes to correspond with a person who is represented by counsel. Make sure the recipient is not represented by counsel before you send the letter.**
- ○ **It is unethical to threaten criminal prosecution if the recipient will not comply with the demand. Review your state's code of professional conduct.**
- ○ **Most states have consumer protection laws regulating demands for payments of certain types of debts. Research your state's consumer debt laws and the Fair Debt Collection Practices Act at 15 U.S.C. §§ 1692-1692p (2006).**

(3) Inappropriate Tone and Content. The letter should be reasonable, firm, and businesslike. Overt threats and name-calling are not only inappropriate but also ineffective. There are two demand letter tactics that are notoriously ineffective: accusing the recipient of fraud and sending copies of the letter to others, such as to a debtor's employer or insurer. These tactics usually produce such outrage in the recipient that chances for settling the dispute amicably will vanish.

(4) Arguing the Case. A demand letter should not present all the evidence you would need to prevail at trial. The recipient will likely know some of the facts relating to the claim, and you need not provide copies of every item of correspondence and the name of every witness who supports the client's version of the matter. If the problem cannot be resolved by direct negotiation, you will have ample opportunity to argue the case during the litigation stage. Don't tip your hand at this juncture. Although a few legal authorities may be cited in some instances, most collection and demand letters rarely include legal analysis.

(5) Failure to Follow Through. If you have told the recipient of the letter that legal action will be instituted by May 15 unless the amount of $10,000 is paid to the client, you must be prepared to follow through on that statement. Nothing jeopardizes credibility more than empty threats. If the client is unsure what action he or she intends to take if the demand is not met, you can create some "wiggle room" by writing one of the following:

- ▪ *We look forward to receiving your response to this letter by May 15;*
- ▪ *Please contact us to discuss this matter further; or*
- ▪ *Unless we receive a satisfactory response from you by May 15, we will take all appropriate legal action.*

Telling the recipient of the letter to make a counterproposal is a serious concession and invites the recipient to play "let's make a deal." See Figure 6-3 for a sample demand letter.

Figure 6-3   Sample Demand Letter

Schillings & Sanders, LLP
1006 Peachtree Street
Atlanta, Georgia 30309
(404) 571-2209

February 8, 2013

Ms. Denise Bailey
1227 Fairview Drive
Atlanta, GA 22055

Re: Fairview Oaks Homeowners' Association
         Conditions, Covenants, and Restrictions

Dear Ms. Bailey:

We represent Fairview Oaks Homeowners' Association (the "Association"), the homeowners' association for Fairview Oaks, the neighborhood in which you live and which is subject to certain Conditions, Covenants, and Restrictions ("CC & Rs") that govern appearance, use, landscaping, and other matters for the homes in Fairview Oaks.

All property owners of Fairview Oaks are subject to these CC & Rs, which are recorded with the county recorder for Fulton County, Georgia, and which were provided to you in 2010 at the time your purchased your home in Fairview Oaks. As you may know, CC & Rs are viewed by courts as enforceable contracts between homeowners and their associations.

Section 4 of the CC & Rs provides as follows: "No temporary house, shack, shed, storage structure, or tent shall be erected, placed, or maintained on property within Fairview Oaks." We have been informed that you have placed a metal shed on your property, which is apparently used to store your lawn and pool equipment. Your placement and maintenance of this shed is a clear violation of the CC & Rs.

Ms. Denise Bailey
Page Two
February 8, 2013

Under Section 20 of the CC & Rs, the Association is required to enforce the CC & Rs and may recover attorneys' fees and costs in any action in which it is successful in enforcing those CC & Rs. Thus, the Association demands that you remove the shed from your property before **March 11, 2013.** If you fail to remove the shed, the Association will bring an action against you seeking an injunction ordering you to remove the shed.

We urge you to comply with the terms of this letter as indicated so you may avoid costly and burdensome litigation, including attorneys' fees and costs, which will be incurred by you if the Association is required to bring an action against you to comply with the CC & Rs.

We look forward to receiving confirmation of your compliance with the CC & Rs by **March 11, 2013.**

Sincerely,

Schillings & Sanders, LLP

SMS/ajk
cc: Fairview HOA

3. Opinion Letters and Their Elements

Letters offering legal advice or opinions can be signed only by attorneys. In some firms, opinion letters can be signed only by a partner after review by another partner or an opinions committee. In many law firms, the opinion letter is signed by a partner on behalf of the entire firm, signaling that the opinion is not provided by any single attorney but rather by the firm itself. Although opinion letters are usually sought by clients seeking advice on a particular matter, sometimes they are requested by a third party, such as an accountant who requires a legal opinion as to a mutual client's progress in litigation before the accountant prepares financial statements.

Opinion letters should contain the standard components of a letter (reference line, salutation, and so forth). Opinion letters should include a legend that they are subject to attorney-client privilege to protect them against later discovery. These letters also share some features in common with research memoranda, although their analysis of legal authorities is more simplified, and they are usually written to a client rather than to another legal professional.

Opinion letters contain the following elements:

a. Date

Although all letters include dates, the date of an opinion letter is especially important because the opinion will relate to the status of the law on that date. Changes in the law after that date may well affect the correctness of the opinion.

b. Introductory Language

It is often a good idea to remind the client why the opinion is being provided. Such an introduction also establishes the scope of the letter by stating the issue that the letter will address. Consider the following introductions:

- *We enjoyed meeting you last week. As you requested, we have researched whether a trademark may be abandoned by nonuse.*
- *Pursuant to our telephone conversation of March 18, 2013, we have reviewed the lease . . .*
- *At your request . . .*
- *You have asked for our opinion whether . . .*

c. Review of Facts

An opinion letter should always set forth the facts on which it is based. Facts are usually given in a narrative (sentence-by-sentence) form rather than in numbered or bulleted list form. Including the facts gives the client the opportunity to correct you if you have misstated the facts. Even a minor factual error, such as in a date or dollar amount, can result in an incorrect opinion. Thus, include the facts so the reader understands that the accuracy of the opinion depends on the specific facts recited. Consider introducing the facts as follows:

- *You have informed us that you signed a written lease on April 30, 2013 . . .*
- *As we understand them, the facts are as follows: On June 24, 2013, you signed a nondisclosure agreement . . .*

d. Opinion

The essence of an opinion letter is the advice given to the client. Clients are particularly interested in the "bottom line," and many writers immediately give their opinion or conclusion after reciting the facts. The conclusion is then followed by an explanation of the opinion. This is an effective technique if the opinion you give is one that is fairly straightforward or will be welcome to the client. On the other hand, if you will be giving the client bad news, such as informing him or her that certain rights have been lost, you may want to lead the reader to this unfavorable news gradually. By explaining the law first, you will be preparing the reader for the unfavorable outcome, so by the time you give the bad news, the reader understands exactly why the outcome is unfavorable. See Figure 6-4. Consider introducing the conclusion as follows:

- *Based upon the facts you provided us and the applicable law in this state, it is our opinion that you may initiate an action for wrongful death against Douglas Sterling.*
- *We have concluded that you may bring an action for wrongful death against Douglas Sterling. Our conclusion is based upon the facts given above and our analysis of Ohio law.*

In any event, be sure your letter answers the client's specific question and is not an abstract discussion of general legal principles.

Figure 6-4   Bad News Bearers

In many instances, letter writers must deliver bad news to clients. In such an event, consider the following approaches:

- If you need to give a client unfavorable news, try to soften the approach by saying *success is extremely unlikely, the chances of a favorable outcome are remote at best,* or *cases similar to yours have been unsuccessful,* rather than a blunt *your case is entirely without merit.*
- Clearly deliver the bad news. Don't soften your approach so much that you haven't accurately conveyed your meaning. Readers often perceive what they want to, and there is no room for ambiguity in delivering unfavorable news to a client. Consider using phrases such as *We regret that the court dismissed your action* or *We are sorry to inform you that the insurance company has rejected your claim.*
- If possible, try to find an alternative avenue for the client, as follows:

    Because the statute of limitations has expired, you will not be able to bring an action against your neighbor for trespass. We would suggest, however, that you attempt to negotiate directly with your neighbor. If this approach is unsuccessful, contact your homeowners' insurance company because it may offer coverage for the damage done to your property.

e. Explanation of Opinion

This portion of the letter explains and summarizes the law on which the opinion is based. Because most opinion letters are written for laypersons who may not be familiar with the law, avoid detailed discussion of statutes and cases. It is usually sufficient to summarize the legal authorities in a general fashion. You should avoid giving citations to cases and statutes unless your reader is sufficiently knowledgeable to understand the citations. Similarly, do not merely retype the text of a statute or case; explain what the case or statute means for this particular matter. Consider the following:

- *Applicable case law provides . . .*
- *We have researched the pertinent statute that governs this matter. It provides . . .*
- *The legal authorities in this state are in agreement that . . .*

If this portion of the letter is long, you may use short headings and subheadings (such as "Damages") to divide your explanation into readable separate sections.

f. Recommendations

After you have explained the law that governs your conclusion, provide a recommendation to the client. Be sure that the recommendation is not unduly optimistic. Phrase advice as a probability rather than a certainty. Thus, write *We believe a court would likely hold that* rather than *Your claim is undoubtedly valid.* Do not include any language that could be construed by the client as a guarantee of success. Conversely, make sure your letter provides an opinion. Wishy-washy phrases such as *It would seem that* or *We are tentatively inclined to think* do not tell the reader anything. Similarly, replace the phrase *We feel* with *We believe* or *It is our opinion that . . . .* It is acceptable to write *We recommend that [or we suggest that] you settle this case.*

g. Instructions

The last portion of an opinion letter is usually a direction to the client to contact the office or take some other action. For example, consider the following:

> *Because the statutes governing this matter require that a claim be submitted to the city within 100 days of the wrongful act, please contact us and provide us with your instructions. Failure to file the claim by **May 1, 2013**, will bar any action against the city.*

If the recipient must take critical action by a certain date, place the date or instruction in bold type or in some otherwise distinctive format.

h. Protection Clauses

On occasion, you may not have all of the information you need to provide a complete opinion. For example, you may be awaiting a copy of a written employment agreement or other document. In such cases, protection clauses (sometimes called *savings* clauses) are used to explain that certain information is lacking or that the opinion may change depending on the information you receive. Similarly, think ahead and consider what defenses or arguments the other party may assert. Prepare your client to meet any challenges. Consider the following examples:

- *This opinion is based upon the facts you have provided us. Once we have had an opportunity to review the addendum to your lease, we will be better able to provide you with our opinion. Assuming the addendum does not materially alter the original lease, however, it is our opinion . . . .*
- *Although your employer may argue his business is not subject to the provisions of the Family Medical Leave Act, we believe such an argument is without merit because . . . .*

See Figure 6-5 for a sample opinion letter.

Figure 6-5   Sample Opinion Letter

Taylor & Aldridge LLP
1401 New Hampshire Avenue, N.W.
Washington, D.C. 20005
(202) 455-1900

July 18, 2012

Privileged and Confidential

Mr. Anthony Fallon
President
WaveLength LLC
5644 Sunset Parkway
Arlington, VA 22201

Re: Monitoring of Employee Internet Use

Dear Mr. Fallon:

We enjoyed meeting you last week. As you requested, we have reviewed whether WaveLength LLC ("WaveLength") may monitor the Internet use of its employees, including their email transmissions.

Mr. Anthony Fallon
Page Two
July 18, 2012

We understand that WaveLength supervisors have observed employees using the Internet during business hours for nonbusiness uses, including shopping, browsing, and personal emailing. Access to the Internet is provided and paid for by WaveLength, and WaveLength owns the computers, laptops, and all electronic systems used by employees at the business premises.

WaveLength is concerned that nonbusiness use of the Internet reduces employee productivity, may subject the company to liability for copyright infringement if employees use the Internet to download software and music illegally, places the company at risk of importing computer viruses, and may subject the company to liability for harassment or defamation if employees engage in such activities using the company's computer systems.

We have reviewed both federal and state law relating to employer monitoring of employee Internet use. The key issues to examine when determining whether an employer may monitor employee Internet use and email messages are whether the employees have a reasonable expectation of privacy at the workplace, and, if so, whether the employer has a justifiable business reason to override that expectation of privacy.

Employers can justify surveillance of employees if employees are informed beforehand of such. Thus, if employers place their monitoring policies in employee handbooks or require employees to sign statements acknowledging the monitoring, such typically precludes employees from asserting that their privacy has been invaded because employees then have no reasonable expectation of privacy. WaveLength's concerns about decreased employee productivity, illegal downloading, and the importing of computer viruses by employees are justifiable business reasons for WaveLength to monitor its employees' use of the Internet.

Accordingly, if WaveLength implements a carefully drafted Internet use policy, presents it to employees who must sign an acknowledgment of receipt of the policy, and consistently enforces the policy, WaveLength should be able to monitor employee Internet use without liability to its employees.

Mr. Anthony Fallon
Page Three
July 18, 2012

Due to the rapidly changing nature of the Internet, the law in this area continues to evolve, and we cannot predict what courts may do in the future. At present, however, if employees are informed of an Internet use and monitoring policy (which is consistently enforced), WaveLength may monitor its employees' Internet use.

Please feel free to call us if you have any questions or comments or if you would like assistance in drafting an Internet use policy.

Sincerely,

Taylor & Aldridge LLP

AMD:fpm

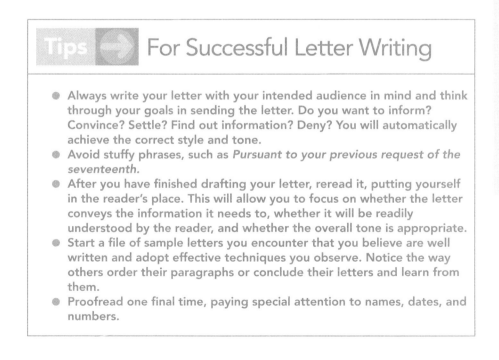

Tips → For Successful Letter Writing

- Always write your letter with your intended audience in mind and think through your goals in sending the letter. Do you want to inform? Convince? Settle? Find out information? Deny? You will automatically achieve the correct style and tone.
- Avoid stuffy phrases, such as *Pursuant to your previous request of the seventeenth.*
- After you have finished drafting your letter, reread it, putting yourself in the reader's place. This will allow you to focus on whether the letter conveys the information it needs to, whether it will be readily understood by the reader, and whether the overall tone is appropriate.
- Start a file of sample letters you encounter that you believe are well written and adopt effective techniques you observe. Notice the way others order their paragraphs or conclude their letters and learn from them.
- Proofread one final time, paying special attention to names, dates, and numbers.

4. Electronic Communications

New forms of communication, namely, electronic communications, have arisen in the past several years, changing the way people communicate in the workplace. Although many of them are great timesavers, others may be traps for the unwary writer. Follow your reader's preferences for communications. If your recipient seldom uses a cell phone or checks email only sporadically, use the telephone instead. To be meaningful, any communication must be received and read.

Some experts advise that any reply to a communication must "meet or exceed" the original communication. Thus, if someone calls you on the telephone, you must either return the call by telephone or "go up one level," such as by sending a letter or meeting personally. If you send a text message in response to a telephone call, it may be viewed as disrespectful.

a. Communicating by Email

StyleLinks

http://writing.colostate.edu/guides/documents/email
This site provides information and tips for effective use of email.

www.emailreplies.com
This site provides helpful information and 32 tips on email etiquette.

Email has become a common method of communication, both within the workplace and with clients. Email creates an air of informality, and the ease with which a message can be composed and sent causes countless errors. We have all heard stories of people who, much to their embarrassment, have mistakenly replied to "all" rather than solely to the sender of a message. Many firms and offices have policies as to the types of communications that may be sent by email, and most include automatically inserted confidentiality notices at the conclusion of each email message.

Email is different from other written communications. Because it is nearly instantaneous, and the time between the sending of a message and receiving a response to it is so reduced, email is more informal and conversational than traditional paper communication. Thus, the communication style for email must be adjusted.

Although email sent to friends on an informal basis probably does not need to be rigorously checked for grammar and compliance with other usage rules, consider the following top 20 tips when using email in a business or office setting (many of which also apply to texting):

- Because email is often dashed off without a great deal of planning, it may result in brusque and abrupt communications. The reader will not be able to see your expression, gauge your body language, or hear any intonation.

Thus, attempts at humor, irony, and sarcasm are often misperceived. Consider receiving a communication saying, *I resent your message.* You may be tempted to fire off a hostile response before you realize the writer meant to say *I re-sent your message.* When in doubt, leave it out. Similarly, be a generous reader. Give the writer the benefit of the doubt and resist overreacting to an email that initially seems abrupt. The writer may have been trying to be brief.

- Understand that the recipient of your email may not use the same software and hardware that you do, and thus the formatting and "look and feel" of the message the recipient sees may appear quite different from what your screen shows. Formatting and visual appearance greatly affect readability.
- Spell-check all email and review it for accuracy. If necessary, print a hard copy of the message, proof it, correct it, and then send it. It is far better to be overly cautious than sloppy.
- Use templates for routine or standard responses, such as directions to your office.
- Reread your completed email to ensure you answered all questions. If you did not, you will simply get another email, causing wasted time.
- Include the original email in your replies. Many people receive numerous emails each day, and they will not be able to make sense of a response such as "No, I did not" without some context, such as the original message.
- Do not request that a recipient confirm delivery or reading of your message. These annoy recipients.
- Be careful in deciding whom to exclude from an email and whom to include as a "cc." There are political ramifications in excluding certain individuals who may believe you are disrespecting them or cutting them out of the loop. Similarly, sending a critical email to a colleague and then "cc-ing" his or her boss is the electronic equivalent of tattling.
- Just as you wouldn't pick up a telephone and start talking without saying *Hello* and you wouldn't hang the telephone up without saying *Goodbye,* use a salutation (such as *Dear Mr. Lee* or *Dear Nicole*) and a closing (such as *Sincerely* or *Best*).
- When sending an attachment, double-check to be sure you really did attach it (and that it is the correct version).
- Follow the same rules of courtesy and tone used in traditional communications. Ask yourself, *Would I say this in person?*
- Avoid overusing email abbreviations (such as IMHO for *in my humble opinion*) in office settings. Similarly, don't use emoticons (emotional icons such as smiley faces) to convey meaning.
- Be brief and to the point. Many people receive a great number of email messages each day and won't bother to read a long, rambling communication.
- Never pass along inappropriate email at your workplace.
- Make the subject or "Re:" line specific. Let the recipient know at a glance what the message discusses. A good subject line is *Taylor v. Reid.* A better one is "Hearing Scheduled in *Taylor v. Reid* for 4.19.13."

- Do not overuse "urgent," and do not use either an overly long subject line or one that merges into the message.
- Control your own email inbox by adding the line *no need to respond* to your email message. This allows others the freedom not to reply to your emails.
- Understand that once you send a message you have no control over its distribution and it may easily be sent to numerous others without your permission or even your knowledge.
- Do not assume that email is confidential. Generally, monitoring of email by employers is permissible if employers have notified employees that such monitoring may occur. Moreover, understand that email is now specifically discoverable in litigation proceedings. Unless material is subject to attorney-client privilege, it may be discoverable. Be careful to maintain client confidentiality.
- Understand that email is not an effective forum for resolving disputes, conveying bad news, or for delicate situations in which tone of voice is important and in which you need to gauge a recipient's reaction so you can tailor your response accordingly. Once a communication or "conversation" becomes even slightly confrontational, end the email and agree to meet in person or speak over the phone. You are far more likely to be more considerate of others when meeting face-to-face than when communicating impersonally by email.

b. Communicating by Facsimile

Sending documents by facsimile is not nearly as commonplace as it was just a few years ago because documents can now be easily scanned and sent by email to others. When sending documents by facsimile, follow these guidelines:

- Be sure to include your office's cover sheet with information about the sender and its confidentiality notice. Include a notice that if the recipient receives the communication in error, he or she should return it to the sender. Such notices are used to preserve attorney-client confidentiality and privilege.
- Send voluminous materials by mail or express delivery; even the best facsimile machines produce a copy that is less readable than an original.
- Preprogram frequently called numbers, or always double-check the facsimile number before pressing "send."
- Call the intended recipient and inform him or her that the document will be sent, especially if the document is confidential or the facsimile machine is in an open location or shared with others. Once the document is sent, it cannot be recalled.

c. Communicating by Telephone and Voice Mail

Although conference calls and voice mail can reduce the time you spend on communications and eliminate certain forms of written communications, there are some guidelines that will assist you:

- When participating in a conference call, treat it as a meeting and be prompt in dialing in to the conference number.
- Make sure that introductions are made for all participants and that all participants can hear each other.
- Always ask for permission before placing someone on a speakerphone.
- Always disclose that another is listening with you if you are on a speakerphone.
- Do not leave overly long or rambling messages on voice mail.
- Clearly and slowly state your name and phone number on voice mail messages. Repeat them at the end of your message for those unfamiliar with you so they do not have to replay the message to obtain your name and number. Spell your name if needed.
- Avoid using voice mail to "dodge" callers, evade bad news, and avoid speaking with the recipient. Nearly everyone will understand you deliberately called when you knew the person was not available.
- Keep notes for the file to confirm that you left (or received) a certain voice mail. Consider the following format: "M/M 4/16/13 re: corp. mtg. date" (meaning that you left a message on the machine on April 16, 2013, regarding the date of the corporate meeting).
- Do not disclose confidential information over a cell phone or on voice mail. Messages may be easily intercepted, and you do not know who may be listening.
- Check your office policy (and state law) to see if cell phones can be used for business while you are driving. After a large law firm was sued in 2001 for an accident allegedly caused by one of its attorneys who was driving while using the cell phone for firm business, many firms now prohibit such use.

d. Communicating by Text Messaging

Text messaging (or *texting*) is the term used for sending short messages (usually fewer than 160 characters) from cell phones or personal digital assistants such as BlackBerrys. Texting has become increasingly popular. Many law firms distribute BlackBerrys or similar devices to their professionals on the first day of work so that everyone can stay in touch at all times. If you text message anyone about a business-related matter, remember that although you may understand certain abbreviations, the recipient might not. Be sure your message is clear. When in doubt, write it out.

Follow these six basic rules for texting in the workplace:

- Texting in front of other people is rude. If your boss is speaking at a meeting, and you are texting, it will be noticed. If you are awaiting critical news and must be "on call," alert the people you are with that you may need to answer your phone or send a text.
- Do not assume that people will read your texts immediately. If you are conveying urgent or time-sensitive information (such as a change in meeting time), follow your text with an email or telephone call.

- Double-check both the recipient's number and the content of your message to ensure that your Auto Correct or Auto Complete feature did not select an unintended recipient or word.
- Avoid informal abbreviations such as PLZ (for *please*) and UR (for *you are*). Do not include emoticons. Remember the difference between personal texting and texting for business purposes.
- If you are texting to someone who may not recognize your number, start with an introduction, such as "I am Lindsey Young, the new associate working with Bill Moss."
- Be considerate of others' schedules and time zones. Sending a text from New York to someone in your firm's Los Angeles office could disturb sleep if it is sent too early.

chapter 7

Legal Memoranda

StyleLinks

http://west.thomson.com/pdf/perspec/how1299.pdf libguides.law.ucla.edu
West provides information about and a template for a legal memorandum.

http://sparkcharts.sparknotes.com/legal/legalwriting/section2.php
This site analyzes the elements of a legal memorandum and provides sample
sections of legal memoranda.

www.alwd.org/publications/pdf/CM2_Appendix6.pdf
This site provides a sample legal memorandum.

http://lawandborder.com/Academic/LW/LW--Samples/SampleMemoSTCL.pdf
This site provides a sample legal memorandum together with information on
formatting.

A. Introduction

A legal memorandum or research memorandum is a research document designed to provide information about a case or matter. Memos are often written by paralegals or junior attorneys for more senior attorneys. You will be asked to research a question, and your answer will be provided in the form of a written memorandum or "memo." It is only by being completely knowledgeable about the strengths and weaknesses of a case that a fully informed decision can be made whether and how best to represent the client, prepare pleadings and motions, settle the case, proceed to trial, or appeal an adverse decision.

The memo is an internal document, meaning it is prepared for use within a law firm, corporation, or agency. Although a copy of the memo may be provided to a client, it is generally protected by the work product privilege and thus is not discoverable by an adverse party. Because it is not discoverable, its distinguishing characteristic is its objectivity.

Focus on the following three guidelines for effective memo writing:

1. Be Objective

The most difficult part of writing a memo is remaining neutral and objective. If you are not objective in pointing out weaknesses and flaws in the client's case, you do the client a disservice. Your goal is to explain the law, not to argue it. Force yourself to play devil's advocate. Role-play being a reporter. Approach the case as your adversary might and closely examine and analyze the authorities that appear unfavorable to your client.

2. Be Specific

If you are asked to determine whether a tenant may sublease rented property when a written lease fails to address such an issue, focus on the specific question. You need not address the issue as if you were writing a textbook on the history of landlord-tenant relations. The academic and scholarly style used for law review writing is not appropriate for legal memoranda, which must be practical and which aim to predict what a court would hold. Because your memo will expressly state the issue it addresses, if you find yourself getting off track, re-focus yourself by rereading your stated issue.

3. Be Thorough

The individual who assigns you the task wants a finished project, not a sheaf of notes or series of printed cases. Your job is to read and analyze the cases and other legal authorities, apply them to the facts of your case, and present this as a finished professional research memorandum together with recommendations or a prediction as to the likely outcome of the matter.

B. Format of Memoranda

Unlike documents filed in court, there is no one rigid format for an internal office memorandum. Some law firms, companies, and agencies have developed their own formats, and you should ask to review memos previously prepared because these will serve as a guide for you. The memo format provided in this Handbook is a very common and standard one. See Figure 7-2.

The components of a memo are each set off by their own headings, which are usually capitalized and centered. Memos are usually single-spaced with double-spacing between components, although double-spacing is common in many writing programs and firms. Always check with the person assigning the memo to see if there are any requirements for formatting the memo. Note that the first page of a memo will usually include the first three major elements: the issues, the answers, and the statement of facts. This presentation style allows a reader to review only a portion of the memo and yet comprehend a total view of the project. The reader does not have to search through the memo to understand the "bottom line." These three elements provide a snapshot of the client's case, and their location on the first page enables a reader to understand at a glance the strengths and weaknesses of the case.

1. Heading

The heading identifies the document, the person for whom the memo is prepared, the author and his or her position, the subject matter of the memo, and the date it is prepared. For ease of retrieval, the subject matter notation (the "Re:" line) should include some descriptive content, such as *Liability of General Partners* rather than merely a case name and file number.

2. Question(s) Presented

This section (also called *Issue(s)* or *Issue(s) Presented*) sets forth the legal issues the memo addresses. If the memo discusses more than one issue, number each one. Do not number a single issue. Most writers use a true question form, such as *Does a landlord have a duty to disclose to tenants information about crimes that have occurred at the leased premises?* Other writers use the "whether" form, as in *Whether landlords have a duty . . . .* Some attorneys dislike this form because questions that begin with the word *whether* result in incomplete sentences. Finally, some writers use the "under" form, as in *Under California Civil Code section 3344, does a celebrity have a cause of action for violation of his right of publicity when his photograph is used in an advertisement without his permission?* This combination of *under, does/is,* and then *when* is a common way of forming issues.

Whichever form of question you use, be consistent and use the same format for all questions. The most important thing in drafting your questions or issues is to be specific. A question such as *What is a trademark license?* is far too broad and unhelpful to a reader. Incorporate significant facts from your case, as follows: *Is a trademark license valid if it imposes no duty on the licensee to monitor quality of the trademarked goods?* In many instances, language in a statute that governs the matter may provide ideas for phrasing the question. If there is more than one issue, list them in order of importance or the order in which they must be proven at trial.

3. Brief Answer(s)

This section of the memo briefly answers the questions you set forth, in the order you presented them (with the same numbering system you used for your questions). Try to avoid answers that merely repeat the question. Your answer should incorporate the reasons for your conclusions; thus, a one-word answer, such as *no*, is inappropriate. Keep your answers brief—no more than one or two sentences. Do not include formal supporting citations, although it is appropriate to write *Under California Civil Code section 3344, a celebrity has a cause of action for violation of the right of publicity when his photograph or likeness is used for commercial purposes without his permission.*

4. Statement of Facts

The statement of facts may precede the issues or follow the brief answers. Some readers prefer the facts to be given first so that they can make sense of the questions the memo will address. Most writers, however, place the statement of facts after the brief answer(s). The statement of facts will be based on what you know about the case, what the client has said, and your review of the file. The factual statement must be objective; therefore, include facts unfavorable to the client's position, and do not tilt the facts in your favor. Include all facts and do not assume that a reader will know all the facts. In some instances, new attorneys may be assigned to the case and your memo may be the first source they review to become familiar with the case. Therefore, the statement of facts should be self-contained and not require reference to other sources. The most common approach in stating the facts is to present them in a chronological approach (in the order in which they occurred) and in a narrative style rather than in a bulleted list. Use the past tense unless facts are developing as you prepare the memo. If there is a dispute about certain facts, include both versions, as follows: *Although the tenant claims she provided written notice to the landlord of the leaky roof, the landlord disputes this.*

Do not include legal conclusions in your statement of facts. Thus, do not write *The partner breached his fiduciary duty by failing to disclose material information about the premises.* Write *The partner did not disclose that the premises were subject to an easement for a right of way.* The word *slapped* conveys a fact; the word *battered* conveys a legal conclusion. Remain neutral and objective in every part of your memo.

5. Analysis or Discussion

The heart of the memorandum is the analysis, or discussion, section. This portion of the memo provides an in-depth analysis of the issues presented. Cases, statutes, and other legal authorities will be discussed. Citations usually appear in the body of the memo rather than as footnotes, although practices vary.

Many experts recommend using a thesis statement as an introduction to the analysis section of a memorandum or other writing. This introductory statement serves to alert readers to the "big picture" that will be addressed in the memo and encapsulates your central argument. A thesis statement is especially helpful in complex projects or those that will address several issues or elements.

Consider using IRAC or its variations (see section b. below) in your analysis of the legal authorities. Thus, provide the issue the memo will address or identify the conclusion, explain the legal rule that governs the issue, apply the legal rule to the facts of your case, and provide a brief conclusion. Other writers believe that IRAC or CRAC (or their variations) are suited only to exam writing.

a. Using a Thesis Statement

A *thesis statement* distills the central ideas and arguments in your project into one or two assertive sentences. It usually appears at the beginning of a project or issue to give focus and direction to the analysis to follow. It encapsulates the argument to follow. It responds to the central question, *My point is that* .... Nonlegal writers often like to build interest and allow readers to draw their own conclusions about characters and plots. Legal writers, on the other hand, must help their readers immediately understand the direction the analysis will take. Sometimes a thesis statement is called an *umbrella statement* because every part of the discussion to follow must fit beneath it. It directs both the writer and the reader by setting forth the rule that will be proved in the analysis to follow.

Some experts refer to this practice of placing an assertive statement at the beginning of a legal document or an issue as *frontloading*. Whichever term is used, whether *thesis statement* or *frontloading*, readers appreciate being given a firm conclusion as they begin a project, especially a complex one.

Although the thesis statement appears early in any discussion, in many instances, you will not be able to draft the statement until after all your research and analysis is complete. It is only then that you will know how to encapsulate your position in one or two sentences. Don't be concerned if you need to revise your thesis statement. It is possible that as you write your project you discover that your original thesis statement is not accurate; simply modify your thesis statement to reflect your argument. In fact, it may take several attempts to get the thesis statement just right.

A thesis statement is not the same as a topic. For example, a topic might be "liability for dog bites," and a thesis statement for this topic would be as follows:

> *Under California Civil Code section 3342, the owner of a dog is liable for the damages suffered by anyone bitten by the dog while in a public place or lawfully in a private place, regardless of the prior viciousness of the dog.*

After providing this thesis statement, the writer should proceed to analyze the various elements of the statute (for example, showing that a party was the owner of the dog, that the victim was in a public place or lawfully on private property when he or she was bitten, and so forth).

Note the decisive nature and specificity of the preceding thesis statement. A much weaker thesis statement would be as follows: *Owners of dogs are generally liable for the behavior of their dogs.*

Similarly, a thesis statement is more assertive than a topic sentence, which generally merely announces the subject matter or theme of a paragraph to follow; a thesis statement, on the other hand, provides a specific conclusion.

Poor Thesis Statement	Better Thesis Statement
A material omission may constitute fraud.	*Failure to disclose significant defects relating to real estate sold to another is fraud.*

The thesis statement should be placed at or near the beginning of each argument or issue, and each issue should have its own forceful thesis statement. Later paragraphs may begin with topic sentences as you proceed to prove your thesis, much the way a scientist proves his or her hypothesis. Sometimes writers are reluctant to provide a thesis statement because thesis statements require a writer to commit to a position. You will need to shed this reluctance and state the conclusion you have reached about a subject.

Consider the following assertive and strong thesis statements:

- To state a cause of action for false advertising, a plaintiff must show that a statement is either literally false or implicitly untrue in that the statement is likely to deceive consumers.
- Jill Taylor, as a director of a corporation, will not be liable for mere errors in her business judgment so long as she had a reasonable basis for her decision and acted in good faith.
- To be enforceable, a noncompetition agreement must be reasonable as to its scope, duration, and geographic area.

In each case, the reader is given the applicable rule and a definitive preview of the analysis that will follow.

Thesis statements for legal memoranda will differ from thesis statements for persuasive documents, such as those submitted to courts. In a legal memorandum, the thesis statement will be neutral and explanatory; it will not advocate for a particular point of view. In contrast, when you prepare court briefs, your thesis statements will be strong and persuasive.

Example of Memo Thesis Statement:

To prevail in a copyright infringement action, a plaintiff must prove that he or she owns the copyright and that the defendant has impermissibly copied the work.

Example of Court Brief Thesis Statement:

The Defendant is liable for copyright infringement because the Plaintiff is the owner of the copyright in the book, and the Defendant has copied the Plaintiff's work without permission.

b. Analyzing Using IRAC and Its Variations

In discussing and analyzing authorities, many writers follow what is referred to as the "IRAC" method. The IRAC method is also a common approach used by students in answering essay examinations. IRAC is an acronym for Issue, Rule, Application or Analysis, and Conclusion. First, the issue is presented (*Does the Uniform Partnership Act govern a partnership that has no written agreement?*). Next, the rule or legal authority that governs the issue is explained. The cases and other legal authorities that provide the rule are discussed. Then the writer analyzes and applies the rule to the client's facts. The facts of the client's particular fact situation will be compared and contrasted with the cases and other authorities. After a thorough analysis, a conclusion is presented.

Other experts suggest a variation of IRAC, usually called "CRAC" (for Conclusion, Rule, Application, and Conclusion). In this type of analysis, the conclusion is given first, followed by the principal rule of law that supports the conclusion. The rule is explained and illustrated through analysis of cases and other legal authorities. The rule is then applied to the client's particular case, and the conclusion is restated. Still another variation of IRAC is "CREAC" (for Conclusion, Rule, Explanation of Rule, Analysis or Application of Rule, and Conclusion).

Some writing experts dislike IRAC and its variations because they believe these methods encourage a rigid and formulaic approach to writing and are better suited to exam writing. Others believe that IRAC is more useful for writing objective projects such as legal memoranda (because it requires the writer to state the issue in a neutral manner) and that CRAC and CREAC (with their assertive conclusions given at the beginning) are more useful in persuasive writings such as court briefs. In any event, IRAC and its variations may be useful tools to help you to remember to include critical elements when you analyze a legal problem.

c. Analyzing the Authorities

Although methods of analyzing cases vary, some techniques are common to all legal analysis:

- Analyze rather than merely summarize the legal authorities on which you rely. Describe the cases you rely on, giving sufficient facts from those cases so the reader may readily see how and why those cases apply to your case.
- Give the holding and the reasoning from the cases you rely on. Then compare and contrast the cases you rely on with the facts of your case.
- Convince the reader by applying the holding and reasoning from the cited authorities to your case. Complete the analysis by giving a conclusion. Don't force the reader to guess at a conclusion.
- When a case is so similar to the client's situation that it will be controlling, give more detail so the reader will understand the importance of the case.
- When cases are "against" you, you may distinguish them from the client's situation (especially in court documents) in a variety of ways. You may argue that such cases are so dissimilar factually that they are inapplicable,

that they are so old that they are no longer relevant, that they are decided by lower courts, or that the language that appears to be contrary to your position is dicta rather than a holding of the court. If these approaches do not work, you will either have to acknowledge the point or ask the court to overrule these prior decisions. Consider making a policy argument that the law should be changed.

Think back to the mathematics and chemistry courses you have taken. It was never sufficient simply to give an answer. The teacher always required that you show your work and demonstrate each and every step you took to get to your answer. The same is true in legal analysis. It is never sufficient to merely give a conclusion. You must show the reader how you arrived at the conclusion.

It is not enough to locate relevant authorities and then summarize them. Anyone can read a case and then restate its holding. You must analyze the authorities and discuss how and why they relate to your situation or case. This requires you to interweave and compare the facts of your case with the authorities on which you rely. Many beginning writers are reluctant to draw a conclusion. They simply summarize the authorities they have found and then move on to the next topic or issue. You will need to synthesize the authorities you discuss by comparing and contrasting them to each other and to your situation. Be sure to give some of the facts from the cases you rely on so readers can see how and why they apply to the client's situation. If a direct quotation is particularly apt, use it. Be careful, however, to ensure that your analysis consists of more than a series of quotations dropped into the memo. Explain their relevance to the client's problem. See "Tips for Using Quotations and Paraphrasing" for information on case analysis.

Use headings and subheadings throughout the Analysis or Discussion section to serve as signposts to the reader that new topics are being introduced. A memo that consists of printed pages with no heading breaks is nearly unreadable. If you have difficulty composing headings and subheadings, review the headnotes in the cases you rely on for ideas (but remember not to quote from the headnotes). Finally, this section of the memo discusses what the legal authorities have to say and not your opinions. Therefore, use the third person only (*A court would likely find*) and not the first person (*I believe a court would find*).

Discuss the issues in the order in which you presented them in your issues or questions section, once again using the same numbering system you used for your questions and your brief answers.

If you find you may be drifting off track, reread your questions or issues presented. Ask yourself *Is this discussion directly responsive to the question I asked?* If not, it can likely be omitted.

6. Conclusion

The conclusion should be brief (probably no more than one paragraph) and should not include formal citations although it may indicate that a certain statute is applicable or inapplicable. In many ways, the conclusion will resemble your brief answer(s), although it will be in narrative form and will not be divided into numbered sections. Be specific and predict what a court would likely hold based on the authorities you analyzed. If you cannot draw a conclusion because the authorities are in conflict, say so. If, during the course of your research and writing, you determine additional information is needed or other issues need analysis, create a new section for these matters called "Recommendations." The conclusion should not introduce any material that has not previously appeared in the body of the memo. See Figure 7-1 for examples of elements in a legal memorandum and Figure 7-2 for a sample legal memorandum.

Tips ➜ For Using Quotations and Paraphrasing

Many beginning legal writers wonder when to use quotations, when to paraphrase, and when to attribute paraphrasing to legal authorities. Use the following guidelines:

- Use a quotation when what has been said is so articulate and apt that to paraphrase it would dilute its meaning, when the words of the quotation themselves are being analyzed in your writing, or when the author of the quotation is so well known that a quotation from this source would provide instant credibility.
- Avoid such long quotations that the reader's reaction is "please don't make me read this." Use quotations sparingly so that their effect is dramatic and they grab the reader's attention.
- Avoid using a quotation to begin discussion of an issue.
- Avoid overuse of block quotations. Some readers skip them.
- You may paraphrase, which is putting someone else's ideas or words into your own language, so long as you properly attribute paraphrases to the source.
- To paraphrase, read the original source several times to make sure you understand it. Then use your own words to "reconstruct" the material without looking at it. Check your finished writing against the original to ensure you have not used too much of the original source's exact structure. Attribute the writing to the original source.
- Paraphrase when the original quotation is difficult to understand or would require so much restructuring (for example, with ellipses and brackets) that it would be distracting to the reader.
- Paraphrase when the quotation is so long that reproducing it in full would invite the reader to skip over it.
- Provide a full citation, with a pinpoint cite to the particular page, for every quotation and paraphrase in your document.
- Avoid dumping quotations into projects without any analysis of how and why they apply to the client's case. Anyone can retype a case or legal authority.

Figure 7-1   Examples of Elements in a Legal Memorandum

Element	Poor	Better
Issue	Does the client have a cause of action for sexual harassment?	Under the Civil Rights Act of 1964, does harassment occur when a supervisor makes a single remark in the workplace, namely, "Hey, babe, you're hot"?
Brief Answer	No	Because courts consistently require that conduct be severe to constitute harassment, the single comment made in this case is highly unlikely to constitute harassment.
Facts	Grace Parks, the client, was subject to intolerable conduct in the workplace when a supervisor teased her by saying, "Hey, babe, you're hot." This comment was made in front of other employees and thoroughly humiliated Grace.	Grace Parks, the client, is an employee of ABC Inc. Two months ago, when Ms. Parks entered a conference room, her supervisor stated to her, in front of other employees, "Hey, babe, you're hot." Ms. Parks would like to know if this remark constitutes sexual harassment.
Discussion	A poor discussion will: – merely summarize cases and fail to include facts from cases relied on – rely on nonsimilar cases, such as those involving physical conduct and touching rather than oral remarks – lack objectivity and examine only cases in which harassment is found and ignore unfavorable cases – provide mere summaries of cases and fail to draw conclusions as to whether harassment is likely to be found	A better discussion will: – provide the text of governing statutes – discuss and analyze cases with similar fact problems, focusing on cases involving oral remarks rather than those involving only physical touching – discuss cases holding that a single remark can constitute harassment and compare and contrast these to client's case – analyze cases in depth – set forth a conclusion for each issue
Conclusion	A poor conclusion will: – be overlong – include citations – introduce new material	A better conclusion will: – briefly summarize the major points of the memorandum

Tips ⇨ For Preparing Effective Legal Memoranda

- Do not number a single issue or question. If there is a *I* or an *A*, there must be a *2* or a *B* following it.
- Do not include formal citations in the Brief Answers or Conclusion sections.
- To eliminate unnecessary facts, reread your Statement of Facts after you have completed your first draft. If the Statement of Facts includes items not later mentioned in the Analysis section, those facts can probably be omitted.
- If each paragraph in your memo discusses a single case, this is a signal that you are merely summarizing cases rather than analyzing them.
- Retain symmetry in your memo. If there are three Questions, there should be three Brief Answers, and three main sections in the Analysis, each corresponding in number and order to the other.
- Use descriptive headings and subheadings. Thus, write *Elements of Fraud* rather than *Issue Two.*
- Review the beginning of each paragraph. If each starts with the same opening, for example, *In* Smith v. Jones, *the court held . . .* the project will have a choppy, stodgy style.
- Do not use first person pronouns. Avoid statements such as *The next case I found* or *I believe.*
- Identify parties in cases by their status or their roles (such as *plaintiff* or *buyer*) rather than by their names.
- If your memo analyzes a complex and lengthy statute, include only its pertinent portions in the body of your memo (rather than setting forth its text in full), and then attach a copy of the statute to your memo.

Figure 7-2   Sample Legal Memorandum

MEMORANDUM

To: James T. Younger, Esq.
From: Ellen T. Carpenter, Esq.
Re: Judith Davidson—Landlord's Liability for Criminal Acts of Third Parties
            Client Number: 0190-001
Date: December 10, 2012

==

ISSUE

   Is a landlord who knows of violent criminal activity at and near its leased premises liable for a sexual assault on a tenant by a third party when it fails to warn the tenant of the prior criminal activity and fails to enhance security measures at the premises?

BRIEF ANSWER

Yes. Although a landlord is not an insurer of its tenants' safety, when a criminal attack is reasonably foreseeable, a landlord may be liable for injury to the tenant by a third party.

FACTS

Our client, Judith Davidson ("Davidson"), is a tenant at Brookside Gardens Apartments. Davidson signed a written lease for the premises on March 1, 2012, after the managing partner of the landlord, Jackson Property Management, LLP ("JPM"), showed Davidson the premises. Two months after Davidson moved into the premises, she was sexually assaulted by a nonresident, Kyle Reynolds, in the common area of the premises. Prior to the assault, JPM had been notified by the local police of increased criminal activity in the neighborhood near the premises. JPM also knew that two robberies and four physical assaults had occurred at Brookside Gardens in the six months before the attack on Davidson. JPM did not notify any tenants of these criminal activities and did not enhance any security measures at the premises.

DISCUSSION

1. Landlords Are Not Insurers of Their Tenants' Safety

Generally, in the absence of statutes or special relationships (such as parent and child), a private person has no duty to protect another from a criminal assault or from physical harm by another. Restatement (Second) of Torts § 315 (1965). Moreover, courts have usually held that landlords are not insurers of the safety of their tenants. Thus, the mere relationship of landlord and tenant does not impose on the landlord a duty to protect the tenant from the criminal activities of third person. Tracy A. Bateman & Susan Thomas, Annotation, *Landlord's Liability for Failure to Protect Tenant from Criminal Acts of Third Person*, 43 A.L.R.5th 207, § 3 (1996). Nevertheless, landlords have been held liable for the criminal acts of third parties when the landlords have breached a contractual or statutory duty or when the criminal occurrence is reasonably foreseeable. *See, e.g., Tedder v. Raskin*, 728 S.W.2d 343, 350-51 (Tenn. Ct. App. 1987). In the present case, because there is no statute requiring JPM to protect its tenants and JPM had no contractual obligation to do so, the question is whether the sexual assault against Davidson was reasonably foreseeable under the circumstances.

2. A Landlord Is Liable for Reasonably Foreseeable Similar Criminal Acts

In many instances, courts have refused to impose liability on landlords for crimes committed against tenants on the basis that the negligence or criminal conduct of a third party constituted an independent, intervening act that was the proximate cause of the tenant's injuries. *Feld v. Merriam*, 485 A.2d 742, 746 (Pa. 1984). More modern cases rely on traditional negligence principles in holding that a landlord's duty to exercise ordinary care to protect tenants against crimes by third parties extends to foreseeable criminal acts. *Days Inn of Am. v. Matt*, 454 S.E.2d 507, 508 (Ga. 1995).

Thus, the central question in this case is whether the assault on Davidson was reasonably foreseeable. As in other negligence actions, a plaintiff alleging that a landlord is liable for the criminal acts of third parties must prove that the landlord was on notice of a likelihood of danger to his or her tenants and thus the harm was foreseeable. The plaintiff must further prove that the landlord's failure to act after receiving notice sufficient to cause a reasonably prudent person to foresee the probability of harm is the proximate cause of the injury. To meet such a burden, the plaintiff tenant must show that the injury was a reasonably foreseeable probability and not merely a remote possibility. *Tedder*, 728 S.W.2d at 348-49.

Some courts have held that for a landlord to be subject to a duty of care to protect tenants from third-party criminal attacks, the injury to the tenant must be "substantially similar" in type to the previous criminal activities occurring on or near the premises such that a reasonable person would take ordinary precautions to protect his or her tenants against the risk posed by that type of activity. *See, e.g.*, *Wojcik v. Windmill Lake Apts. Inc.*, 645 S.E.2d 1, 3 (Ga. Ct. App. 2007). In *Wojcik*, a pizza deliveryman was murdered by a nonresident at an apartment complex while delivering pizza. The court affirmed summary judgment in favor of the apartment owner, holding that although there was evidence that there were certain property crimes on the premises (such as vehicle break-ins), no murders had occurred at the complex. Thus, the landlord could not have reasonably anticipated the occurrence of the murder.

Similarly, prior property crimes (primarily, automobile thefts and vandalism in an apartment building garage) were held insufficient to make a landlord reasonably anticipate that a violent sexual assault on a tenant might occur in the garage. *Doe v. Prudential-Bach/A.G. Spanos Realty Partners, L.P.*, 492 S.E.2d 865, 867 (Ga. 1997). Moreover, criminal incidents in the neighborhood surrounding a building were not sufficient to put a landlord on notice that a sexual assault of a tenant at the leased premises was foreseeable. *Rozhik v. 1600 Ocean Parkway Assocs.*, 617 N.Y.S.2d 535, 536 (App. Div. 1994).

3. Identical Criminal Activity Is Not Needed to Show Foreseeability

Although the injury to a tenant must be substantially similar to the type of previous criminal attacks in order for liability to be imposed on a landlord, the crime committed by the third party need not be identical to prior criminal acts. In *L.A.C. v. Ward Parkway Shopping Center Co.*, 75 S.W.3d 247, 256-57, 259 (Mo. 2002), the court held that a sexual assault of a female shopping mall customer was foreseeable when seventy-five violent crimes had occurred on the mall property in the three years preceding the attack (more than 60 percent of which involved female victims), and a security audit had noted that the area where the sexual assault occurred was frequented by unruly youths. Thus, although there was no evidence of an identical crime in an identical location, the mall owners and operators owed a duty to protect their customer from the sexual assault. The court specifically noted that foreseeability does not require identical crimes in identical locations. *Id.* at 259.

Other courts have permitted evidence of crimes in the neighborhood as bearing on the issue of foreseeability. *See, e.g., Holland v. Liedel*, 494 N.W.2d 772, 775 (Mich. Ct. App. 1992). In *Holland*, the court noted that of more significance than whether crimes had occurred previously at the premises was whether the premises as a whole were located in a high-crime area. *Id.* Similarly, several courts have endorsed the court's statement in *Paterson v. Deeb*, 472 So. 2d 1210, 1219 (Fla. Dist. Ct. App. 1985) that it was not willing to give a landlord "one free ride . . . and sacrifice the first victim's right to safety upon the altar of foreseeability by slavishly adhering to the now discredited notion that at least one criminal assault must have occurred before the landlord can be held liable."

In *O'Hara v. Western Seven Trees Corp.*, 142 Cal. Rptr. 487, 490-91 (Ct. App. 1977), a tenant sued her landlord and others seeking damages for injuries suffered when she was raped in her apartment. The court held that her complaint stated a cause of action against the defendants because of their alleged negligence in failing to provide adequate security, in misrepresenting security measures in effect at the premises, and in failing to warn the tenant of the danger of rape where it was alleged that the defendants knew of rapes near the premises and had been given composite drawings of the suspect by the police.

In the present case, although there had been no prior sexual assaults on the premises, there had been numerous incidents of violent crime at the premises. The landlord had been informed of criminally violent acts in the neighborhood by the police and knew of six violent acts at the premises itself within the prior six months. Crimes had occurred both in the area *and* at the premises, not merely in the surrounding neighborhood, as was the case in *Rozhik*, 617 N.Y.S.2d at 536. In *In re World Trade Center Bombing Litigation*, 776 N.Y.S.2d 713, 735 (Sup. Ct. 2004), the court held that whether a landlord's knowledge of prior criminal incidents is sufficient to make injuries to its tenants foreseeable depends on the location, nature, and extent of those previous criminal acts and their similarity, proximity, or other relationship to the crime in question. The court stated that a landlord does not need to have had a past experience with the exact criminal activity before liability can be imposed. Where "ambient crime" has infiltrated a landlord's premises, or where the landlord is otherwise on notice of a serious risk of such infiltration, the duty to protect the tenants arises. *Id.* Thus, in the present case, after receiving notice of violent crimes in the neighborhood and at the premises, a reasonably prudent person would have taken ordinary precautions to protect his or her tenants against a known risk of violent acts. JPM knew of violent criminal activity at its premises and in the area and yet failed to take any action to protect its tenants. In such a case, Reynolds's criminal conduct was reasonably foreseeable.

An identical crime need not have been committed at the premises to impose a duty on a reasonable person to take ordinary precautions to protect his or her tenants against the type of risk posed by criminal acts. Only the general risk of harm need be foreseen, not the specific harm. *Sharp v. W.H. Moore, Inc.*, 796 P.2d 506, 510 (Idaho 1990). The risk to be prevented is criminal activity — not exclusively sexual assault. In fact, the court in *Sharp* specifically noted that the "solid and growing national trend has been toward the rejection of the 'prior similar incidents' rule." *Id.*

4. Landlords Are Best Able to Protect Tenants from Harm

Many courts have noted that landlords are in the best position to take appropriate protective measures to protect tenants. *Kline v. Mass. Ave. Apt. Corp.*, 439 F.2d 477, 481 (D.C. Cir. 1970). In *Kline*, 439 F.3d at 482, the court noted that the most analogous relationship to that of modern apartment dwellers is that of innkeepers and guests. Other courts have also noted that similar to guests at inns, tenants in apartment buildings whose leases are often of short duration cannot be expected to make the expenditures necessary to secure a building's common areas or take other precautionary measures. *See, e.g., Tedder*, 728 S.W.2d at 347. Because landlords retain control over apartment common areas and grounds, they are in a superior position to take appropriate measures to secure the premises for the safety of the tenants. *Id.*

CONCLUSION

Although the mere relationship of landlord and tenant does not impose upon JPM the duty to protect Davidson against criminal acts by third parties, in this case, because the landlord knew of multiple violent crimes both in the area and at the premises, the attack on Davidson was a reasonably foreseeable probability. Thus, the landlord will likely be liable for the injuries suffered by Davidson because it failed to take steps to avoid a predictable risk.

chapter 8

Legal Briefs

StyleLinks

http://supreme.lp.findlaw.com/supreme_court/briefs
Many briefs filed with the U.S. Supreme Court since 1999 are available at this website.

www.llrx.com/features/briefsonline.htm
LLRX.com provides numerous links to sites providing state and federal court briefs.

http://howappealing.law.com
This blog is devoted to appellate litigation with interesting articles and more.

www.ca4.uscourts.gov/pdf/briefchecklist.pdf
The Fourth Circuit Court of Appeals offers an excellent checklist for the content and the format of briefs filed with federal courts.

www.legaline.com/freebriefslinks.html
Attorney Robert J. Ambrogi provides a number of links to free briefs available on the Internet.

www.zielkelaw.com/profile/articles-publications/trial-brief.asp
This site offers an excellent article on preparing trial court briefs.

A. Introduction

The initial documents submitted to courts in litigation cases, such as complaints and answers, are called *pleadings*. Pleadings are discussed in Chapter 9. This chapter discusses legal arguments made in support of or in response to motions in pending cases. When a party requests action from a court (for example, an order changing venue or dismissing a case), he or she makes a motion requesting the action.

Note that most motions include three core elements: the actual motion (a straightforward one- or two-page document formally requesting or moving the court for the desired action, such as moving the court to compel the defendant to answer interrogatories); a proposed order granting the motion (which will be signed by the judge if he or she grants the motion); and the legal argument in support of the motion (generally consisting of several pages with citations to legal authorities). This legal argument is generally called a *brief*, although it can be called a Memorandum of Law or Memorandum of Points and Authorities, perhaps to emphasize that each legal point made in the document must be supported by legal authority. Be careful not to confuse this type of memorandum with the internal office memoranda discussed in Chapter 7. Be careful not to confuse briefs submitted to courts with *case briefs*, which are summaries of the key elements in published cases, often prepared by students in preparation for law classes. A sample of a case brief is provided as Appendix G.

Briefs differ from letters and memoranda in their purpose and audience. Whereas letters and memoranda are intended primarily to inform and explain, briefs are intended to persuade judges. The writing techniques used for briefs are therefore different because each element of a brief should be drafted with its objective in mind: to persuade a court to rule in the client's favor. Trial briefs are submitted in pending cases, and appellate briefs are used to appeal an adverse decision (or submitted in support of a decision) made by a lower court. Moreover, the format for trial briefs is generally simpler than that for appellate briefs.

B. Five Tips for Effective Briefs

1. Be Persuasive

In some ways, you may find it easier to prepare a brief than an internal office memo. It is easier and more natural for most writers to advocate the client's position in a court brief than to maintain the objectivity required in an interoffice research memo. Aim at being persuasive throughout every portion of the brief. Even identifying the parties provides an opportunity to win over the audience. For example, when representing a corporation, personalize it by referring to the individuals involved (the directors and officers) rather than repeatedly calling it *the company*. Use the client's name (*Fran Nelson*) rather than *Defendant*. Similarly, the table of contents and headings provide an opportunity for you to persuade the court. Consider the following two headings. You can easily see the difference in the persuasiveness of the headings.

Neutral Heading	Persuasive Heading
Punitive Damages	*Defendant's Reckless Conduct Entitles Plaintiff Leigh Ryan to Punitive Damages*

The most persuasive headings consist of a single sentence. They are numbered (using either Arabic or Roman numerals) and may appear in all capital letters centered on the page (although longer headings presented in all capital letters are difficult to read and may be ignored by the reader). Use parallel structure so that if a reader reads only these point headings in a brief, they provide a clearly written summary and outline of the argument. Don't alternate between phrases and complete sentences. Maintain consistency in your headings.

2. Be Concise

Judges and law clerks are almost always overworked. Moreover, judges are often unfamiliar with the area of law in a brief; they may not be experts in immigration law or civil rights as your firm or practice group may be. Similarly, law clerks are often inexperienced. Thus, it is critical for the writer to clearly and concisely explain the law and specifically apply it to the facts of the case. The reader wants to know only two things: what relief you are requesting and why you deserve it. Use a thesis statement (see below) at the beginning of your brief to answer these questions and set the stage for the analysis to follow.

3. Use a Thesis Statement

Recall from Chapter 7 that a thesis statement distills an argument into one or two assertive and conclusory sentences placed at the beginning of a project or issue. Always use a thesis statement in brief writing. It is a preview or roadmap for your reader of the argument and analysis to follow. Remember that legal writing is entirely unlike creative writing: Readers do not want suspense; rather, they need a conclusion up front to lead them through your analysis. A thesis statement provides structure to your project and controls your analysis to follow.

Remember that a thesis statement is far more emphatic than a topic sentence. Consider the following:

Topic Sentence:	This brief addresses the business judgment rule.
Thesis Statement:	The business judgment rule protects the corporate directors in this case because their actions in opposing the hostile takeover were directed to maximizing shareholder value rather than enriching themselves.

If you find it helpful in crafting your thesis statement, in your first draft use the words *In a nutshell, my client should win because . . .* and then delete these unpolished words in your next draft. Recall that it is possible that you will not be able to finalize your thesis statement until near the end of your writing when you are certain of your conclusions. Refining and modifying a thesis statement throughout the writing process is common.

Remember that the thesis statement is also called an umbrella statement because each and every point you make thereafter fits under it. Think of your thesis statement as a campaign or ad slogan. It provides the overarching theme of your document. Every part of your brief must remind your reader of and advance this theme.

Using a thesis statement will not only guide your reader but also help you retain focus. As you draft each section of your brief, reread your thesis statement and then test your analysis against it to ensure that your argument is advanced by and is consistent with your thesis statement. See Chapter 7 Section B.5 for more information about thesis statements.

4. Be Honest

Although you need not present the adversary's argument, you have an ethical duty to be honest and bring to the court's attention anything that would assist the court in reaching a decision. If you discover cases that do not support the client's position, address them in a straightforward fashion, and then show the reader why they do not apply. Neutralize their effect by showing that the unfavorable cases are factually or legally distinguishable from your case. Argue that these adverse cases should be narrowly interpreted. Act on the assumption that your adversary will discover these cases and that if you introduce these problem areas yourself, you decrease the effect of the adversary's "smoking gun" and have the opportunity to take the lead rather than being forced to respond defensively (or, in a worst case scenario, not have the opportunity to respond at all). Moreover, the integrity shown by an honest and direct discussion of these issues will carry over to the rest of your argument. Don't overstate or exaggerate your own case.

5. Know the Rules

Nearly all courts issue rules relating to documents submitted to them. Some of these rules relate to the paper used, citation form, length of the document, and the elements required in a brief. Many courts now establish maximum page, word, or character limits. For example, a newly revised federal rule has reduced the page allowance for principal briefs filed in the U.S. courts of appeal from fifty pages to thirty pages. Fed. R. App. P. 32. A failure to comply with the rules can be fatal. For example, in December 1997, the *National Law Journal* reported that after attorneys submitted a brief three times in the incorrect type size (using 10-point rather than 12-point font, as required by court rules), a court dismissed the case. Nearly all courts, including the U.S. Supreme Court, have posted their rules on their websites. Table T.1 of *The Bluebook* and Appendix 2 of *ALWD* provide each state's judicial website. Additionally, you may always contact the court clerk to obtain a copy of the court's rules.

Ethics Alert: Follow the Rules

Always check the court's rules to ensure your brief complies with all requirements as to form, contents, and filing. In a recent case, an appeal brief was filed six minutes late, and the court dismissed the appeal as untimely. *Alva v. Teen Help*, 469 F.3d 946, 950 (10th Cir. 2006). Thus, failure to comply with even seemingly minor court rules and requirements may well be malpractice.

> When a point is asserted without argument and authority for the proposition, it is deemed to be without foundation.
>
> *In re S.C.*, 41 Cal. Rptr. 2d 453, 464 (Ct. App. 2006).

C. Trial Court Briefs

1. Introduction

Briefs submitted to trial courts may be written in support of a certain position or in response or opposition to an argument. As in all legal writing, remember your audience. The judge who will read the brief will be busy and will be frustrated with a lengthy and repetitive document. Opposing counsel will scrutinize the brief looking for errors and mischaracterizations of the law. Although it is futile to believe you can persuade opposing counsel, aim at presenting a brief that at least cannot be attacked by opposing counsel. A sample trial court brief is found in Figure 8-2 at the end of this chapter.

2. Elements of a Trial Court Brief

The elements of a brief submitted to a trial court will vary from jurisdiction to jurisdiction. The following elements are found in most briefs, but always review your local court rules to determine if there is a required format.

a. Caption

Because the brief submitted to the court is a form of pleading, it must display the *caption* of the case. The caption identifies the pertinent information about the case: the court, the parties, the docket number, and the title of the document, such as *Defendant's Memorandum of Law in Support of Motion to Change Venue*. Rule 8 of *The Bluebook* and *ALWD* Rule 3 provide instructions for abbreviations and capitalization in headings and titles of court documents.

b. Introductory Statement

The party submitting the brief typically begins with a short statement identifying what the party is requesting, such as the following: *Defendant Vincent T. Parker respectfully submits the following Memorandum of Law in support of his Motion to Change Venue.*

c. Statement of Facts

To save the judge the time of reviewing all the pleadings submitted to the court to determine what the case is about, the brief should include a statement of facts. Although these facts must be accurate, strive to present them in a manner most favorable to the client. Use active voice and descriptive facts to emphasize facts supporting the client's position. Most facts are presented in chronological order, although you may discuss them by topic if you wish to emphasize certain facts. Present the facts in the third person and in the past tense unless the facts are still unfolding. Be careful not to jump the gun and argue your case. Thus, focus solely on the facts, not on legal theories or analysis. Don't overlook the importance of a well-written statement of facts. Because most judges have a thorough understanding of the law, they may begin forming impressions and drawing conclusions even as they read the facts.

d. Argument

The argument section is the heart of the brief. This section contains the analysis of the legal authorities that support the client's position. Use a thesis statement for each issue to provide an assertive encapsulation of your analysis and "set the stage" for the discussion to follow. As discussed in Chapter 7, many writers use the IRAC approach in writing. Other writers believe that IRAC is not well suited for persuasive writing because a neutral statement of the issue (the *I* in IRAC) is ineffective in a document that should be forceful in every regard. Thus, these experts prefer the CRAC (or CREAC) approach with an assertive conclusion given first, followed by explanation of the legal rules governing the subject matter, application of the rules to the specific fact situation, and a summing-up conclusion. Still other experts avoid using either IRAC or its variations, believing they are suited only to exam writing, especially because IRAC places the conclusion at the end of the analysis or project rather than at the beginning of an issue or section.

Divide your argument into sections, giving each section a persuasive heading and an Arabic or Roman numeral and centering the heading on the page. Use subheadings if needed, making sure all headings of the same type are presented consistently. Discuss authorities in the past tense as in *The court held that* . . . . When discussing statutes with several elements or a test used by the courts, discuss each element in the order provided in the statute or case. Watch the use of the phrase *this case;* a reference to *this case shows* may be interpreted as a reference to the client's particular case rather than a published authority. Be definite. Avoid expressions such as *it seems* or *it is likely,* which immediately convey the message that the author is not sure of the position taken. Do not use the first person. Thus, do not write *We argue,* or *We will show.* Instead use expressions such as *Defendant will show* or *Plaintiff has contended.* This keeps the focus on the parties, not on you as the writer. Discuss your strongest arguments first when the reader is most attentive. Try to bury weaker arguments about two-thirds of the way through the brief, and then end with a strong argument. As always, be sure to do more than merely summarize case holdings. Analyze cases and tell the reader how and why they apply to the client's particular fact situation. Be sure that each section of your brief ends with a strong conclusion before you move to the next section or topic. Finally, although the aim of your brief is to persuade, you need not denigrate the adversary's position. A logical and well-reasoned argument will command respect. A hostile and sarcastic diatribe will destroy your credibility.

e. Conclusion

The conclusion should be a very brief recap of the highlights of the argument. Use the conclusion as your final opportunity to deliver your message. Because it is a summary, no citations should be included. The last sentence of the brief should remind the reader of the relief requested, as in *For the foregoing reasons, Defendant Vincent T. Parker respectfully requests the Court grant his Motion for Change of Venue.*

f. Signature and Date

The brief is typically "closed" much like a letter, although the complimentary close is usually *Respectfully submitted,* and a date is included together with the attorney's bar number, signature, and identification of the firm.

g. Certificates of Service and Compliance

A certificate of service is placed at the conclusion of a pleading to verify that a copy of the document has been served on all parties. The method of service, such as hand delivery or first class mail, and the date of service must be specified. Many courts also require a certificate of compliance by the attorney or preparer of the document to verify that the document complies with all court rules, including those relating to page or word count limits.

h. Exhibits

A number of exhibits may be attached to the brief, such as transcripts of deposition testimony, declarations, answers to interrogatories, and so forth. Make sure that the titles and labeling of the actual exhibits are consistent with how they have been titled and labeled in the brief itself. Use a style sheet (a list that shows how you will present certain terms or titles) to ensure consistency. Style sheets are discussed in Chapter 11.

i. Order

Most courts require the parties to submit a proposed order with the brief so that if the judge agrees with a party, an order is ready for the judge's signature.

See Figure 8-2 at the end of this chapter for a sample trial court brief.

Tips ➡ **Responding to an Adversary's Brief**

- When you are responding to briefs filed by adversaries, review the authorities cited in their briefs. Dissents in the cases cited by your adversary often provide good ammunition for drafting a reply or response brief.
- Always submit a reply brief to any brief filed by your opponent.
- Take the opportunity to have the last word.

D. Appellate Briefs

1. Introduction

An appellate brief seeks reversal, affirmance, or some modification of a lower court's action. Although the trial court judge who rules on a motion may be familiar with the case and the facts presented in a trial brief and may, in fact, have been assigned to a case from its filing, appellate judges will have no such familiarity with cases before them. You will thus have to be as articulate and persuasive as possible to convince the appellate court to rule in your client's favor.

Appellate work is highly complex and is often carried out by law firms whose practices are devoted solely to appellate work. Because the focus of an appeal is so different from that of a trial (in that its focus is on determining whether a prejudicial error in law occurred at the trial rather than in determining whether given facts occurred), in many instances the appealing parties obtain new counsel exclusively for the purposes of preparing the appellate brief and conducting the oral argument. Because appellate work is so specialized and is a field in which few attorneys are engaged, a sample appeal brief is included as Appendix C rather than in this chapter.

2. Elements of Appellate Briefs

Many of the elements of an appellate brief are the same as the elements of a trial brief. Following are the elements typically found in an appellate brief, although their order may vary.

a. Cover Sheet

The cover sheet is a title page identifying the court hearing the appeal, the identities of the appellant and appellee (sometimes called the petitioner and the respondent), the docket number of the case, the lower court that handled the trial or prior appeal, the title of the document, and the attorneys representing the parties submitting the brief.

b. Identification of Parties

Unless all of the parties are identified on the cover sheet, a list of all parties to the lower court proceeding usually must be provided to allow judges or justices to review it for conflicts of interest. This identification of parties is often called a corporate disclosure statement.

c. Table of Contents

A table of contents or index must be included to identify for the reader the page location of each element in the brief. Most software programs automatically generate a table of contents. The table of contents will include all headings and subheadings so phrase these as persuasively as possible. This will be your first opportunity to persuade the reviewing court to rule in your favor.

d. Table of Authorities

An appellate brief (and some trial briefs, depending on court rules) must include a list of all authorities cited in the brief together with an indication of the page(s) in the brief on which the authority appears. As with the table of contents, many software programs automatically generate a table of authorities. Follow court rules as to citation form. Few courts have rules relating to how tables of authorities should be structured, so follow these guidelines:

- Organize your authorities by category, so that all of your cases are listed together (alphabetically) under the heading "Cases," all of the statutes are listed together under the heading "Statutes" (listing federal statutes first by ascending order and then listing state statutes alphabetically by state and then by ascending number or alphabetically by title), and all of the secondary authorities are listed together (alphabetically) under their own heading, often called "Other Authorities."
- Include the full citation (and any subsequent history) for all cases. Be consistent. Either present all case names in full or use abbreviations (such as *Acad.* for *Academy*), but don't mix and match the two styles.
- You need not include pinpoint cites or signals for the cases you have cited.
- Include a page reference for any cases cited in short form (as in *Id.* at 423).
- Review other briefs (for example, those filed with the U.S. Supreme Court, available at www.supremecourt.gov) as models.

e. Jurisdictional Statement

The appellate brief should include a concise statement of the grounds upon which the court's jurisdiction rests, including a reference to the pertinent authority. The jurisdictional statement simply tells the appellate court which statute allows the appeal. A simple jurisdictional statement might read *This Court of Appeals for the Eighth Circuit has jurisdiction to hear this appeal pursuant to 15 U.S.C. § 1071(b) (2006)*.

f.   Constitutional and Statutory Provisions

If the court's determination of the issues requires the study of constitutional provisions, statutes, or regulations, they must be set forth in full together with their citations. If the provisions are especially lengthy, you may set forth their pertinent parts. Many courts allow the relevant constitutional and statutory provisions to be set forth in an appendix to the brief.

g.   Question(s) Presented

Most courts require the parties to present the issues the court is being asked to address. In some briefs, such as those submitted to the U.S. Supreme Court, the question(s) presented is set forth immediately after the cover sheet, thus immediately signaling to the reader the focus of the argument to follow. These issues are presented in question format and are somewhat similar to the questions presented in an office memorandum but should be drafted in such a persuasive manner that the desired answer is obvious. For example, a petitioner's question may begin *Did the trial court err when it held* . . . whereas the respondent's brief may begin *Did the trial court properly hold* . . . .

h.   Statement of the Case

The statement of the case includes a brief overview of the case's procedural history, namely, a review of what happened below and how the case arrived at this reviewing court.

i.   Statement of Facts

The statement of facts includes only the facts that have been proven at trial. Thus, each factual statement is followed by a reference to the location in the lower court record or clerk's transcript where such fact was established. To some degree, the statement of facts will parallel the statement of facts for a brief submitted to a trial court. Be honest and straightforward. Establish credibility by being accurate and including all facts, even those unfavorable to the client's position. Remember the techniques of passive voice and placement to de-emphasize unfavorable facts. Present the statement of the case in narrative form, in chronological order, and in the past tense.

j.   Summary of the Argument

A concise summary of the argument is often included. This is a preview of the argument to follow. This is the first section of the brief that allows advocacy and you should take advantage of this opportunity to persuade the reader to rule in favor of the client.

k. Argument

Like the argument in a trial court brief, the argument in an appellate brief is the heart of the document. This section analyzes the authorities and convinces the reviewing court to rule for the client. Divide the brief into separate sections with each section receiving its own persuasive point heading. The headings should correspond to the questions set forth earlier and should be parallel to each other. Use subheadings as needed. Read in sequence, the headings should provide an outline of the argument. If possible, discuss topics in the order discussed in the statement of facts. Use an assertive thesis statement (see Chapter 7 Section B.5 and Section B. of this chapter) for each issue in the argument section, and include a strong conclusion for each section before you move on to a new section or topic.

l. Conclusion

The conclusion of an appellate brief often does not summarize the argument section. This summary has already been given before the argument. Instead, the conclusion often merely specifies the relief sought, such as requesting the court to affirm or reverse the lower court's decision. Avoid formal citations in the conclusion.

m. Signature and Date

The document is signed and dated, and the firm name, address, telephone number, and bar number of the attorney representing the party are set forth after the conclusion.

n. Certificates of Service and Compliance

The certificate of service demonstrates to the court that the brief has been provided to all parties and specifies the date and manner of service, such as hand delivery or first class mail. The certificate of compliance demonstrates to the court that the document complies with all court rules, including those relating to typeface and length limitations.

o. Appendix

Appellate briefs nearly always include an appendix, which may consist of portions of the trial court transcript, jury instructions, pleadings, and other documents from the lower court action. Make it easy for the reader by using exhibit tabs, including a table of contents for the appended material, and highlighting relevant material. You cannot be sure a reader will thoroughly review materials in an appendix, so keep the focus of your argument in the body of the brief. Moreover, frequent references to extraneous material disrupt the flow of the argument. See Figure 8-1 for a chart comparing elements of trial and appellate briefs.

Figure 8-1   Elements of Trial and Appellate Court Briefs

Trial Court Briefs	Appellate Court Briefs
Caption	Cover Sheet
Introductory Statement	Identification of Parties
	Table of Contents
	Table of Authorities
	Jurisdictional Statement
	Constitutional and Statutory Provisions
	Questions Presented
	Statement of the Case
Statement of Facts	Statement of Facts
	Summary of the Argument
Argument	Argument
Conclusion	Conclusion
Signature and Date	Signature and Date
Certificates of Service and Compliance	Certificates of Service and Compliance
Exhibits	Appendix
Order	

Tips for Effective Brief Writing

- Know and follow the rules of the court to which the brief will be submitted.
- Do more than summarize cases. Show the reader how and why the authorities you rely on apply to the client's case.
- Write from the client's perspective. Do not use first person. Do not write *We argue*, and so forth. Use third person only, as in *The Commissioner will show*.
- Avoid a rote method of writing. If each paragraph discusses one case and ends with a citation, the brief will have a rigid appearance and tone. Variety in analyzing cases will enhance readability.
- Avoid sarcasm, humor, or irony. These techniques are often misinterpreted in written documents because they largely depend on voice inflection and body language to convey meaning. Maintain a respectful tone toward the court and the other party.
- Review your table of contents to ensure that it persuasively and concisely previews your argument.
- Avoid the overuse of quotations, especially block quotations. A well-chosen quotation can give force to your writing; continual quoting dilutes the strength of the quotations. Avoid merely dropping quotations into the project. Explain their relevance.

(continued)

Tips → Tips for Effective Brief Writing

- Avoid string citing (citing several authorities in support of a proposition). They clutter your document. If you must cite several authorities, give a brief parenthetical explanation as to the relevance of each, as in the following: *Smith v. Jones*, 540 U.S. 32, 39 (2006) (holding that trademarks can be abandoned by nonuse).
- Keep the focus on your argument. Fully develop the client's position before responding to the opposition.
- Do not distort or overstate your position. If any portion of the brief is not supported by valid authority, the entire brief is undermined.
- Focus on your best arguments. If some arguments are "long shots," do not include them. Including weak arguments causes readers to question the writer's credibility.
- Write clearly. In 2000 the Kentucky Supreme Court suspended a lawyer for sixty days for a "virtually incomprehensible" brief and dismissed his client's case.
- Avoid confusing labels such as *Cross-Respondent*. Use either the party's name (*Doyle*) or a functional description (*the employer*). In fact, federal court rules specifically require brief-writers to minimize the use of the terms *appellant* and *appellee* and to use actual names or descriptive terms such as *the employee* or *the taxpayer*. Fed. R. App. P. 28(d).
- Review only your headings for both parallel structure and content. If your brief is well written and well organized, they should provide an overview and an outline of the argument to follow.
- Study and review other briefs. Briefs submitted to the U.S. Supreme Court may be accessed at www.supremecourt.gov.

Footnotes or Not? Pros and Cons

Citations to legal authority can appear throughout the narrative text or in footnotes. There are two schools of thought on using footnotes in legal memos and court briefs.

Pros. Some experts advocate moving citations out of the body of text and into footnotes to unclutter the narrative. In fact, some judges are experimenting with writing citation-free opinions, placing all citations and extraneous comments in footnotes to create more readable and less distracting opinions.

Cons. Other experts believe that the placement of a footnote number at the end of a sentence jars curious readers who are then compelled to glance at the bottom of the page, abandoning important arguments in the body of the text as they look to find the date of a case or determine what court decided it. These experts suggest that if the point of a logical argument is to carry the reader

(continued)

Footnotes or Not? Pros and Cons

seamlessly from the first sentence to the last, footnotes disrupt this objective. These experts point out that legal readers readily understand citation form and can easily skip over citations in the body of the text.

Rules for Footnotes

- Never use footnotes to circumvent court rules on page limits.
- Check your firm or office practice as well as court rules regarding the use of footnotes. Some courts require footnotes to be in the same size type as the body of a brief whereas others, such as the U.S. Supreme Court, require smaller type. Supreme Court Rule 33.1(b) requires 10-point type for footnotes and 12-point type for the body of briefs submitted to the Court.
- Don't assume all readers will read all footnotes. Thus, use footnotes to cite to legal authorities or to elaborate but never to set forth a main argument. Avoid these "talking" footnotes. If an argument deserves to be made, it deserves to be made in the body of the document.
- Avoid footnotes that wrap from one page to the next (or beyond). Many readers will leave the narrative discussion, read the footnote, turn the page, and then resume reading where they are, rather than returning to the page on which the footnote began.
- Never use endnotes.

Having to read a footnote resembles having to go downstairs to answer the door while in the midst of making love.

Noel Coward

Figure 8-2   Sample Trial Court Brief

Following is an actual brief submitted to the United States District Court for the Southern District of California. Portions of the brief have been edited. The author wishes to apologize to the authors of the original brief for any revisions.

Seyamack Kouretchian (State Bar No. 171741)
Robert Berkowitz (State Bar No. 227888)
Rachel Lipsky (State Bar No. 239128)
COAST LAW GROUP LLP
169 Saxony Road, Suite 204
Encinitas, California 92024
Tel: (760) 942-8505
Fax: (760) 942-8515
Attorneys for Defendant,
Shawn Hogan

UNITED STATES DISTRICT COURT
SOUTHERN DISTRICT OF CALIFORNIA

UNIVERSAL CITY STUDIOS PRODUCTIONS LLLP, a Delaware limited liability limited partnership, Plaintiff, vs. SHAWN HOGAN, an individual Defendant.	))))))))))))))	Case No. 06 CV 0545 W WMc **DEFENDANT'S MOTION TO DISMISS FOR LACK OF SUBJECT MATTER JURISDICTION** **(Fed. R. Civ. P. 12(h)(3))** Judge: Hon. Thomas J. Whelan Date: November 27, 2006 Courtroom 7 10:00 a.m.

I.

SUMMARY OF ARGUMENT

The Plaintiff's Complaint for Copyright Infringement must be dismissed for lack of subject matter jurisdiction. Evidence recently obtained from the Plaintiff through discovery has revealed that the Copyright Certificate of Registration ("Copyright Registration") upon which the Plaintiff is relying is patently invalid. In addition, this evidence has revealed that the Plaintiff lacks standing to bring or maintain this action before this Court. Either of these circumstances—an invalid federal copyright or lack of standing—is sufficient, as a matter of law, to preclude this Court from asserting subject matter jurisdiction. For this reason, Defendant Shawn Hogan seeks an order dismissing the Plaintiff's Complaint.

II.

STATEMENT OF FACTS

On March 14, 2006, Plaintiff Universal City Studios Productions, LLLP filed suit against San Diego County resident, Defendant Shawn Hogan (hereinafter "Hogan"). In its Complaint, which consists of only one cause of action, the Plaintiff alleges that Hogan infringed the Plaintiff's Copyright Registration in the motion picture *Meet the Fockers* (hereinafter "Movie") by making a copy of it available over the Internet. Attached to the Plaintiff's Complaint is a copy of the Copyright Registration, which makes no reference whatsoever to the Plaintiff. Rather, the Copyright Registration identifies a third party, Universal City Studios, LLLP, (a Delaware limited liability limited partnership, which is neither a parent nor subsidiary of Plaintiff) as the copyright claimant and the author.

The Copyright Registration contains the following statements, all of which were certified under law to be correct:

1. that third party Universal City Studios, LLLP is a co-author of the Movie;
2. that third party Universal City Studios, LLLP submitted the copyright application;
3. that third party Universal City Studios, LLLP is the copyright claimant; and
4. that the individual signing the application is the authorized agent of third party Universal City Studios, LLLP.

The application was signed on January 20, 2005, by third party Universal City Studios, LLLP and received by the United States Copyright Office on January 25, 2005. Notably, the Plaintiff never alleges in its Complaint how it came to own the Copyright Registration, so Hogan was initially unable to contest the issue of subject matter jurisdiction and was thereby forced to file an answer.

In order to establish whether the Plaintiff actually had any rights in the Copyright Registration, on or about August 10, 2006, Defendant propounded and served upon the Plaintiff the Defendant's Request for Production of Documents and Things, pursuant to Fed. R. Civ. P. 34. In his Request No. 3 of the Defendant's Request for Production of Documents and Things, Hogan requested that Plaintiff produce "any and all documents that evidence or relate to a transfer of ownership of copyright registration no. PA-1-255-623."

On or about September 15, 2006, the Plaintiff responded to Hogan's said request as follows: "Universal will produce, or has produced, the following document evidencing the transfer of ownership of copyright registration no. PA-1-255-623: the operative assignment agreement related to the copyright."

Included with Plaintiff's response was a copy of the "operative assignment agreement" ("Assignment Agreement"). The Assignment Agreement indicated that third party Universal City Studios, LLLP had assigned all of its "right, title and interest in and to . . . " the Movie, "including . . . the copyright in and to [the Movie] . . . ." The Assignment Agreement further indicated that third party Universal City Studios, LLLP had divested itself of any and all rights in the Movie by assigning them to the Plaintiff on November 29, 2004.

Based upon the evidence recently uncovered, the following facts are now known:

1. On November 29, 2004, third party Universal City Studios, LLLP transferred all of its rights in the Movie to the Plaintiff;
2. At the time of the said assignment, there was no Copyright Registration;

3. Some two months after having assigned all "right, title and interest" in the Movie to the Plaintiff, third party Universal City Studios, LLLP applied for the Copyright Registration in its own name as an author and claimant;

4. At the time of the Copyright Registration, third party Universal City Studios, LLLP did not own any right, title, or interest in the Movie;

5. The Plaintiff has not identified any document other than the Assignment Agreement that it purports to evidence or relate to a transfer of ownership in or to the Movie or to the Copyright Registration; and

6. The Plaintiff's Complaint for Copyright Infringement against Hogan is specifically based upon the Copyright Registration.

In light of these facts, which expose the lack of subject matter jurisdiction by this Court, Hogan has filed this Motion to Dismiss.

III.

ARGUMENT

A. This Court Must Dismiss the Plaintiff's Complaint for Lack of Subject Matter Jurisdiction Because the Defendant's Purported Copyright Registration is Invalid and Unenforceable.

Whenever it appears by suggestion of the parties or otherwise that the court lacks jurisdiction of the subject matter, the court shall dismiss the action. Fed. R. Civ. P. 12(h)(3). An action for infringement may not be brought unless registration of the copyright claim has been made in accordance with the Copyright Act. 17 U.S.C. § 411 (2000). Thus, "[a] copyright registration is a jurisdictional prerequisite to an infringement action." *In re Napster, Inc. Copyright Litig.*, 2005 U.S. Dist. LEXIS 7236 (N.D. Cal. 2005) (citing 17 U.S.C. § 411); *see also* 2 Melville B. Nimmer & David Nimmer, *Nimmer on Copyright* § 7.16 (2002) (citing *Chicago Bd. of Educ. v. Substance, Inc.*, 354 F.3d 624, 631 (7th Cir. 2003), *cert. denied*, 543 U.S. 816 (2004)).

Only "the owner of copyright or of any exclusive right in the work may obtain registration of the copyright claim . . . ." 17 U.S.C. § 408 (2000). Once an author assigns its common-law copyright in a work, it thereby divests itself of all right to claim copyright in such work. *See* Nimmer, *supra*, § 5.01 (citing *Ripley v. Findlay Galleries, Inc.*, 155 F.2d 955 (7th Cir. 1946)); *see also Grandma Moses Props., Inc. v. This Week Magazine*, 117 F. Supp. 348 (S.D.N.Y. 1953).

For this reason, a copyright registration obtained by a party other than the owner has no legal effect. *Warren v. Fox Family Worldwide, Inc.*, 328 F.3d 1136, 1143 (9th Cir. 2003) (citing 17 U.S.C. §§ 201(b), 501(b) (2000)) (holding that a copyright registration is invalid when obtained by the work's creator pursuant to a work-for-hire relationship); *Morgan, Inc. v. White Rock Distilleries, Inc.*, 230 F. Supp. 2d 104, 108 (D. Me. 2002). Thus, a claim based upon such a copyright registration must be dismissed for lack of subject matter jurisdiction. *Warren*, 328 F.3d at 1143.

It is a plaintiff who bears the burden of demonstrating that the court has subject matter jurisdiction to hear the action. *Warren v. Fox Family Worldwide, Inc.*, 171 F. Supp. 2d 1057, 1060 (C.D. Cal. 2001), *aff'd*, 328 F.3d 1136 (9th Cir. 2003). The general rule is that "[i]n any judicial proceedings the certificate of a registration . . . shall constitute *prima facie* evidence of the validity of the copyright *and of the facts stated in the certificate.*" 17 U.S.C. § 410 (2000) (emphasis added). However, the evidence recently disclosed by the Plaintiff to support its claim of ownership proves exactly the opposite conclusion—that the Copyright Registration has no legal effect.

The sequence of events as documented by the Plaintiff's evidence makes it clear that third party Universal City Studios, LLLP assigned *all* of its rights in the Movie two months *before* it applied for the Copyright Registration. Thus, at that time of registration, third party Universal City Studios, LLLP was not the owner of the copyright; nor was it the owner of any of the exclusive rights in the Movie. In other words, at the time of registration, third party Universal City Studios, LLLP had as much authority to apply for the Copyright Registration as did Hogan—absolutely none. For this reason, the Copyright Registration upon which the Plaintiff is relying is simply not enforceable.

Federal courts have unwaveringly enforced the statutory ownership requirement by giving no legal effect to copyright registrations obtained by anyone other than the actual owner of the copyright in the underlying work. Where, as here, the Copyright Registration upon which the pending action is based was obtained by somebody other than the actual owner in the copyright, the registration is plainly and fatally defective, invalid, and unenforceable. In fact, the Copyright Office would not have registered the subject copyright had it have known that third party Universal City Studios, LLLP was not the rightful copyright claimant at the time it submitted the application. *See* 37 C.F.R. § 201.7(c)(4)(vi) (2005), which states that a completed registration will be cancelled where "the 'claimant' named in the application does not have the right to claim copyright." The Plaintiff's attempt to nevertheless maintain this action before this Court is plainly improper and must, by order of this Court, cease because the Copyright Registration upon which the Plaintiff is relying is fatally defective, invalid, and unenforceable. For these reasons, Defendant Hogan requests that this Court grant this Motion to Dismiss the Plaintiff's Complaint for lack of subject matter jurisdiction.

B. This Court Must Dismiss the Plaintiff's Complaint Because the Plaintiff Does Not Have Standing to Bring or Maintain This Action.

The law is clear. "Standing is a jurisdictional requirement, and the court must dismiss an action for lack of subject matter jurisdiction if it determines that plaintiff lacks standing to assert a claim. *Warren*, 171 F. Supp. 2d at 1063. With regard to copyright infringement actions, the law is equally clear that only the legal or beneficial owner of an exclusive right under copyright has standing to assert a claim for infringement. "The legal or beneficial owner of an exclusive right under a copyright is entitled, subject to the requirements of section 411, to institute an action for any infringement of that particular right committed while he or she is the owner of it." 17 U.S.C. § 501(b). Section 411 provides that "no action for infringement of the copyright in any United States work shall be instituted until registration of the copyright claim has been made in accordance with this title."

If a plaintiff is not the author of the copyrighted work then he or she must establish an ownership interest through the chain of title in order to support a valid claim of copyright infringement. *Religious Tech. Ctr. v. Netcom On-Line Commun. Servs.*, 923 F. Supp. 1231, 1241 (N.D. Cal. 1995) (citing Nimmer, *supra*, § 12.11[C]); *see also Motta v. Samuel Weiser, Inc.*, 768 F.2d 481, 484 (1st Cir. 1985). If the plaintiff cannot establish this ownership interest, then he or she does not have standing to bring an action for copyright infringement. *Maljack Prods. v. Goodtimes Home Video Corp.*, 1994 U.S. Dist. LEXIS 5838 (C.D. Cal. Apr. 26, 1994); *see also Motta*, 768 F.2d at 484.

Once again, it is the evidence recently disclosed by the Plaintiff in support of its claim of copyright ownership that conclusively establishes that it lacks standing to bring or maintain the subject action. This is because this evidence shows that either the underlying Copyright Registration is invalid or that the Plaintiff does not have any right in the Movie that it can allege was infringed by Hogan. Whatever the case, the evidence is clear that the Plaintiff lacks standing to bring or maintain this action.

1. If the Assignment Agreement Is Valid, Then the Plaintiff Lacks Standing to Bring This Action Because the Copyright Registration Is Invalid.

The Copyright Act confers standing only upon those Plaintiffs who are asserting their rights under a valid copyright registration. By requiring compliance with 17 U.S.C. § 411, the Copyright Act expressly requires compliance with the entire title, including the requirement in 17 U.S.C. § 408 that the party applying for the copyright registration be the owner of the copyright. When the party that applied for the copyright registration is not the owner at the time of registration, then the registration has not been obtained in compliance with the Copyright Act, and the registration is invalid and unenforceable. The Plaintiff appears to claim that it has acquired rights in the Movie under the Assignment Agreement. However, the Assignment Agreement was executed two months *before* the Copyright Registration was applied for. If, therefore, the Assignment Agreement is effective to establish chain of title, then the document is also effective to prove that third party Universal City Studios, LLLP had divested itself of all rights, title, and interest in the Movie and, therefore, did not have any right to apply for and obtain the Copyright Registration.

The Plaintiff cannot have it both ways. Either third party Universal City Studios, LLLP assigned all "right, title and interest" in the Movie and then mistakenly or fraudulently obtained the Copyright Registration in its own name, or the Assignment Agreement is somehow invalid and third party Universal City Studios, LLLP properly applied for the Copyright Registration.

In bringing this action, the Plaintiff is relying upon an invalid Copyright Registration if it alleges that the Assignment Agreement is valid. Therefore, because the Plaintiff has failed to identify another valid copyright registration for the Movie, it lacks standing to bring or maintain this action for copyright infringement against Hogan. For this reason, this Court must dismiss this action for lack of subject matter jurisdiction.

2. If Plaintiff Alleges That the Copyright Registration Is Valid, Then the Plaintiff Lacks Standing to Bring This Action Because It Has Failed to Establish Chain of Title in the Movie.

The law requires that a plaintiff asserting an ownership interest in a copyrighted work document the chain of title by which it obtained its rights. The burden is on the Plaintiff to prove its ownership rights. If the Plaintiff alleges that the Copyright Registration is valid, then the Assignment Agreement is invalid because, according to the terms of the Copyright Registration, third party Universal City Studios, LLLP is the owner of the copyright in the Movie. If, therefore, the Assignment Agreement is invalid, then the Plaintiff has failed to set forth any evidence to document the chain of title through which it allegedly acquired rights in the Movie. Without any showing of how the Plaintiff acquired rights in the Movie, the Plaintiff lacks standing to bring this suit because it has failed to establish the ownership of any right which it can claim was infringed by Hogan. For this reason, this Court is respectfully urged to dismiss the Plaintiff's Complaint for lack of subject matter jurisdiction.

IV.

CONCLUSION

For the reasons set forth above, Hogan moves this Court for an order dismissing the Plaintiff's Complaint, without leave to amend, for lack of subject matter jurisdiction.

Dated: October 19, 2006   s/Seyamack Kouretchian
                            Seyamack@CoastLawGroup.com
                            Coast Law Group, LLP
                            Seyamack Kouretchian
                            Attorney for Defendant, Shawn Hogan

chapter 9

Pleadings and Transactional Documents

StyleLinks

http://topics.law.cornell.edu/wex/pleading
Cornell University Law School's Legal Information Institute offers some basic information on pleadings and links to other sources.

www.courtinfo.ca.gov/forms.htm
The California Judicial Council offers a variety of litigation forms, many of which may be filled out electronically.

www.kinseylaw.com
The website of the law offices of Eugene E. Kinsey of California provides numerous forms for complaints, answers, motions, and other pleadings, as well as transactional documents.

www.justia.com
Justia provides links to hundreds of litigation forms for both state and federal practice.

A. Pleadings

1. Introduction

A pleading is a document submitted to a court in the course of litigation. In federal cases, the only pleadings are a complaint, an answer, an answer to a counterclaim, an answer to a cross-claim, a third-party complaint, and a third-party answer. Fed. R. Civ. P. 7(a). In some jurisdictions, the term *pleading* encompasses almost anything filed with the court in the course of a pending action.

Court rules today have eliminated older requirements that made pleading so complex and technical that a failure to follow rules could lead to a dismissal of the case. The current approach is called *notice pleading,* which generally means that a pleading must be sufficiently clear as to notify another party of the nature of one's claims or defenses.

2. Format of Pleadings

All jurisdictions have rules relating to the content and format for pleadings. Many state rules of civil procedure are patterned after the Federal Rules of Civil Procedure. For example, most state courts follow Fed. R. Civ. P. 8(d)(1) requiring allegations to be "simple, concise, and direct." Some courts have preprinted and fillable forms available on the Internet. For example, the Judicial Council of California provides a variety of pleading forms at its website at www.courtinfo.ca.gov/forms.htm. Some of the more common rules imposed by courts for pleadings are as follows:

- **Caption.** All pleadings start with a caption that identifies the court, the docket number assigned to the case by the court, an identification of the parties to the case, and the title of the document, such as "Answer to Plaintiff's Complaint."
- **Introductory Matter.** Introductory paragraphs often identify the parties and state the basis for the court's jurisdiction (for example, there is often a reference to the particular statute that allows for the filing of the pleading).
- **Numbering.** Paragraphs are numbered consecutively.
- **Pleading in the Alternative.** Parties are allowed to plead in the alternative and inconsistently. For example, a complaint may allege that the same conduct is both a breach of contract and negligence.
- **Citations.** Pleadings routinely cite statutes but never cite cases.
- **Paragraph Content.** Most paragraphs include only a single allegation so that the other party can readily deny or admit the allegation. Most pleadings "tell a story" in that they set forth the party's claim or defense in a chronological fashion. For example, a complaint for breach of contract generally begins by alleging that a contract was entered into by the parties, then states that the contract was breached by the defendant, and then concludes by stating that the breach caused damage to the plaintiff.

- **Endings.** Most pleadings end with a *prayer*, which is the party's request for relief. Thus, a complaint usually requests money damages or some other relief, and an answer usually requests that the plaintiff's complaint be dismissed.
- **Incorporation by Reference.** Pleadings routinely incorporate other information by reference. Thus, paragraph 16 of a complaint might incorporate the allegations from paragraphs 1 through 5 so that the plaintiff does not have to repeat the information.
- **Responding to a Complaint.** Each allegation in a complaint must be responded to by the defendant. If the defendant does not expressly deny a fact or allege that he or she has no knowledge about the fact, it will be deemed admitted. Moreover, if a defendant does not specifically raise certain defenses in the answer, these defenses may be waived.
- **Attachments.** Pleadings may attach other documents. Thus, a complaint that alleges a breach of a contract may attach of the copy of the contract. The terms of the attachment are often incorporated by reference in the pleading.
- **Amendments.** Don't count on being able to amend a sloppy pleading. Although leave to amend pleadings can be granted by a court, in some instances, a failure to plead a matter may preclude proof of it at trial, and all courts eventually refuse to allow amendment of pleadings without good cause.
- **Certificate of Service.** All court pleadings after the complaint must be accompanied by a certificate of service, verifying that the pleading was provided to all parties, usually by mail or personal service. The complaint is accompanied by a summons issued by the court that will indicate how the defendant was served. The summons is then returned to the court with this information completed, usually by a professional process server.

3. Using Form Books

Form books provide suggested forms and models for various documents. There are some excellent form books for preparing pleadings. Most states have state-specific form books, and law firms that engage in litigation have numerous sample forms that can be used as guides. Make sure that you do not view forms as mere fill-in-the-blank documents. Use the form books or samples as helpful guides but modify or update them when needed. In addition, be careful when using a prior pleading as a form so you don't import errors and irrelevant allegations. Although preparing a pleading does not usually require the same level of creativity as an appellate brief, it does provide an opportunity to advocate for the client. Consider the following form books:

- *Federal Practice and Procedure* by Charles Alan Wright and Arthur R. Miller (usually called "Wright and Miller") is an excellent multivolume set relating to practice in federal courts that includes many forms.

- *American Jurisprudence Pleading and Practice Forms, Annotated.* This set consists of more than thirty volumes of forms and provides more than 40,000 forms relating to litigation, including forms for complaints, answers, discovery procedures, motions, and jury instructions.
- *Bender's Federal Practice Forms.* This twenty-volume set includes forms for use in federal practice.

See Figure 9-1 for a sample pleading.

Anna T. Carr
Carr & Nelson, LLP
1010 Second Avenue
Suite 1700
San Diego, CA 92110
State Bar No: 12898
(619) 276-1090
Attorney for Plaintiff

SUPERIOR COURT OF THE STATE OF CALIFORNIA

COUNTY OF SAN DIEGO

Liberty Associates, LLC	)	CASE NO: 08-1088
	)	
Plaintiff,	)	COMPLAINT FOR
	)	BREACH OF
	)	CONTRACT
v.	)	
	)	
	)	
Jackson Enterprises, Inc., and	)	
	)	
Does 1 through 10	)	
	)	
	)	
	)	
	)	
	)	
Defendants		

Plaintiff complains and for causes of action alleges as follows:

FIRST CAUSE OF ACTION

(For Breach of Contract Against Jackson Enterprises, Inc.)

1. Plaintiff Liberty Associates, LLC ("Plaintiff") is a Limited Liability Company organized and existing under the laws of the State of California with its principal offices in the City of San Diego, County of San Diego.

2. Defendant Jackson Enterprises, Inc. ("Defendant") is a corporation organized and existing under the laws of the State of California with its principal offices located at 1800 Pomerado Road, in the City of San Diego, County of San Diego.

3. Plaintiff is ignorant of the true names and capacities of Defendants sued as Does 1 through 10, inclusive, and therefore sues these Defendants by such fictitious names. Plaintiff will amend this Complaint to allege their true names and capacities when ascertained.

4. Plaintiff is informed and believes and thereon alleges that each of the Defendants was the agent and employee of each of the remaining Defendants and was at all times acting within the purpose and scope of such agency and employment.

5. On or about February 15, 2013, in the City of San Diego, County of San Diego, State of California, Plaintiff and Defendant entered into a written agreement, a copy of which is attached hereto as Exhibit "A" and made a part hereof. By the terms of the written agreement Defendant agreed to pay Plaintiff for certain construction services performed by Plaintiff for Defendant.

6. The consideration set forth in the agreement was fair and reasonable.

7. Plaintiff has performed all conditions, covenants, and promises required by it on its part to be performed in accord with the terms and conditions of the written agreement.

8. On or about May 1, 2013, the Defendant breached the agreement by failing and refusing to pay Plaintiff for the services provided by Plaintiff to Defendant.

9. By reason of Defendant's breach of the contract as alleged in this Complaint, the Plaintiff has suffered damages in the sum of Seventy-Five Thousand Dollars ($75,000).

10. By the terms of the written agreement, the Plaintiff is entitled to recover reasonable attorney fees incurred in the enforcement of the provisions of the agreement. By reason of the aforementioned breach of the Defendant, the Plaintiff has been forced to secure the services of the law firm Carr & Nelson LLP to prosecute this lawsuit.

WHEREFORE, Plaintiff requests judgment against Defendants, and each of them, as follows:

1. For compensatory damages in the sum of $75,000;

2. For interest on the sum of $75,000 from and after May 1, 2013, to date of judgment;

3. For reasonable attorney fees according to proof;

4. For costs of suit incurred; and

5. For such other and further relief as the court may deem proper.

Date: _____

_____
Anna T. Carr, Esq.
Carr & Nelson, LLP
Attorneys for Plaintiff

4. Legalese

Although this Handbook has discussed the importance of writing in plain English, you will find that the language used in pleadings tends to be more legalistic. For example, the prayer usually states "WHEREFORE, this Plaintiff respectfully prays that . . ." rather than the plainer statement "Therefore, the Plaintiff requests the following relief." The reliance on legalese is perhaps understandable given that many pleading forms have existed for hundreds of years. Moreover, many law firms use pleadings similar to the ones they used twenty years ago. Finally, although pleadings will be reviewed by clients and are often verified by clients (meaning that the client verifies by signature that he or she has read the pleading and that it is truthful and accurate), pleadings are primarily intended for a legal audience and thus there has been no aggressive movement to modernize them. For example, the sample complaint shown as Figure 9-1 uses far more terms of art and outmoded expressions than would be advisable in other legal writings, such as letters or memos. Experienced legal readers, however, are easily able to cut through these expressions to understand their meaning.

B. Transactional Documents

www.allaboutforms.com
This website offers more than 2,000 free forms for contracts, employment agreements, leases, deeds, and other documents.

www.lectlaw.com
The site of The 'Lectric Law Library offers a variety of forms, including some sample letters and checklists for motions.

www.onecle.com
OneCle provides links to hundreds of forms used in "real life" business and other transactions.

1. Introduction

The term *transactional documents* usually refers to documents used in various transactions, such as contracts, leases, employment agreements, and corporate minutes. Legal professionals seldom draft these documents "from scratch." Generally, they rely on forms or models that have proven useful in other instances.

In many cases, there is not a great deal of creativity in transactional documents, nor should there be. Later readers of a lease may examine it carefully trying to find a loophole so they can terminate the lease. The employee may later contend that he or she is not bound by a noncompetition provision in an employment agreement because the provision is unreasonable as to its duration. Thus, because the document must protect the client in the future against interpretations that were unforeseen at the time the document was drafted, transactional documents tend to be overlong as they attempt to foresee and forestall every possible future problem raised by a hostile reader.

2. Drafting Considerations

There are a variety of considerations and objectives to keep in mind when preparing transactional documents.

- **Review applicable statutes.** In many instances, statutes control the content or form of documents. For example, most statutes require that a disclaimer of a warranty be printed "conspicuously." Similarly, an assignment of a registered trademark must be in writing and must include a statement that the goodwill relating to the mark is being assigned with it. 15 U.S.C. § 1060

(2006). Thus, some preliminary research may be needed to ensure that the document complies with all legal requirements. Although courts give great latitude to parties in structuring their transactions, and generally will not substitute their judgment for the judgment of the parties, applicable statutory and common law provisions must be followed.

- **Volunteer to draft the document.** The party who creates the initial draft of a document has certain advantages in selecting the structure and word choice. Some adverse parties will only perform a cursory review of a document presented to them to ensure it includes the basics of a transaction. Although there is no place for deceit or trickery, there is nothing wrong with trying to draft a document that protects the client to the greatest extent possible. On the other hand, it is a standard legal principle that any ambiguity in a document is construed against the party who drafted it.
- **Avoid making business decisions.** It is the legal professional's job to draft a document that memorializes the transaction and sets forth the parties' duties. Although attorneys can and should offer advice to clients, it is not appropriate for the drafter to insert himself or herself into the negotiations in such a way that the deal breaks apart.
- **Avoid overreaching.** A good drafter will protect the client's interests but will not draft the agreement in such a lopsided way that the other party immediately rejects it and negotiations stall. Be fair and accurate. Consider using the tools on your word processor (namely, the "track changes" tool) to show the changes you have made to a document sent to you by another party, a technique called *redlining* because the changes usually show up in red on your computer screen. You can easily accept or reject changes.
- **Use headings.** Because many agreements can be long, use descriptive headings for each section so the reader can readily find a needed provision. Similarly, consider using a table of contents for long documents. If the document will include several definitions, include a separate alphabetized definition section at the beginning of the document for all the defined terms.

3. Elements of Transactional Documents

Although the elements of transactional documents vary greatly, some common components are as follows:

a. Introductory Matter

Most documents begin with an introduction, identifying the name of the document, the parties who will sign it, and its effective date.

b. Recitals

Many documents include a recitals clause, indicating the purpose of the document. For example, a partnership agreement might provide *It is the intent of the parties to form a partnership under California law . . . .*

c. Consideration

Because all contracts require consideration, contractual documents usually include a statement similar to the following: *For valuable consideration, the receipt and sufficiency of which are hereby acknowledged, the parties agree as follows* . . . . This recital then prevents any party to the agreement from challenging the agreement on the basis that there was no consideration supporting it.

d. Operative Terms

The body of the document will include the terms of the parties' agreement, their duties, obligations, and the consequences of noncompliance.

e. Standard Provisions

Most agreements include a number of standard provisions, such as clauses stating the applicable law under which the agreement will be governed, whether the agreement is assignable, that the agreement can only be modified by another agreement in writing, how notice of default will be given, that references to the masculine *he* and *him* are meant to include the feminine, and so forth. These standard provisions are often called *boilerplate* because they routinely appear in most transactional documents.

f. Signatures

Agreements end with the parties' signatures.

4. Using Form Books

There are numerous well-known form books that provide suggested forms, language, and checklists for transactional documents. As with all form books, use the forms as a guide and feel free to modify the forms when needed. Most law firms and offices have numerous standard forms that have served clients well, and these are excellent starting places. Create your own form files of documents so you have samples on hand. Indicate who drafted the document so you can contact the drafter if you have questions. Be aware of the following limitations in using forms for drafting transactional documents:

- Using forms slavishly often results in importing unneeded material, including incorrect names, pronouns, and labels. Proofread carefully.
- Create defined terms to identify parties and issues and use these consistently throughout the document. Use your word processor's "find and replace" feature to ensure consistency.
- Avoid cross-referencing to so many provisions that a reader is hopelessly confused. For example, avoid statements such as *Tenant shall provide notice as provided in Paragraph 11(a)(ii); however, as provided in Paragraph 14(b)(iii), such notice must comply with all provisions of Paragraph 15 hereof.*

■ Avoid legalese when you can. Like pleadings, forms tend to use more archaic language than some other legal writings. Trim away stuffy expressions when you can but realize that many law firms are wedded to their tried and true forms and are resistant to making changes. Some lawyers have seen so many agreements start with the word *Witnesseth* that they never question its use. Nevertheless, use expressions such as *lessee* rather than *party of the first part* and *as provided in paragraph 4* rather than *as provided hereinabove*. For example, consider the following two paragraphs:

Legalese	Improved
Lessee shall make and deposit as and for rent the sum of $850 per month, which payment shall be made on the first day of each and every month throughout the term of the lease. Payment shall be made to the Landlord at the address provided hereinabove in this Agreement.	Lessee must pay rent of $850 per month. Payment must be made to the Landlord on the first day of each month at the address provided in Paragraph 2.

■ Make the document readable. Give your document a descriptive title such as *Employment Agreement* rather than *Agreement*. Use lists and consistent numbering to present the information logically. Make sure the information is presented in a parallel structure.
■ Move bulky information into attachments. Use attachments or exhibits to identify long lists of items (for example, a list of assets purchased or a list of partners) rather than including such information in the body of the document.

Ethics Alert: Preserving Client Confidentiality

An emerging issue relating to client confidentiality is the duty to "scrub" documents so as to eliminate metadata, which is information relating to the creation, management, and tracking of an electronically created document. For example, if you use a law office form lease that was originally created for client Smith for new client Jones, metadata would reveal that the lease was originally created for client Smith and would reveal its critical terms and provisions. Metadata mining also allows readers to view changes and deletions made through the course of a document's drafting, the sequence of those changes, comments made by the drafters, and other possible confidential information. Failure to "scrub" metadata out of confidential client documents can lead to a waiver of attorney-client privilege or work product privilege. Ethics opinions about metadata mining are still evolving, with some jurisdictions holding that recipients of documents cannot mine for metadata because it invades another attorney's client confidences but other jurisdictions holding that senders have a duty to scrub metadata, and if they fail to do so, the recipient is free to mine for it. Most law firms are now using sophisticated software that scrubs or strips metadata out of confidential documents.

Following are some well-known form books used in drafting transactional documents:

- *American Jurisprudence Legal Forms, 2d.* This set consists of more than twenty-five alphabetically arranged volumes of more than 20,000 forms and provides forms for contracts, wills, and leases as well as for hundreds of other topics.
- *West's Legal Forms 3d, 4th, and 5th.* This set of books, consisting of more than sixty volumes, contains a variety of forms for general law practice, including bankruptcy forms, forms for the purchase and sale of real estate, and forms relating to business organizations such as partnerships and corporations.
- *Current Legal Forms with Tax Analysis* by Jacob Rabkin and Mark H. Johnson is a thirty-four-volume set of forms for law practice, with an emphasis on business forms. The forms are excellent and include a number of checklists and practice guides and tips for drafting transactional documents.

See Figure 9-2 for a sample partnership agreement.

Figure 9-2   General Partnership Agreement

THIS AGREEMENT is entered into on _____, 20___, among Ann Myers ("Myers"), an individual residing at _____, Gregory Kelly ("Kelly"), an individual residing at _____ _____, and Philip Hendrix ("Hendrix"), an individual residing at _____.

Myers, Kelly, and Hendrix are sometimes referred to individually as "Partner" and collectively as "Partners."

RECITALS

WHEREAS, the Partners desire to form a partnership for the purpose of _____ and have decided that it is in their best commercial interests to do so.

NOW, THEREFORE, for good and valuable consideration, the receipt and sufficiency of which are hereby acknowledged, the Partners agree as follows:

1. *Formation and Purpose of Partnership.* The Partners hereby form a general partnership (the "Partnership") under the laws of the State of _____ for the purpose of _____ _____ and the carrying on of any and all activities necessary and incident thereto.
2. *Partnership Name and Address.* The name of the Partnership is "MKH Enterprises" and its principal place of business shall be located at _____ _____, in the City of

_____, State of _____, and at such other places as may be mutually agreed upon by the Partners in writing.

3. *Term.* The Partnership shall commence on _____, 20___, and shall continue until dissolved by mutual agreement of the Partners or as provided in Paragraph 13 below.

4. *Capital Contributions.*

(a) *Initial Capital Contributions.* Each Partner shall contribute the following amounts in cash ("Initial Capital Contribution") on or before _____, 20___, or this Agreement shall be void.

Name	Amount
Myers	$ _____
Kelly	$ _____
Hendrix	$ _____

(b) *Additional Capital Contributions.* At such times as the Partners agree by majority vote of the Partners in accordance with their Partnership Interests that additional capital is necessary to operate the business of the Partnership, the Partners shall contribute additional capital in accordance with their respective Partnership Interests (as defined in Paragraph 5) at the relevant time and in accordance with the agreed amount of the additional capital contribution and the method of payment thereof determined by the Partners. If any Partner fails to make an additional capital contribution required to be made under this Agreement within the time period prescribed, such Partner shall be deemed to be a "Defaulting Partner" and a non-defaulting Partner shall be entitled to make the contribution on behalf of the Defaulting Partner and such contribution shall be a personal debt due and owing to the non-defaulting Partner from the Defaulting Partner(s) with interest at the rate of _____ percent (__%) per annum until paid. No money or assets shall be distributed by the Partnership to a Defaulting Partner until the Defaulting Partner shall have paid in full the amount owed to the non-defaulting Partner(s), together with interest. The term "capital contribution" shall mean a Partner's Initial Capital Contribution together with any additional capital contribution.

(c) *Return of Capital Contribution.* No interest shall be paid on any Partner's capital contribution. No Partner has a right to receive a return of all or any part of his or her capital contribution except as expressly provided in this Agreement or in the event of liquidation or dissolution of the Partnership, and then only to the extent of the net assets of the Partnership available for distribution.

5. *Interest of Partners in Partnership.* The Partners shall own the following interest in the Partnership ("Partnership Interest" or "Partnership Interests"):

Name	Interest in Partnership
Myers	_____%
Kelly	_____%
Hendrix	_____%

Any change in the Partnership Interest of any Partner shall be reflected in writing and signed by all Partners.

6. *Profits and Losses.* Partners shall share in the profits and losses of the Partnership in accordance with their respective Partnership Interests.

7. *Voting.* The Partners shall be vested with voting rights in the Partnership equal to their respective Partnership Interests. Except as otherwise agreed by the partners in writing or except as otherwise provided in this Agreement, actions of the Partnership shall require majority action of the outstanding Partnership Interests.

8. *Management.* In the general operation of the Partnership business, all the Partners must be consulted and their advice must be obtained as much as is practicable. However, for the purpose of ensuring continuity in the conduct of the Partnership business, the general management of the Partnership business shall vest solely in Myers who shall be the Managing Partner. Myers is entitled to enter into agreements on behalf of the Partnership for the conduct of partnership operations in the ordinary course of business. Persons dealing with the Partnership are entitled to rely on the power and authority of Myers.

   Notwithstanding the foregoing, nothing in this Agreement is intended to grant Myers the authority to make all decisions regarding the business of the Partnership. The authority vested in Myers pertains only to the right to bind the Partnership, without the consent or approval of any other Partner, for contracts or obligations in the ordinary course of business that are necessary, appropriate, or incidental to the Partnership's business.

   Myers shall not undertake any of the following business activities without the majority vote of the Partners in accordance with their Partnership Interests:
   (a) borrow money in excess of _____Dollars ($____);
   (b) purchase or sell any real estate;
   (c) enter into any agreement that would require the Partnership to make any payment of more than _____Dollars ($____) per year;
   (d) compromise any claim or institute any litigation or other proceeding on behalf of the Partnership; or
   (e) sell all or substantially all of the Partnership's assets.

9. *Duties of Partners.* Each of the Partners shall give his or her undivided time and attention to the Partnership business and shall use his or her best efforts to promote the interests of the Partnership. Partners shall have fiduciary duties to each other and to the Partnership.

10. *Books of Account.* Books of account of the transactions of the Partnership shall be kept at the principal place of business of the Partnership and shall be available at all reasonable times for inspection by any Partner. Financial statements shall be prepared on a quarterly basis and shall include a statement of cash flow. The financial statements shall be prepared by independent certified public accountants selected by the Partners. The tax and accounting year of the Partnership shall be the calendar year. Any Partner, at his or her sole expense, may cause the books of the Partnership to be audited at any time. No later than thirty (30) days after the close of the fiscal year, an annual accounting shall be prepared by the Partnership's independent certified public accountants.

11. *Bank Accounts.* The funds of the partnership shall be kept in such bank accounts or in such manner designated by the Partners. Checks drawn on Partnership funds in any account shall be signed by Myers or such person or persons as the Partnership shall designate from time to time.

12. *Withdrawals, Distributions, and Expenses.*

(a) *Withdrawals.* Each Partner shall be permitted to withdraw from the funds of the Partnership _____ Dollars ($_____) per _____ for the Partner's living expenses. The sums so drawn shall be charged to the Partner and at the annual accounting shall be charged against that Partner's share of the profits. If the Partner's share of the profits is insufficient to equal the sum drawn, the Partner must pay the amount of the deficiency within ten (10) days after notice from the Partnership, and said deficiency shall draw interest at the rate of _____ percent (__%) per year until paid.

(b) *Distributions.* So far as is practicable, the net cash flow, if any, of the Partnership (after allocation of an amount agreed upon by the Partners for working capital obligations and contingencies) shall be distributed among the Partners in accordance with their respective Partnership Interests at least annually or on a more frequent basis as decided by the Partners.

(c) *Expenses.* Partners who have incurred expenses on behalf of the Partnership in the ordinary course of Partnership business shall be reimbursed therefor upon submission to the Partnership of appropriate evidence of such expenses, as determined in the sole discretion of the Partners.

13. *Dissolution.* The Partnership shall be dissolved upon the agreement of all Partners or the sale or other disposition of all or substantially all of its assets. Upon dissolution of the Partnership, the Partners shall proceed with reasonable promptness to liquidate the assets of the Partnership. Thereafter, the assets of the Partnership shall be used and distributed in the following order: first, to pay or provide for the payment of all Partnership liabilities to any

person (other than Partners) and liquidating expenses; second, to pay or provide for the payment of all liabilities to any Partner; and third, to distribute to the Partners, in accordance with their respective Partnership Interests, the remaining assets of the Partnership.

14. *Change of Partners.* Any change of Partners shall be done only in the manner set forth in this Paragraph and any attempt to transfer otherwise shall be void.

(a) *Withdrawal of Partner.* Any Partner may withdraw from the Partnership by giving to each of the other Partners and the Partnership at least thirty (30) days' prior written notice of the Partner's intent to withdraw. On withdrawal of a Partner, that Partner's Partnership Interest shall be determined by appraisal of the value of the Partnership, and the withdrawing Partner shall be repaid his or her capital contribution as follows: After deduction for any draw or indebtedness, the withdrawing Partner shall receive cash payments in _____ (__) equal installments, commencing immediately after the end of the fiscal year for the Partner's Interest in the Partnership's profits. The withdrawal of a Partner under this Paragraph 14(a) shall have no effect upon the continuance of the Partnership or its business.

(b) *Bankruptcy, Death, or Permanent Disability.* The bankruptcy, death, or permanent disability of a Partner (an "Event") shall not result in the dissolution of the Partnership, unless required by law. An Event shall immediately terminate all right, title, and interest of that Partner in the Partnership. The deceased, bankrupt, or permanently disabled Partner's share of the Partnership shall be established based on the date of the Event and, after deduction for any draw or any indebtedness of the Partner, the Partner's estate, trustee in bankruptcy, or the permanently disabled Partner shall be paid a cash payment representing the Partner's capital contribution to the Partnership, the Partner's share of the net profits or losses for the current fiscal year to the date of the Event and the Partner's share of the current Partnership business as of the date of the Event.

(c) *New Partners.* New partners may be added to the Partnership by invitation from the then-existing Partners or by purchase of a withdrawing, deceased, bankrupt, or permanently disabled Partner's Interest. An invitation to a new partner may be extended on a vote of existing Partners representing at least _____ percent (__ %) of the Partnership Interests. When a Partner's interest is to be sold to a third party by a Partner leaving the Partnership, a vote on the acceptability of the proposed new partner shall be made by a vote of existing

Partners representing at least _____ percent (_____%) of the outstanding Partnership Interests. A new partner must execute an amendment to this Agreement agreeing to the terms of this Agreement. In the event a proposed new partner is not found acceptable as provided in this Agreement, the Partnership must purchase the departing Partner's interest at the price and upon the terms offered by the third party, and the Partnership may resell the interest to a candidate acceptable to the Partners as provided in this Paragraph 14.

15. *Miscellaneous Provisions.*

(a) *Valuation.* Any valuation or appraisal of the Partnership or any Partner's interest in the Partnership shall be conducted by an independent appraiser selected by Partners representing a majority of the outstanding Partnership Interests.

(b) *Notices.* All notices required by law or this Agreement shall be in writing and may be delivered to the Partners personally or may be deposited in the United States mail, postage prepaid, addressed to the Partners at their addresses identified in this Agreement.

(c) *Disputes.* Any dispute arising under the terms of this Agreement that cannot be resolved amicably by the parties shall be submitted to binding arbitration in accordance with the rules of the American Arbitration Association.

(d) *Amendments to Agreement.* No modification of this Agreement shall be valid, nor shall any waiver of any term or provision be valid unless such modification or waiver is in writing and signed by all of the Partners.

(e) *Time of Performance.* Whenever performance by a Partner or the Partnership is required under this Agreement, time shall be of the essence.

(f) *Counterparts.* This Agreement may be executed in one or more counterparts, but all such counterparts shall constitute one and the same Agreement.

(g) *Severability.* In the event any provision of this Agreement is declared invalid or unenforceable, then such provision shall be deemed severable from this Agreement, and the remainder of this Agreement shall remain in force and effect.

(h) *Successors and Assigns.* Subject to the provisions hereof, this Agreement shall inure to the benefit of and be binding upon the heirs, personal representatives, successors, and assigns of the parties.

(i) *Entire Agreement.* This Agreement contains the entire understanding of the parties hereto with respect to the subject matter hereof, and there are no other agreements or understandings, whether written or oral, with respect to the subject matter hereof.

(j) *Applicable Law.* This Agreement shall be governed under the laws of the State of _____.

IN WITNESS WHEREOF, the Partners have executed this Agreement at _____, _____, as of the date and year given in this Agreement.

_____
Ann Myers

_____
Gregory Kelly

_____
Philip Hendrix

chapter 10

Legal Conventions and Legal Writing Blunders

StyleLinks

http://libguides.law.ucla.edu
UCLA's School of Law offers helpful guides to legal writing. Select "Legal Writing."

http://law.tm/froomkins-legal-writing-tips-2
Professor Michael Froomkin offers numerous excellent writing tips.

www.plainlanguagenetwork.org/legal/legalwriting.pdf
Judge Mark Painter of Ohio offers 30 suggestions to improve readability in his excellent source *Legal Writing 201*.

http://law.lclark.edu/programs/legal_analysis_and_writing/resources.php
Lewis & Clark Law School's Legal Analysis and Writing Program offers links to several excellent legal writing sites and resources.

A. Legal Conventions

There are a few customs or practices routinely seen in legal writing that are not commonly encountered in other forms of writing. For example, the language in certain documents such as wills, contracts, and deeds remains traditional and somewhat legalistic despite efforts to write in plain English. Recognize that in some instances, you will not be successful in fighting such customs and practices. Some other customs or conventions commonly seen in legal writing include the following.

1. Defined Terms

Because many terms or names are long and may have to be repeated throughout a legal document, legal writers tend to identify fully a term or name when it is first used and then label it by indicating in parentheses the shorthand way they will refer to it later. For example, consider the following shorthand label for *Plaintiff's Supplemental Responses to Defendant's Third Set of Interrogatories ("Supplemental Responses")*. If two parties will be labeled, consider the following form: *Patricia Allen and Maria Lopez (collectively, "Plaintiffs")*. The reference in the parentheses is now called a *defined term*, and the writer must use it consistently in every later reference. Some writers use quotation marks around the defined term the first time it is used; others do not. It is not necessary to use the word *hereinafter*. Thus, avoid a reference such as the following: *Plaintiff Sterling Appliance and Repair, Inc. (hereinafter referred to as "Sterling")*. Although defined terms are useful in many documents, they may not be needed. For example, if a complaint identifies one plaintiff only, establishing a label or defined term for the party is unneeded. When using defined terms, make sure the term appears after being defined (there's no point in identifying Josephson Manufacturing Associates Inc. as *Josephson* if the party will not be referred to again). Also, be careful when using initials so that you don't confuse your reader with language such as the following: *JMAI later refused to deliver the goods to CACB and instead returned them COD to PRBL*. If there are references to two parties or cases with the same name, label them with a number, as in *Ford I* and *Ford II*.

2. Repetitive Terms

The consistent use of defined terms will result in some repetition in your writing. Resist the urge to achieve variety in your writing by selecting new words for established terms. It is better to be thought of as boring than confusing.

3. Labels

Note that the actor and the person acted upon are usually referred to by the signals *-or* and *-ee*, as in *offeror-offeree* and *franchisor-franchisee*, although many nonlegal dictionaries would spell the terms *offerer* and *franchiser*.

4. *Including But Not Limited to* Phrases

When introducing a list, the word *including* is probably sufficient because it signals that the list is not exhaustive; however, in nearly all instances, to be safe, most legal writers will write *including but not limited to* in contracts and other documents, as in the following: *The employee must perform all assigned duties, including but not limited to . . . .* Such language is intended to prevent the employee from claiming that he or she was required to perform only the listed duties . . . . The word *namely* and phrase *consisting of* signal a complete list. Thus, a statement that *The employee must perform the following duties, namely . . .* would require the employee to perform only the identified duties and no others. Consequently, to allow "wiggle room," most lists are introduced by the phrase *including but not limited to.*

5. Money Amounts

To reduce errors it is customary in legal writing to spell out a money amount and then identify the figures in parentheses, as in *Defendant will pay the sum of Forty Thousand Dollars ($40,000).* In 1999, the Financial Times reported that a comma in the wrong place in a sales price figure cost Lockheed Martin $70 million. The comma (used in Europe to mark decimal points rather than periods) was misplaced by one decimal point. Combining both the figure with the words may have saved the company this loss.

6. Numbers

Legal writers usually spell out all numbers and then identify the number in parentheses, as in *There will be twelve (12) directors' meetings this year.* This practice is somewhat outmoded. Moreover, on occasion, this style can produce odd-looking and difficult to read sentences, as in *Only one (1) report was prepared by the two (2) members.* Note that both *The Bluebook* (R. 6.2) and *ALWD* (R. 4) provide that numbers from zero to ninety-nine should be spelled out in text. Most writers (and the *Style Manual*) write out only the numbers one through nine and use figures for larger units, such as 14 and 54.

7. Initial Phrases

Many legal writers capitalize the first word or two in many documents or sections. Thus, many contracts begin with the words THIS AGREEMENT, and many corporate resolutions begin with the words RESOLVED THAT. Similarly, many pleadings, such as complaints, are introduced by the archaic phrase COMES NOW THE PLAINTIFF.

8. The *Whether* Clause

Many issue statements begin with the word *whether*, as in *Whether a trademark may be abandoned by three consecutive years of nonuse.* Such a phrase is an incomplete sentence but is acceptable to most attorneys.

9. d/b/a References

The abbreviation *d/b/a* is short for *doing business as* and indicates that one or more persons are doing business under a business name rather than their personal names. Thus, a plaintiff might sue *Dan Greenwood, d/b/a Creative Caterers of Charleston.* Do not include *d/b/a* in formal case citations.

10. Law Firm Names

Punctuation and presentation of law firm names varies widely. Some firms use commas and others do not. A current trend is to reduce the four or five names in a firm to two, as in *Jones Day.* Follow the firm practice as shown by its letterhead or on its website.

11. Ordinals

In legal citations, use *2d* and *3d* rather than *2nd* and *3rd.* All other ordinals, such as *1st, 5th,* and so forth, follow the generally accepted presentations. Present these ordinals "on line" as in *5th,* rather than in superscript form (as in 5th). Outside of the legal context, use the generally accepted presentations, as in *The theater is on 42nd Street.* Note that per *Bluebook* R. 6.2(b), in a "stand-alone" citation, you would use the presentation *102d Cong.*, but in a textual sentence, you would use *102nd Congress* as in, *The 102nd Congress produced little legislation, leaving much work for the 103rd Congress.*

12. Pagination

It is common to omit any number on the first page of a legal writing. In a brief, the main section or argument often begins as page number one (1). Introductory pages, which include the Table of Contents and Table of Authorities, are often numbered with romanettes (small roman numerals, as in *i, ii, and iii*).

B. Common Legal Writing Blunders

There are several blunders commonly committed by beginning legal writers. Some are oddly phrased constructions; others are defects in reasoning and analysis. Thus, pay careful attention to the following topics:

1. Labels and Numbering

Never label or number an item *A* or *I* unless a *B* or *II* will follow.

2. Defined Terms

Once you define a term or use a label, it must be used consistently. Thus, once you tell a reader that the defendant Kyle Walters will be referred to as *Walters,* you must continue this reference, and not later refer to the defendant as *Mr. Walters.*

Figure 10-1   Plagiarism

Plagiarism is taking another's ideas, thoughts, or expressions and representing them as your own. The word *plagiarism* is derived from the Latin for *literary thief* or *kidnapper*. Plagiarism is a serious ethics violation. It is perfectly acceptable, however, to paraphrase another's material. Paraphrasing is taking the ideas or expressions of another and putting them in your own words. Nevertheless, even paraphrased material must be attributed to the original author. Follow these guidelines in legal writing, as in all writing:

- When you quote from any authority, use quotation marks and give the full citation and the pinpoint, namely, the page on which the specific material appears.
- When you paraphrase an authority, give the full citation and the pinpoint.
- When an entire paragraph includes paraphrased material and the sentences in the paragraph are closely connected, it is acceptable to give the citation at the end of the paragraph, rather than giving citations at the end of each sentence. Similarly, it is permissible to give a citation to a legal authority, such as a case, and give the facts from that case in several sentences without repeating the citation at the end of each sentence.
- Do not assume that material in the public domain (for example, statutes and cases) can be used without attribution. When you rely on such materials, give the full citation and the pinpoint.
- Using material from the Internet is not only an ethics violation, it may also be a copyright violation. Just as it is easy for a writer to find material on the Internet and "cut and paste" the material into a writing, it is easy for the reader to locate the original source on the Internet and realize that you have plagiarized.
- Understand that in law firms and office settings, professionals routinely share their writings, memos, and briefs with each other. This sharing of materials is considered practical and cost-effective for clients. Such use with the permission of another is not plagiarism.
- When in doubt, err on the side of caution and give a citation.

3. Supporting Authorities

Do not conclude that a test or element of an argument is satisfied without supporting authority. Every assertion you make or conclusion you provide must be supported by some legal authority. See Figure 10-1 for information about citing to authorities and plagiarism.

4. Conclusory Language

Avoid conclusory language. Simply writing *The defendant's conduct was reckless* is not persuasive. You must tell the reader why the defendant's conduct was reckless; give specific facts and reasons that support this conclusion.

5. Including Facts

Be sure to include facts from the cases you rely on so the reader can easily see why the authorities you cite apply to your case. Thus, a statement such as *The present case is governed by* Powell *because of its similarity* . . . without any discussion of the facts of *Powell* will leave the reader in the dark as to why *Powell* is controlling. Compare and contrast the facts of *Powell* to your case, and show the reader why the result in reached in *Powell* compels a similar result in your case.

6. Other Legal Authorities

Let experts help. In many instances, A.L.R. annotations, law reviews, and treatises provide depth and texture to a discussion. Don't think that a document can cite only to cases and statutes.

7. Tone in Court Documents

Although it is important to be persuasive in court documents, arrogantly telling a court what it must do is inappropriate. Thus, write *The Plaintiff respectfully urges this Court to grant this Motion* . . . rather than *This Court must grant this Motion* . . . . Also, be sure your tone in court documents is not too informal or conversational. Thus, write *The Court further stated* . . . rather than *The Court goes on to state* . . . .

8. Title Headings in Statutes

When discussing a statute, it is generally not necessary to give the title of the statute. For example, avoid the following construction: *Under 17 U.S.C. § 201 (2006), Ownership of Copyright, the authors of a joint work are co-owners of copyright in the work.* Omit the title *Ownership of Copyright.* It is distracting and unneeded. On the other hand, it is perfectly acceptable to refer to a specific act by its name, as in *The Lanham Act prohibits counterfeit use of trademarks.*

9. Complete Discussion

If your argument asserts, for example, that three elements of a certain test must be satisfied, you must discuss all three elements (in the order you listed them), and each section must be supported with legal authorities. When discussing the three elements, either discuss each one separately or discuss them all together. For example, it is awkward and unparallel if you combine elements one and two and then discuss element three in its own section. Similarly, your argument is incomplete if you analyze only some of the elements of the test or merely recite the elements of the test and then jump to the conclusion that the test is satisfied. If for some reason you do not need to address one element or one portion of a test, say so, rather than leaving the reader wondering where the discussion is.

10. Concurring and Dissenting Opinions

Do not rely too heavily on a concurring or dissenting opinion. Recognize that these opinions are persuasive at best. Start your argument and analysis with the majority opinion. Bolster it with sparing use of concurring or dissenting opinions, if you like, but don't lead with these. Similarly, plurality opinions (those in which no single rationale enjoys the agreement of the majority of voting judges) are of limited precedential value. If you rely on a dissenting, concurring, or plurality opinion, you must indicate such in a separate parenthetical in your citation. *Bluebook* R. 10.6.1, at 100; *ALWD* R. 12.11(a), at 104.

11. The Complete Package

Include all the information the reader will need. Don't make the reader search through other pleadings or files to make sense of your document.

12. Use of Headnotes

Never quote from headnotes in a case. Headnotes are summaries of what the publisher of the case believes the court said. Rely on the majority opinion itself. The headnotes are meant to be guides or an index to the information in the case. Relying on a headnote in a case would be the equivalent of relying on a table of contents in a book. When you read a case, find the author of the majority opinion. The author's name is a signal that every word thereafter was written by the court. Similarly, be careful that you are relying on the majority opinion and not on a dissenting or concurring opinion. It is easy to drift into a dissenting or concurring opinion, especially when reading cases on Lexis or Westlaw, where the screen doesn't display page breaks as cleanly as they are shown in books.

13. Addressing Readers

Do not address the reader of a document by name. Thus, in a letter, do not write *Mr. Lee, you should therefore . . . .* It is sufficient to write *You should therefore . . . .* The only legal document in which a reader is directly addressed by name is in the salutation in a letter. Briefs do not address the reader, the judge, by indicating *Your ruling of June 10 . . . .* Similarly, memos do not address readers directly.

14. Authors of Court Opinions

Do not continually mention the author of a case. It is sufficient to write *The Court held* . . . . It is not necessary to write *Justice Thomas noted that* . . . . The author of an opinion is often immaterial. It is a court, acting as a collective unit, that states the law, not a particular justice or judge. Similarly, when discussing the *Harris v. Jackson* case, for example, avoid references to the *Harris Court*, which many writers dislike. Write *The Court in* Harris *held that* . . . . In fact, the U.S. Supreme Court's guidelines for counsel arguing before the Court state, "Do not refer to an opinion of the Court by saying: 'In Justice Ginsburg's opinion.' You should say: 'In the Court's opinion, written by Justice Ginsburg.'" Sup. Ct. Guide for Couns. 11 (2011), *available at* www.supremecourt.gov/oral_arguments/guideforcounsel.pdf. You may, however, refer to a court by the name of its presiding judge or chief justice, as in *the Roberts Court*.

15. New Topics

Don't introduce any new issues or topics in a conclusion that have not been previously analyzed in the document. A conclusion summarizes material previously presented; it does not introduce new topics.

16. Citations

Use case citations to tell a reader what a court held in a published case. For example, assume the client's name is Smith. It would be inappropriate to write *Smith's conduct is reasonable.* Young v. Carr, *435 U.S. 36, 42 (1998).* Such a statement implies that the Supreme Court case *Young v. Carr* analyzes Smith's conduct. Additionally, all citations must be correct according to *The Bluebook, ALWD,* or local rules. Always include pincites to relevant pages in cases and to specific subsections for statutes.

17. Over-Quoting

Don't give so many quotations from legal authorities or so many citations to the authorities that it appears that your project was assembled from a hodgepodge of authorities rather than being the result of your own analysis. Don't just drop quotations into a project without explaining their relevance to your analysis. Use block quotations sparingly. Many readers skip them.

18. Mini-Conclusions

Analyze throughout a memorandum or brief. Do not discuss all the legal authorities in one section and then give your conclusions as to how and why they apply in another section. Make your presentation seamless, and for each point you make, give the law, apply it, and provide a mini-conclusion. Only then should you move on to the next point.

19. Headings

Always give sufficient headings that the reader can readily determine the topic that will be next addressed. Review each heading to make sure each is parallel and that each advances your argument. Although many writers use all uppercase letters for major point headings, some experts suggest that the easiest way for something to be ignored is to place it in a heading in all uppercase letters. Consider whether your heading will be more visible if you use underscoring or bolding.

20. Use of First Person

Do not use the first person (*I, we*) in any document other than correspondence. In briefs, do not write *We will show that* but rather *The Plaintiff will show that*. In most instances you are writing on behalf of the client; thus, third person is appropriate.

21. Use of Party Names

When discussing the litigants in a case, in most instances, you should identify them by their legal status rather than by their names. Thus, write *The Plaintiff argued* rather than *Ms. Davis argued*. On the other hand, if their legal status is confusing (for example, they are cross-complainants or cross-respondents) or if several parties share the same legal status, consider identifying them by their roles, such as *buyer*, *landlord*, or *employee*. As noted earlier, this is the approach of the federal courts. Fed. R. App. P. 28(d). When referring to a party in a case precedent, it is typical to refer to that party as *the plaintiff* or *the defendant* (with the definite article *the*). In contrast, when you refer to a party in the matter that is the subject of your document, it is typical to refer to that party as follows: *Plaintiff has alleged* or *Defendant has offered*, without the definite article *the* and with an initial capital letter. *Bluebook* B7.3.2; *ALWD* R. 3.3.

Correct Example:	In *United States v. Dixon*, 413 F.3d 520, 522 (5th Cir. 2005), the defendant alleged she acted under duress at the time of her illegal purchase of a firearm. In the present case, however, Defendant has alleged . . . .

22. Tense

Use correct tense. Use the past tense when describing the facts, procedural background, and holding of a case. Use present tense when discussing what the law is, whether you discuss a statute, case, or regulation. Thus, for example, write *The Miller Act provides that* . . . . Do not shift tenses unless there is an actual change in time.

23. Writing *This Case*

Watch the use of the expression *this case*. When you are analyzing case law in a memo or court document, references to *this case* are confusing because readers are unsure whether you are referring to the published precedent or the client's case.

24. Abbreviations

Do not use abbreviations in text. Thus, do not write *The defendant lived in Los Angeles, CA until Nov. 2012.* Spell out *California* and *November*.

25. Collective Nouns

Always refer to corporations, groups, and other similar entities as *it* or *its* rather than *they* or *their*. Thus, write *The corporation held its meeting* or *The committee released its report*. If you wish to refer to the members of these entities, write *The members of the board of directors held their meeting*.

26. Cross-References

If your document includes numerous instances of *as explained below* and *as discussed previously*, this is a strong signal that your writing is poorly organized. These references require readers to either jump ahead or back in your document, disrupting your narrative and confusing your reader. Use your word processor's "find" feature to locate such phrases and then work to keep all related issues and discussion points together in the same section rather than scattered throughout your project.

27. Recycling Documents

Using previously prepared documents in a later case or transaction is an efficient use of your time. If you recycle documents, however, you will need to redouble your proofreading efforts to make sure that cases are still good law, that the names of parties are correct, that you haven't imported irrelevant information, and that pronoun references are correct.

28. Sentence Starters

The first word of any sentence must be spelled out. *Bluebook* R. 6.2(c). Thus, do not start a sentence with a dollar amount, a number, or an abbreviation. It is incorrect to begin a sentence with *U.S. law requires* or *200 documents are missing*. Change to *United States law requires* and *Two hundred documents are missing*.

29. The Biggest Blunder—Violating Court Rules

Remember that courts have the power to enforce strict compliance with their rules. Courts routinely dismiss cases or refuse to accept documents that do not comply with their rules, including those regarding length, cover colors, and timeliness. Remember *Alva v. Teen Help*, 469 F.3d 946, 950 (10th Cir. 2006), in which the court dismissed an appeal that was filed six minutes too late.

Postwriting Steps and Document Design

■ After writing, the real work begins: proofreading and editing. These are among the most difficult tasks in writing. This section of the Handbook provides you with some techniques for effective proofreading and for revising your writing. Additionally, although no amount of "tricks" can make up for a poorly written document, there are several strategies you can adopt to make your project more visually appealing and thus more readable. This section describes methods of displaying your writings so that they present a polished and professional appearance.

chapter 11

Postwriting Steps

StyleLinks

Purdue University's Online Writing Lab provides an excellent review of the steps in editing and proofreading.

The Writing Center of the University of North Carolina offers a thorough overview of the proofreading process.

Chapter One of the Government Printing Office *Style Manual* provides a list and explanation of the standard proofreaders' marks.

Merriam-Webster's site displays illustrations of proofreaders' marks.

A. Introduction

One of the most difficult writing tasks begins only when most writers think they have finished a project. Steps taken in the postwriting stage provide a final opportunity to ensure a document is correct in all respects. Don't underestimate the difficulty of postwriting. All major publishers require that writings be reviewed by professional editors and proofreaders for the very reason that writers are notoriously unlikely to catch their own errors.

You cannot review (literally, "re-see") for all errors and flaws in a project at the same time. Thus, divide your review into two parts. During stage one, often called *editing*, review for content and meaning. During stage two, often called *proofreading*, review for technical errors, such as errors in spelling, punctuation, and formatting. The task of cite-checking, namely, checking the format and validity of your citations, is a separate task and should not be combined with any revising or polishing of your document. Before you do anything, however, take three critically important steps:

- **Get some distance from the project.** Try to allow at least a few hours (and, if possible, overnight or longer) to pass between the completion of your first draft and your initial review. It is extremely difficult to review effectively a project with which you are too familiar. If you can come to the review "cold," you will be better able to detect flaws (just as the project's ultimate reader will be able to locate errors easily). A harsh reality of today's busy law office environments, however, is that legal professionals do not always have the luxury of putting aside a project for a few days and then returning to it to proofread it. Even a short break, however, may help refresh you and allow you to approach the project with a more critical eye.
- **Work on a hard copy.** Never engage in a full review while the document is on the screen of your computer. It is too difficult to see the flow of the project when you can only see part of a page at a time. Moreover, you need to see the document the way it will appear to the reader.
- **Enlarge your project.** For better reviewing, copy your document on 11″ x 17″ paper or enlarge it to 120 percent of its size. This gives you room to make notes and reduces the eyestrain caused by on-screen revision. Moreover, changing the look of the document may trick you into thinking you are looking at an unfamiliar project and thus help you catch errors.

Remember to expect the unexpected. Allow time for human error or machine malfunction. Don't work so close to the deadline that a jammed printer causes you to miss a deadline. Understand that someone else's project may bump yours. People will get sick. Leave some margin for error.

B. Stage One Reviewing: Editing for Content and Meaning

Your initial review should focus on whether you have accurately conveyed all the information needed (and no more than what is needed). Focus on content. Consider the following strategies:

- Review the project from the perspective of the reader and ask if the reader will understand the writing.
- Review your thesis statement. Does it fully encapsulate the argument or discussion to follow?
- Keep the purpose of the writing in mind. If the project is a brief, its purpose is to persuade. If the project is a memorandum, its purpose is to inform. Check to see if the writing meets these goals. Review to ensure the tone is appropriate for the reader and whether the project is either too formal or too breezy.
- Review to ensure the writing flows smoothly and that its organization assists the reader's comprehension. Move paragraphs and sections to other locations if you believe they would be better placed elsewhere.
- Stay focused on your task. Ask someone to hold your calls and find a quiet space where you can concentrate on your project.
- Make sure the first page of each draft includes a date and a time. Often, several versions of a project will accumulate, and some drafts will vary only slightly from each other. Identifying each version with the date and time will help you keep them straight.
- Read the project aloud. This will help you locate awkward phrasing, repetitive sections, and missing transitions.
- Read only the headings and topic sentences to ensure they advance your message and that taken alone they provide a complete mini-view of the content of the document.
- Ensure your headings, numberings, and presentations of lists are consistent and that their structure is parallel, especially if you have worked on the project with others.
- Focus on one or two problem areas at a time, such as overlong sentences or legalese. Work on correcting these, and then move on to other weak spots. Remember some easy tips to focus on problem areas: You can detect passive voice by looking at a noun introduced with the word *by* (as in *The complaint was filed by the plaintiff*); you can detect nominalizations by looking for words ending in *-ent, -ant,* and *-ion*; and you can detect wordiness by looking for prepositional phrases such as *during the time that* and changing them to one-word replacements, such as *during* or *when*. To obtain visual cues about your problem areas, use a colored marker to highlight every nominalization or use of passive voice. Do patterns emerge?
- Consider using a revision or writing checklist to remind you to check for certain errors. A writing checklist is found on the inside back cover of this Handbook.

C. Stage Two Reviewing: Proofreading for Technical Errors

1. The Effect of Technical Errors

The best argument in the world can be quickly sabotaged by what most writers think of as minor errors, namely, errors in grammar, punctuation, and spelling. These types of technical or surface errors in legal documents have a disproportionately negative effect on a reader. Thus, no review is complete without a final run-through to make sure that there are no technical or mechanical errors that will detract from the message of your writing.

2. Using a Style Sheet

Most professional editors develop a style sheet that they rely on when editing. The style sheet is their blueprint for the correct spelling of names, how they intend to present headings, how issues will be numbered, and so forth. For example, will the writer use "Section I" or "Section One"? Will the writer use "email" or "e-mail"? During the process of review, they then have a quick guide they can consult to ensure accuracy and consistency. Develop your own style sheet and include a list of planned exhibits so you can readily ensure consistency in their names and numbering. Similarly, many writers use a project checklist to remind themselves to check various items during the proofreading stage. See Figure 11-1 for a sample project checklist you can use to ensure all projects are in final form.

Tip → Style Sheets

For a quick and speedy style sheet, use the notepad gadget on your computer desktop to show how you will present certain terms and names.

---

3. The Limitations of Spell-Checkers

As always, do not over-rely on your computer's spell-checker. Spelling checkers are wonderful tools, but they have their limitations because they cannot tell you to use *form* rather than *from* because both words are properly spelled. There is no substitute for human proofreading, as shown by the fact that a review of some recently published court decisions disclosed 23 cases referring to "Santa Clause" and 817 cases referring to the "trail court." Similarly, in 2012, the *Washington Post* reported the results of a study that found students caught fewer spelling errors and grammar mistakes when they relied on their spelling checkers because they placed so much confidence in this tool that they failed to catch errors that weren't flagged.

Figure 11-1   Project Checklist

Moving target _____   Type of project _____

Nearing final form _____   Client _____

Final form _____   File/Billing No. _____

Due date _____   Supervisor _____

Spell Checked   _____

Proofread   _____

Cite-Checked   _____   *Bluebook/ALWD*/Other _____

Shepardized/KeyCited   _____

Quotations Checked   _____

Defined Terms Consistent   _____

Consistency in Headings   _____

Numbering Is Accurate   _____

Consistency in Exhibits   _____

No Widows or Orphans   _____

All Exhibits Attached   _____

Court Rules Checked   _____

Create Table of Authorities   _____

Create Table of Contents   _____

Special Filing/Mailing Notes   _____

Other   _____

4. Techniques to Slow Down

Because a standard reading of your project will naturally focus on content and you will read groups of words and phrases rather than isolated words, you must force yourself to slow down and focus on each word.

Try these techniques:

- Slide a ruler or piece of paper under each line as you read the document. This will prevent you from jumping ahead to the next sentence or idea and force you to focus on each word.
- Point at each word with a pencil. This technique will help you focus on individual words.
- Read the project backward, from the last page to the first page and from right to left. Although this technique is excellent for finding spelling errors and typos, it will not help you locate a missed word or ensure that you used *complaint* rather than *compliant*. Moreover, it is very time consuming.
- Read the document aloud by yourself or read with a partner who has a copy of the document. Reading aloud allows a double check because you not only see what is being read but also hear it. Additionally, if you or your partner stumbles over certain sections, you will know these need more work.
- Read sections of the document out of order to make sure you stay focused on the mechanics of spelling, grammar, and punctuation, and do not begin concentrating on content.
- Read or do something else for a while as a quick break and then switch back to your project.
- If your project is a short one, cut it into separate sections (using your computer's "cut" tool) and read each one carefully.
- Dictate complicated materials (such as patent claims or descriptions of real property) into a tape recorder or iPhone. Then play back the recording, listening and proofreading against your text.

5. Asking for Help

You can ask someone to proof the project for you. Having someone else review the document can be extremely helpful because the newcomer will have no familiarity with the project. He or she will then review the writing with a fresh approach and no preconceived ideas or expectations. Note, however, that each reviewer of a document will tend to add rather than to delete language. If you want the reader to review only for technical errors, say so, or you may receive a project with substantial corrections and suggestions. If you have asked for help, give the reviewer the courtesy of being open to his or her comments or suggestions without becoming defensive.

6. Using Templates and Forms

Using a sample document prepared for an earlier transaction or case increases the risk of importing incorrect terms into later documents. Thus, a document prepared for a tenant needs to be scrupulously checked when it is later used for a subtenant. Use the "find and replace" feature in your word processor to locate terms and names and ensure they are uniformly presented and that pronouns are correct.

7. Using Technology to Help with Proofreading

A number of software programs can help with proofreading. Thomson Reuters's new program Deal Proof is specially tailored to help with the proofreading of complex documents. With the click of a button you can make sure that terms are defined only once, that each defined term is used in the document, that numeration is correct, and that phrases are used consistently.

Proofreading Exercise

Count every "F" in the following example:

FRANK FILED THE RE-
SULT OF HIS STUDY OF SCIENTIFIC
PRINCIPLES TOGETHER WITH
THE LAB RESULTS OF HIS FINAL
PROJECT.

Case Illustration: Competent Representation Extends to Proofreading

In *Devore v. City of Philadelphia*, No. Civ. A. 00-3598, 2004 WL 414085, at *3 (E.D. Pa. Feb. 20, 2004), the court slashed an attorney's rate from $300 per hour to $150 per hour because of his careless writing and numerous typos. The court noted that the writer's "complete lack of care in his written product shows disrespect for the court." Thus, the duty to represent a client competently is broad enough to encompass even seemingly minor matters such as proofreading, editing, and cite-checking.

D. Proofreading for Others

No passion in the world is equal to the passion to alter someone else's draft.

H.G. Wells

If you are asked to review someone else's work, obtain clear instructions so you know if you should review for content or review only for mechanics, such as typos and spelling errors. Reviewing for technical errors in someone else's writing is generally quite easy. If you are not familiar with the content, the errors will jump out at you (just as they will for the ultimate reader, such as the client or judge).

If you are asked to review for content, consider the following:

- Be realistic. Recognize that each writer has a unique style. Just because an idea is not expressed in the exact way you would express it does not mean it is inaccurate or vague.
- Limit your corrections to meaningful changes. It is unproductive to change *glad* to *happy* or *but* to *however.* Your credibility as an effective reviewer will be jeopardized if you make such meaningless changes.
- Be specific. Comments such as "weak" or "expand" placed beside a paragraph are nearly useless. Specifically explain why the section is weak and give a suggestion for improving it.
- Be diplomatic. Harsh comments such as "What are you thinking?" are inappropriate. Try phrasing suggestions diplomatically, such as "Have you considered . . . ?" or "Let's discuss some alternatives." These approaches focus on the two of you as colleagues in the writing process rather than on the writer's perceived inadequacies. Focus on the reader and suggest "Will the reader know what this means?" rather than writing "This is unclear."

E. Proofreaders' Marks

Although there is some variety in the marks writers use to show errors, most legal writers employ the standard marks, called proofreaders' marks, used by professional editors. Many attorneys learned these marks while in law school, so their use among legal professionals is common.

Most dictionaries (including online dictionaries) will provide descriptions and illustrations of proofreaders' marks. These marks are designed to show support staff where and how to make corrections in your project. Be sure all of your working drafts are double-spaced and have generous margins so you will have sufficient room to note corrections. The most commonly used proofreaders' marks are shown in Figure 11-2.

Figure 11-2   Commonly Used Proofreaders' Marks

Mark	Explanation	Example
≡	Capital letters	president obama
/	Lowercase letters	the eleventh Juror
∿	Boldface	April 16, 2012
⌒	Close up space	in as much
¶	Begin new paragraph	¶ The plaintiff
ℓ	Delete	The hearing was was
Stet	Let original text stand	Many courts have concluded
∧	Insert	The plaintiff his attorney argued
#	Add space	to the court.The defendant then
∿	Transpose	complaint
⊏	Move left	any jury
⊐	Move right	any jury
↗	Insert comma	the plaintiff Josh Brownell stated
∨	Insert apostrophe	its a sad day
⊙	Insert period	to the court The jury also requested
○	Spell out	Newport, RI

F. The Final Run-Through

Just before your writing is sent to the reader, check these five items:

- **Widows and Orphans.** A *widow* or an *orphan*, respectively, is a heading or isolated line occurring at the top of a page or an isolated line or heading occurring at the bottom of a page. Omit this awkward placement. Many software programs now protect against widows and orphans. Always keep at least two lines together.
- **Numbering.** Quickly scan the project to make sure the page numbering is correct. If the document has a table of contents, review it to make sure all page references are correct. If footnotes are used, check their numbering for accuracy. Make sure the numbering of headings and subheadings is accurate.
- **Dates, Names, and Amounts.** Do one final check to make sure dates, names, and money amounts are correct.
- **Exhibits.** Make sure all exhibits or attachments to the project are included and are properly marked and that their titles and labeling are consistent with the way they are presented in the document itself.
- **Page-By-Page Review.** Look at each page in your document to ensure there are no missing, blank, or upside-down pages.

▶ Tip: Approach cite-checking as a task distinct from revising. First, check the format of the citations to ensure they are in *Bluebook or ALWD* (or local) form. Then check your primary authorities (either by Shepardizing or KeyCiting) to ensure the law you rely on is still valid.

Tips ➡ For Successful Reviews

- Energy levels are usually higher in the morning, so try to schedule your review as the first thing you do in the day.
- Devote extra attention to the parts of the project that were prepared last. More errors occur when you are tired.
- Watch for substitutions of letters in small words, such as *now* for *not*.
- Pay extra attention to your known problem areas. For example, if you tend to misspell the word *judgment*, watch for this. Use your word processor's "find" feature to locate your typical errors.
- Consider preparing a "lessons learned" memo to yourself, noting the techniques that worked well and those that did not so that your next project can benefit from what you learned.
- Always ask yourself the most important question for any writing project: *Will my reader understand my writing?*

Challenge ? Proofreading

Correct the errors.

In general, all securities offered in the Untied States must be registered with the SEC or must gualify for an exemption from the registration requirements, The securities to be issued by the corporation are usally in the form of equity securities (stock representing onwership interest in the corporation) or debt securities (bonds representing money owed by a corporation to a creditor).

The generally excepted test used to determine if a "security" is being issued hinges or whether the person is investing money in a common enterprise and is lead to expect any profits from the the mangerial efforts of others. If so, a security is being offered and, unless exemptions exist, the issuer must comply with the Securities Act of 1933.

The form of registation statement provided by the SEC is From S-1. The SEC has adopted regulations requiring the use of "plain English" in the registration form so that in is clear and understandable to the average investor. Since 1993, registration forms must be filed electronicly with the SEC through its EGDAR (Electronic Data Gathering and Retrieval) database. The main part (or Part I) of the registration statement is called the prospectus. The prospectus describes the securifies being sold, provides background information about the issuing corporation and its directors and officers and describes the investment so that all inventors can fully evaluate the potential risks involved it purchasing the security. Section II of the registration statement includes "additional information" about the company and the offering and remaining on file with the SEC for public inspection.

chapter 12

Document Design

StyleLinks

www.sec.gov/pdf/handbook.pdf
See Chapter 7 of the SEC's *A Plain English Handbook* for information on document design, use of graphics, font size, and so forth.

http://writing.colostate.edu/guides/documents/desktop_publishing/list3.cfm
Colorado State University offers information on preparing figures, illustrations, tables, and other layout and design elements.

www.ca7.uscourts.gov/Rules/Painting_with_Print.pdf
The excellent article *Painting with Print*, prepared by the Association of Legal Writing Directors, discusses incorporating concepts of layout design into legal writings.

www.typographyforlawyers.com
This excellent website provided by attorney and graphic designer Matthew Butterick offers tips and strategies for improving the appearance of legal documents.

A. Principles of Document Design

1. Introduction

Even if your project is well written, clear, and readable, it should be presented in such a manner that it creates a favorable impression on the reader. One of the reasons that some appellate courts insist that a brief submitted must be professionally printed rather than merely typed is that printed briefs are easier to read and present a uniform appearance. A good document reflects careful design choices. On the other hand, no amount of design techniques can overcome a poorly written document. Thus, use document design to enhance your writing, not obscure it.

The term *document design* refers to the conventions that determine the way that a written project looks, including quality of paper, typeface, formatting, and headings and other visuals. Visually appealing documents are easier to understand.

2. Paper

Use the highest quality paper possible. Some courts require that the paper used for documents be of a certain quality. For example, the U.S. Supreme Court requires all booklet-format documents to be produced on unglazed opaque white paper. Sup. Ct. R. 33.

Select a paper of sufficient weight so that page two of a document doesn't show through to page one. Although some law firms and offices use cream or ivory-colored paper, most use white. White is the more traditional color, and many readers find it easier to read because black type provides a greater contrast on white paper than on cream paper.

3. Typeface

There are several decisions to make about typeface, including whether the typeface should be serif or sans serif, monospaced or proportionally spaced, and what size of typeface should be selected.

a. Typeface or Font Style

Typeface selection can dramatically affect the readability of your document. Typefaces (called *fonts* on word processors) come in two styles: serif and sans serif. A serif typeface has small lines or wings at the top or bottom of each letter. This Handbook is printed in serif typeface. Most newspapers and magazines use a serif type because the small connecting lines draw the reader's eye from letter to letter and word to word, making the text easier to read. Sans serif typefaces (*sans* means *without* in French) do not have the connecting lines or added strokes. Almost all experts agree that a serif typeface should be used for text. Sans serif is acceptable for headings or emphasis. Consider the following:

This is Times New Roman, a serif font, in 12-point size.

This is Century Schoolbook, a serif font, in 12-point size.

This is Courier New, a serif font, in 12-point size.

This is Arial, a sans serif font, in 12-point size.

This is Calibri, a sans serif font, in 12-point size.

Do not use a decorative style of font, such as Comic Sans, or one that uses script or cursive, in legal writing.

b. Mixing Typefaces

Generally, do not mix more than two typefaces in a document. In fact, most experts recommend using one typeface throughout a document, selecting its Roman, italic, and bold styles as needed. Too many variations will make your writing look like an advertisement rather than a serious work. Moreover, readers assume that headings in the same size and font signal information of the same importance. Switching fonts confuses readers and obscures the significance of the headings.

c. Roman Typeface

Writing may be presented in ordinary Roman letters (as most of this Handbook is), *italics*, or **boldface**. Use ordinary Roman type for most of your writing. Italics or underscoring are generally used only for emphasis (except for their use in citation form, which is discussed in Appendix A). Use boldface only for headings or special purposes, such as emphasizing a deadline date in a letter to a client.

d. Proportional or Monospace Typeface

Some typefaces, such as Courier, are monospaced, meaning that every letter takes up the same amount of space, whether it is a capital *M* or a lower case *i*. Times New Roman and Garamond are proportionally spaced, meaning that a capital *M* takes up more space than a lowercase *i*. Courier type uses about 30 percent more space than Times New Roman. Generally, proportionally spaced typefaces are easier to read. Consider the following:

This sentence, in Times New Roman font, is proportionally spaced.

This sentence, in Courier New font, is mono-spaced.

There are three reasons to use a proportional typeface such as Times New Roman rather than a monospaced typeface:

- Proportional typefaces are easier to read;
- They eliminate the need for two spaces after a period at the end of sentences; and
- They take up less space, helping writers more easily comply with court-imposed page limits.

e. Size of Typeface

Type size is measured in "points," such as 10-point type or 12-point type, with a larger number showing larger print. Review the fonts shown earlier and note that although all are presented in 12-point size, they are not all equal in size. Some courts require documents to be printed in a certain size type. Similarly, some statutes require certain information, such as language disclaiming a warranty, to be of a specified type size. Unless there are rules you must follow, select 12-point because it is the most readable size. Larger type sizes in text appear artificial and convey a sense of shouting, although they may be effective for headings, if used consistently. United States Supreme Court rules require that the text of booklet-format documents be typeset in a "Century" family (for example, Century Schoolbook) in 12-point type. Sup. Ct. R. 33.1(b).

On occasion a client may insist that certain information be included in a contract, invoice, or other form. To fit all the information or terms in the document, you may need to use a much smaller type size, such as 6-point or 8-point. Alternatively, most photocopy machines can reduce the size of an image. These reductions, however, impair readability and convey the message *this is fine print.*

Tip → **Using Underscoring or Italics for Emphasis**

Underscoring is a relic from the days when typewriters could show emphasis only by underscoring. Italics are viewed as more modern and more elegant. Moreover, when you underscore, you obscure certain characters, namely, the descending parts of the letters *g, j, p, q,* and *y,* as well as punctuation marks, as shown in the sentence *Paul jumped very quickly, and moved out of the way.* Thus, most modern writers use italics for emphasis (and in citations) rather than underscoring.

B. Formatting and Layout

Designers give careful consideration to the way text looks on a page, including white space, justification, paragraph length, and so forth.

1. White Space and Margins

Pages filled with a solid block of text cause eyestrain and frustration. Using adequate white space (space where no words appear) will make the project more readable and cause headings and quotations to be more easily noticed. Using white space shows readers which items in a project are related; greater distance between sections indicates separation, and proximity indicates correlation. Although the technique of leaving ample white space on a page, including adequate or generous margins, may seem like an artificial device, reading studies have shown that it results in a more readable project, particularly in legal documents, which often feature dense blocks of complex text. Margins should be at least one inch on all sides and should be larger than one inch if the project will be bound along the top or left side or if the reader will be making notes in the margins.

2. Justification

Research has shown that the easiest text to read is text that is left justified (meaning the text is aligned, or flush, at the left margin) and ragged right (meaning the text at the right margin has a ragged edge, such as a typewriter would produce). A *fully justified* text is one in which both the right and left edges are flush, or even, with all words starting and ending at the same location in each line. This text is fully justified. Although full justification presents a clean and crisp-looking document, it may be more suited for transactional documents, such as contracts, than for legal correspondence and briefs. The disadvantage of full justification is that the spacing between words may be either cramped or stretched out to ensure the text is even, inhibiting the flow of reading and causing "rivers" of white space to cascade downward vertically through the text. Although word processors are improving, only a professional typesetter can reduce the uneven spacing that occurs with full justification. The current trend is to use left justified and right ragged edges in legal correspondence and court documents.

3. Spacing

Line spacing (or *leading*, which rhymes with *sledding*) refers to the amount of space between each line of text in a document. Correspondence is single-spaced with double-spacing between paragraphs. Single-spacing is easy to read and allows the reader to comprehend at a glance the structure of a document. Headings and indented quotations are then more noticeable. Many courts (and the Federal Rules of Appellate Procedure) require documents submitted to them to be double-spaced. Double-spacing is helpful when editing and proofing a document because it allows room for edits to be made on the page.

As to word spacing, leave one space between words and one space after most punctuation marks, such as commas. As discussed in Chapter 2, the current trend is to use one space after a period rather than two, as was common when typewriters were used, although many writers still use two spaces after a period. Whichever approach you use, be consistent. In most documents, paragraphs are indented five spaces.

Most word processing programs protect against odd line breaks by ensuring that words are not hyphenated at the end of a line, that a line will not begin with a period or comma, and so forth.

4. Document Length

Many courts impose limitations on document length. For example, the federal rules provide that a principal brief cannot exceed 30 pages or 1,300 lines of text (if it uses a monospaced type) or 14,000 words (with headings and footnotes counting toward line and word limitations). Fed. R. App. P. 32(a)(7).

If your project exceeds a maximum length requirement, you can revise the project and omit needless words, use smaller margins, drop textual material into footnotes (which are often in smaller type), or use smaller point type size. Two easy ways to reduce the length of a document are to use one space rather than two after a sentence-ending period and to eliminate any indents for paragraphs (assuming paragraphs are separated by double spaces).

Check court rules to make sure you comply with any requirements as to margins and type size. For example, U.S. Supreme Court rules flatly require margins of at least three-fourths of an inch, impose word count limits, and insist on 12-point type for text and 10-point type for footnotes. Sup. Ct. R. 33.1. Another disadvantage of squeezing material into a document is that it creates a more cramped appearance, and few, if any, readers will be fooled by artificial techniques adopted to meet length requirements. Some word processing programs, including some WordPerfect versions, include a feature called "Make It Fit," which will shrink margins and reduce font size and line spacing to ensure that a document fits on one page (or a prescribed number of pages). Similarly, in some version of Microsoft Word, select "File," Print Preview," and then "Shrink to Fit." The danger of using such techniques, however, is that you may well violate court rules on formatting and margins.

One common cause of excessive document length is having too many editors. Nearly every reader of a document will make changes, and the changes are nearly always additions rather than deletions. Ask for help from a colleague, but understand that if too many readers review the project, it will grow in length.

To enhance readability, keep paragraphs less than one-half page in length. Although paragraph length is dictated by content, the use of more frequent, shorter paragraphs improves reader comprehension.

5. Headings

Headings not only provide the reader with a signal as to what will follow, but also create visual drama on a page. The number of headings you use will be determined by the content of the document. Most legal writers use more than one technique for headings. Headings in the same location, typeface, or font style signal information of the same importance. Headings and subheadings should be consistently numbered, as shown in Figure 12-1. Do not use a *1* or an *A* unless a *2* or a *B* will

Figure 12-1   Headings

- Main headings are often centered and single-spaced. Each is usually given a Roman numeral. Some writers use boldface print to make headings stand out. Remember that headings (especially longer headings) that use all capital letters are harder to read and may be ignored.
- Subheadings that occur within a main heading should be flush left and use capital letters only for the first letter in each major word. Do not capitalize articles, conjunctions, or prepositions of four or fewer letters. *Bluebook* R. 8. Each subheading should be labeled with a capital letter and should be underlined or boldfaced for emphasis.
- Separate all headings and subheadings from the text by double-spacing above and below.
- Following is a common structure for headings and subheadings:

I.

A.

B.

    1.

    2.

        a.

        b.

        c.

II.

A.

B.

III.

follow. Proofread only your headings to make sure their structure is parallel and that you haven't skipped over or repeated a letter or number.

a. Placement

Headings and subheadings may be centered, placed flush left, or indented. Main section headings, such as "STATEMENT OF FACTS," are typically centered and single-spaced. Subheadings are usually set flush left. Again, maintain parallelism in the headings. If one subheading is flush left and boldfaced, all other subheadings of the same level should be flush left and boldfaced.

b. Phrasing

Headings should be concise and descriptive. They can be single words (such as *Argument*), phrases (such as *Jury Selection*), or sentences (*Failure to Provide Adequate Notice of Shareholders' Meetings Violates California Law.*). Whatever the selection, headings at the same level must be stated in parallel terms and must appear in the same format. For example, all subheadings could be phrases or complete sentences. If the heading or subheading is a complete sentence, follow it with a period. Make sure there are no page breaks immediately following any heading; move the heading to the next page, if needed.

In persuasive documents, such as briefs submitted to courts, use persuasive headings rather than neutral ones. Thus, write *Quoting Excerpts of Copyrighted Material in News Reports Is a Permissible Fair Use* rather than *The Fair Use Doctrine.*

c. Emphasis

Each heading can be emphasized by centering or by using all capital letters, underscoring, italics, or boldface type. Use all capital letters sparingly because they are more difficult to read than lowercase letters, and many experts believe they are easy to ignore. Thus, it may be acceptable to use all uppercase letters for a short heading such as "CONCLUSION," but do not use all uppercase letters for longer phrases or sentences because the shapes of the words disappear, impairing readability and encouraging readers to ignore the material. Again, each level of heading should be consistent with other equivalent levels. This approach will help readers recognize how you approach important information.

d. Lists

The guidelines applicable to headings apply equally to lists. The elements of a list must be parallel, and the formatting should be consistent. Don't use bullets in some lists and dashes in others. When using parentheses, use a full set, not a single parenthesis. Thus, use (a), rather than a).

6. Visuals

Visuals, such as tables, graphs, charts, or figures, are not as commonly used in legal writing as in other types of writing although they may be used to illustrate financial and statistical results. When used sparingly, they can make a point far more effectively than words can. Note that color is seldom used in legal documents. If you use such visuals, follow these guidelines:

- Keep the design simple;
- Place each visual as close as possible to the text section discussing the information;
- Show time moving forward if the visual shows information that occurs over a period of time; and
- Use your "eye" and sense of judgment to determine if the visual is helpful or merely a form of eye candy.

Citation Form

A. Introduction

A critical part of the writing process in many documents is citing to legal authorities. Every legal assertion made in a document must be supported by legal authority. These supporting authorities appear as citations in your document. Citations must appear in a standard and consistent format so that any reader will be able to retrieve the legal authority you cited and verify that you have accurately represented the status of the law. Thus, legal writers communicate using the same "language" or citation form. Errors in citation form will cause the reader to lose respect for the author of a document and conclude that if an author cannot be depended on to cite correctly, the author likely cannot be depended on to conduct thorough analysis.

Case Illustration: Court Complaints About Citation Form

Recently, courts have been complaining that too many briefs are riddled with citation errors. *See, e.g., Edison Mission Energy, Inc. v. FERC*, 394 F.3d 964, 969 n.1 (noting that failure to indicate relevant pages in citations in briefs is sanctionable under the Federal Rules of Appellate Procedure); *Hurlbert v. Gordon*, 824 P.2d 1238, 1245-46 (Wash. Ct. App. 1992) (stating that counsel's errors in briefing and poor citation form made it impossible for the court to find information in the record, hampering the work of the court, and justifying the imposition of monetary sanctions against counsel).

Professor Peter W. Martin of Cornell University Law School offers excellent explanations of citation form with examples of citations in both *Bluebook* and *ALWD* format at www.law.cornell.edu/citation.

B. Citation Systems

There are two primary guides to citation form in the United States:

- *The Bluebook.* The oldest and best-known system of citation is found in *The Bluebook: A Uniform System of Citation* (Columbia Law Review Ass'n et al. eds., 19th ed. 2010) (*The Bluebook*). *The Bluebook* is complex, and the rules are often poorly worded with few examples. Nevertheless, because most judges and practicing professionals were taught to use *The Bluebook* for citation form, it is the most commonly used citation manual.
- *ALWD.* ALWD & Darby Dickerson, *ALWD Citation Manual* (4th ed., Aspen Publishers 2010). In 2000, the Association of Legal Writing Directors and Professor Darby Dickerson produced an alternative to *The Bluebook*. Called *ALWD* (pronounced "all wood"), the citation system was intended to provide an easy-to-learn and user-friendly alternative to *The Bluebook*. In many instances, the *ALWD* format is identical to *Bluebook* format. For example, the format for most lower court cases, statutes, constitutions, journals and periodicals, and encyclopedias is identical. Rules for spacing are identical, and most short forms are identical. There are, however, differences in many abbreviations, and although the presentation and numerous examples in *ALWD* make it easier to use than *The Bluebook*, it is more than 150 pages longer than *The Bluebook*.

Although there are other guides to citation form, the most notable of which is the *University of Chicago Manual of Legal Citation*, usually referred to as the *Maroonbook*, and used primarily in the Chicago metropolitan area, *The Bluebook* is probably the best-known system at this time, although *ALWD* continues to attract a great deal of interest because of its sensible rules and approach. Follow your school, firm, or office practice. Note, however, that if local citation rules exist for a court or jurisdiction, they must be followed and will supersede any citation system. For example, California requires citation to either the *California Style Manual* or *The Bluebook*. Cal. R. Ct. 1.200.

C. Law Reviews

According to *Bluebook* Rule 2.2, the main text of law review pieces contains no citations; instead, citations appear in footnotes. The presentation of citations in law review footnotes differs greatly from the style of citations used by practitioners. Thus, *The Bluebook* is primarily directed to showing how to cite in law review footnotes and presents information for practitioners in a separate section called the Bluepages. Although there are many differences between the two methods, the most noticeable are the following:

- Law review footnotes usually use large and small capitals (as shown in the word PATENT) for many citation forms, such as the authors and titles of books, whereas practitioners never use large and small capitals and always use ordinary Roman typeface (as shown in the word *Patent*).

- Full case names are not italicized in law review footnotes whereas they are always underscored or italicized by practitioners.

ALWD does not differentiate between citation form for law review footnotes and for practitioners; it endorses ordinary type and does not use any form of LARGE AND SMALL CAPITALS.

D. Using This Appendix

This appendix is intended to provide a quick reference only to citation form and thus the focus is on the most commonly encountered types of citations and their examples rather than on explanations of the underlying rules for citation form. Consult *The Bluebook* and *ALWD* for explanation of the rules. Most examples in this section are fictitious.

E. Quick Reference for Citations (*Bluebook and ALWD* Forms)

Note that references to the Bluepages in *The Bluebook* are shown as "B."

Type of Citation and *Bluebook* and *ALWD* Rule	*Bluebook* Law Review Footnote Form	*Bluebook* Practitioner Form (Note that underscoring may be substituted for italics in any example.)	*ALWD* Form (Note that underscoring may be substituted for italics in any example.)
State Cases (if court rules require parallel citations) (*Bluebook* B4.1.3, Rule 10.3, and Table T.1.3; *ALWD* Rule 12.4)	Not applicable	*Allen v. Carr,* 201 N.C. 118, 429 S.E.2d 16 (1984); *Harris v. Lee,* 101 N.C. App. 12, 409 S.E.2d 90 (1982)	*Allen v. Carr,* 201 N.C. 118, 429 S.E.2d 16 (1984); *Harris v. Lee,* 101 N.C. App. 12, 409 S.E.2d 90 (1982)
State Cases (in all other instances) (*Bluebook* B4.1.3, Rule 10.3, and Table T.1.3; *ALWD* Rule 12.4)	Allen v. Carr, 429 S.E.2d 118 (N.C. 1984); Harris v. Lee, 409 S.E.2d 90 (N.C. Ct. App. 1982)	*Allen v. Carr,* 429 S.E.2d 16 (N.C. 1984); *Harris v. Lee,* 409 S.E.2d 90 (N.C. Ct. App. 1982)	*Allen v. Carr,* 429 S.E.2d 16 (N.C. 1984); *Harris v. Lee,* 409 S.E.2d 90 (N.C. App. 1982)

Type of Citation and *Bluebook* and *ALWD* Rule	*Bluebook* Law Review Footnote Form	*Bluebook* Practitioner Form (Note that underscoring may be substituted for italics in any example.)	*ALWD* Form (Note that underscoring may be substituted for italics in any example.)
U.S. Supreme Court Cases (*Bluebook* B4.1.3, Rule 10.4, and Table T.1.1; *ALWD* Rule 12.6)	Daley v. Fisk, 520 U.S. 103 (1998)	*Daley v. Fisk*, 520 U.S. 103 (1998)	*Daley v. Fisk*, 520 U.S. 103 (1998) (*ALWD* permits but does not prefer parallel citations)
U.S. Courts of Appeal Cases (*Bluebook* B4.1.3, Rule 10.4, and Table T.1.1; *ALWD* Rule 12.6)	Lawrence v. Mather, 103 F.3d 114 (8th Cir. 1999)	*Lawrence v. Mather*, 103 F.3d 114 (8th Cir. 1999)	*Lawrence v. Mather*, 103 F.3d 114 (8th Cir. 1999)
U.S. District Court Cases (*Bluebook* B4.1.3, Rule 10.4, and Table T.1.1; *ALWD* Rule 12.6)	Blakely v. Yost, 742 F. Supp. 2d 942 (C.D. Cal. 2000)	*Blakely v. Yost*, 742 F. Supp. 2d 942 (C.D. Cal. 2000)	*Blakely v. Yost*, 742 F. Supp. 2d 942 (C.D. Cal. 2000)
U.S. Constitution (*Bluebook* B6, Rule 11; *ALWD* Rule 13)	U.S. CONST. amend. IV	U.S. Const. amend. IV	U.S. Const. amend. IV
State Constitution (*Bluebook* B6, Rule 11; *ALWD* Rule 13)	CAL. CONST. art. XX, § 4	Cal. Const. art. XX, § 4	Cal. Const. art. XX, § 4
Federal Statutes (*Bluebook* B5, Rule 12, and Table T.1.1; *ALWD* Rule 14)	17 U.S.C. § 101 (2006); 17 U.S.C.A. § 101 (West 1998); 17 U.S.C.S. § 101 (LexisNexis 1996)	17 U.S.C. § 101 (2006); 17 U.S.C.A. § 101 (West 1998); 17 U.S.C.S. § 101 (LexisNexis 1996)	17 U.S.C. § 101 (2006); 17 U.S.C.A. § 101 (West 1998); 17 U.S.C.S. § 101 (Lexis 1996)
State Statutes (*Bluebook* B5, Rule 12, and Table T.1.3; *ALWD* Rule 14 and App. 1)	ARIZ. REV. STAT. ANN. § 10-401 (1992); CAL. EVID. CODE § 521 (West 1998)	Ariz. Rev. Stat. Ann. § 10-401 (1992); Cal. Evid. Code § 521 (West 1998)	Ariz. Rev. Stat. Ann. § 10-401 (West 1992); Cal. Evid. Code Ann. § 521 (West 1998)

Type of Citation and *Bluebook* and *ALWD* Rule	*Bluebook* Law Review Footnote Form	*Bluebook* Practitioner Form (Note that underscoring may be substituted for italics in any example.)	*ALWD* Form (Note that underscoring may be substituted for italics in any example.)
Federal Rules (*Bluebook* B5, and Rule 12.9.3; *ALWD* Rule 17.1)	FED. R. CIV. P. 12(b)(6)	Fed. R. Civ. P. 12(b)(6)	Fed. R. Civ. P. 12(b)(6)
Federal Regulations (*Bluebook* B5 and Rule 14.2; *ALWD* Rule 19.1)	Cheese Import Regulations, 42 C.F.R. § 131 (2012); or 29 C.F.R. § 605.89 (2010) (include title if helpful)	Cheese Import Regulations, 42 C.F.R. § 131 (2012); or 29 C.F.R. § 605.89 (2010) (include title if helpful)	42 C.F.R. § 131 (2012); or 29 C.F.R. § 605.89 (2010) (include title if helpful)
Federal Register (*Bluebook* Rule 14.2; *ALWD* Rule 19.3)	Standard Industrial Codes, 64 Fed. Reg. 27812 (Dec. 6, 2012)	Standard Industrial Codes, 64 Fed. Reg. 27812 (Dec. 6, 2012)	64 Fed. Reg. 27812 (Dec. 6, 2012) (title is optional)
Administrative Decisions (*Bluebook* Rule 14.3 and T.1.2; *ALWD* Rule 19.5)	Network Solutions, Inc., 18 F.C.C.2d 909 (2000); Stevens Textile Co., 403 N.L.R.B. 120 (1985)	*Network Solutions, Inc.*, 18 F.C.C.2d 909 (2000); *Stevens Textile Co.*, 403 N.L.R.B. 120 (1985)	*Network Solutions, Inc.*, 18 F.C.C.2d 909 (U.S. Fed. Commun. Commn. 2000); *Stevens Textile Co.*, 403 N.L.R.B. 120 (U.S. Natl. Lab. Rel. Bd. 1985)
Looseleaf Services (*Bluebook* Rule 19 and Table T.15; *ALWD* Rule 28.1)	*In re* Walmart Stores, Inc., 5 Bus. Franchise Guide (CCH) ¶ 42,201 (D.N.J. Aug. 12, 1995)	*In re Walmart Stores, Inc.*, 5 Bus. Franchise Guide (CCH) ¶ 42,201 (D.N.J. Aug. 12, 1995)	*In re Walmart Stores, Inc.*, 5 Bus. Fran. Guide (CCH) ¶ 42,201 (D.N.J. Aug. 12, 1995)
Attorneys General Opinions (*Bluebook* T.1.2; *ALWD* Rule 19.7, 20.7)	Recess Appointments, 23 Op. O.L.C. 4 (2010); Forefeiture of Pension Benefits, Op. Ill. Att'y Gen. 11-003 (2011)	Recess Appointments, 23 Op. O.L.C. 4 (2010); Forefeiture of Pension Benefits, Op. Ill. Att'y Gen. 11-003 (2011)	23 Op. Ofc. Leg. Counsel 4 (2010); Ill. Atty. Gen. Op. 11-003 (2011)

Type of Citation and *Bluebook* and *ALWD* Rule	*Bluebook* Law Review Footnote Form	*Bluebook* Practitioner Form (Note that underscoring may be substituted for italics in any example.)	*ALWD* Form (Note that underscoring may be substituted for italics in any example.)
Books (*Bluebook* B8 and Rule 15; *ALWD* Rule 22.1)	2 J. THOMAS MCCARTHY, MCCARTHY ON TRADEMARKS AND UNFAIR COMPETITION § 4:13 (4th ed. 1998); 7 SAMUEL WILLISTON, TREATISE ON THE LAW OF CONTRACTS § 901 (Walter H. Jaeger ed., 3d ed. 1964)	2 J. Thomas McCarthy, *McCarthy on Trademarks and Unfair Competition* § 4:13 (4th ed. 1998); 7 Samuel Williston, *Treatise on the Law of Contracts* § 901 (Walter H. Jaeger ed., 3d ed. 1964)	J. Thomas McCarthy, *McCarthy on Trademarks and Unfair Competition* vol. 2, § 4:13 (4th ed., West 1998); Samuel Williston, *Treatise on the Law of Contracts* vol. 7, § 901 (Walter H. Jaeger ed., 3d ed., West 1964)
Periodical Materials and Law Reviews (*Bluebook* B9 and Rule 16 and Table T.13; *ALWD* Rule 23.1)	David J. Hayes, Jr., *Due Process*, 41 EMORY L.J. 164 (1997); Janet R. Sanders, *Corporate Takeovers*, 12 J. BUS. L.18 (2001)	David B. Hayes, Jr., *Due Process*, 41 Emory L.J. 164 (1997); Janet R. Sanders, *Corporate Takeovers*, 12 J. Bus. L. 18 (2001)	David B. Hayes, Jr., *Due Process*, 41 Emory L.J. 164 (1997); Janet R. Sanders, *Corporate Takeovers*, 12 J. Bus. L. 18 (2001)
Dictionaries (*Bluebook* B8 and Rule 15.8; *ALWD* Rule 25.1)	BLACK'S LAW DICTIONARY 791 (9th ed. 2009)	*Black's Law Dictionary* 791 (9th ed. 2009)	*Black's Law Dictionary* 791 (Bryan A. Garner ed., 9th ed., West 2009)
Legal Encyclopedias (*Bluebook* B8 and Rule 15.8; *ALWD* Rule 26.1)	76 AM. JUR. 2D *Trademarks* § 13 (1986); 95 C.J.S. *Trial* § 32 (1988) 14 CAL. JUR. 3D *Contracts* §§ 14-18 (1994)	76 Am. Jur. 2d *Trademarks* § 13 (1986); 95 C.J.S. *Trial* § 32 (1988); 14 Cal. Jur. 3d *Contracts* §§ 14-18 (1994)	76 Am. Jur. 2d *Trademarks* § 13 (1986); 95 C.J.S. *Trial* § 32 (1988); 14 Cal. Jur. 3d *Contracts* §§ 14-18 (1994)
Restatements (*Bluebook* B5 and Rule 12.9.5; *ALWD* Rule 27.1)	RESTATEMENT (SECOND) OF TORTS § 13 (1986)	Restatement (Second) of Torts § 13 (1986)	*Restatement (Second) of Torts* § 13 (1986)

Type of Citation and *Bluebook* and *ALWD* Rule	*Bluebook* Law Review Footnote Form	*Bluebook* Practitioner Form (Note that underscoring may be substituted for italics in any example.)	*ALWD* Form (Note that underscoring may be substituted for italics in any example.)
A.L.R. Annotations (*Bluebook* Rule 16.7.6; *ALWD* Rule 24.1)	James W. Gray, Annotation, *Nuisance Theory*, 56 A.L.R.4TH 145 (1990)	James W. Gray, Annotation, *Nuisance Theory*, 56 A.L.R.4th 145 (1990)	James W. Gray, *Nuisance Theory*, 56 A.L.R.4th 145 (1990)
Electronic Databases (*Bluebook* B4 and Rule 18; *ALWD* Rule 12.12)	Bowes v. Capital Inc., No. 94-1765, 1995 U.S. App. LEXIS 1202, at *2 (4th Cir. Oct. 8, 1995)	*Bowes v. Capital Inc.*, No. 94-1765, 1995 U.S. App. LEXIS 1202, at *2 (4th Cir. Oct. 8, 1995)	*Bowes v. Capital Inc.*, 1995 U.S. App. LEXIS 1202 at *2 (4th Cir. Oct. 8, 1995)
	Green v. Taylor, No. 97-CAS-120, 1998 WL 44102, at *1 (D.N.J. Feb. 10, 1998)	*Green v. Taylor*, No. 97-CAS-120, 1998 WL 44102, at *1 (D.N.J. Feb. 10, 1998)	*Green v. Taylor*, 1998 WL 44102 at *1 (D.N.J. Feb. 10, 1998)
Internet Source (article available solely on Internet) (*Bluebook* Rule 18; *ALWD* Rule 40.1)	Mike Scarcella, *DOJ Fights over Privacy*, LAW.COM (July 30, 2012), http://www.LAW.COM/jsp/nlj/PubArticleNLJ.jsp	Mike Scarcella, *DOJ Fights over Privacy*, Law.Com (July 30, 2012), http://www.law.com/jsp/nlj/PubArticleNLJ.jsp	Mike Scarcella, *DOJ Fights over Privacy*, http://www.law.com/jsp/nlj/PubArticleNLJ.jsp (July 30, 2012)

F. Special *Bluebook* and *ALWD* Citation Issues

1. General Comments

- Practitioners never use LARGE AND SMALL CAPITALS in citations in their court documents or legal memoranda. They always use ordinary Roman type. LARGE AND SMALL CAPITALS are used only for law review footnotes in *The Bluebook* system and other similar academic writings. *ALWD* does not recognize LARGE AND SMALL CAPITALS as appropriate for any citation.
- Practitioners may underscore or italicize case names, book titles, names of articles in journals, and so forth. Select one method and be consistent. Use this same method for signals (such as *see* and *id.*). Italics are far more common in law practice than underscoring.

- In citations, use the abbreviations "2d" and "3d" rather than "2nd" and "3rd." All other ordinals (4th, 5th, and so forth) are the same as in general use. Do not use a superscript. Thus, use "8th" rather than "8th."

2. Abbreviations in Case Names: *Bluebook* and *ALWD*

- Under *Bluebook* Rule 10.2.1(c), when a citation appears in a textual sentence (meaning that the citation is needed to make sense of the sentence), you may abbreviate only well-known acronyms (such as FBI and CIA) and the following abbreviations in case names: "&," "Ass'n," "Bros.," "Co.," "Corp.," "Inc.," "Ltd.," and "No." *ALWD* Rule 12.2(e) follows the same general approach but also allows the abbreviation "Assn."
- When a citation appears as a stand-alone citation, for example, after a declaratory sentence, you must abbreviate any of the nearly 180 words identified in Table T.6 of *The Bluebook*, such as "Hosp." or "Cas." even if the word is the first word in a party's name. Many of *The Bluebook* and *ALWD* abbreviations differ from each other. *ALWD* Rules 12.2(e)(3) and 12.2(e)(5) state that you *may* abbreviate words in its Appendix 3 when the case name appears in a stand-alone citation and that it is traditional to spell out virtually all words in a case name when it appears in text.

Correct Example for Law Review Footnotes

Trademarks may be abandoned by nonuse. Bates Constr. & Div. Auth. v. S. Maint. Found., 499 U.S. 16, 19 (1999).

Correct Example for Practitioners *(for Bluebook and ALWD)*

Trademarks may be abandoned by nonuse. *Bates Constr. & Div. Auth. v. S. Maint. Found.*, 499 U.S. 16, 19 (1999).

3. Spacing (*Bluebook* Rule 6.1(a), *ALWD* Rule 2.2)

- Close up adjacent single capital letters. Treat an ordinal (2d, 3d, 4th, and so forth) as a single capital letter.

  Correct Examples: U.S.
  F.3d
  N.W.2d

- Place spaces before and after multiple letter abbreviations.

  Correct Examples: F. Supp. 2d
  Fed. R. Crim. P.
  Cal. 4th

- Be careful with the abbreviations for the names of periodicals. Their spacing is odd. Mimic the spacing shown in *Bluebook* Table T.13 and *ALWD* Appendix 5.

Bluebook Correct Example
for Law Review Footnotes: 46 B.C. L. Rev. 190

Bluebook Correct Example
for Practitioners: 46 B.C. L. Rev. 190

ALWD Correct Example
for Any Purpose: 46 B.C. L. Rev. 190

- Always place a space after a section or paragraph symbol, as in 35 U.S.C. § 102 (2006). To pluralize sections, use two symbols, as in §§ 102–104, and include all digits.

4. Punctuation

- If the citation supports or contradicts a previous declaratory sentence, follow it with a period.
- If the citation is used as a clause within a complete sentence, set it off with commas.
- If the citation is used in a "string" of other citations, separate the citations from each other with semicolons and follow the order required in *Bluebook* Rule 1.4 and *ALWD* Rule 45. The ordering systems for *The Bluebook* and *ALWD* differ, especially with regard to the order of lower federal court cases.

5. Pinpoints

Give a pinpoint citation (a reference to the page on which specific material appears) for all citations (*Bluebook* Rule 3.2; *ALWD* Rule 5.2). See the following examples and *The Bluebook* and *ALWD* for rules relating to the citation of multiple pages.

Bluebook Correct Example for Law Review Footnote

Hardy v. Bailey, 520 U.S. 118, 124 (1992)
Jackson v. Emerson Inc., 691 N.W.2d 145, 150-51 (Wis. 1994)
Steven Mills, *Bankruptcy Law*, 31 Stan. L. Rev. 308, 314-15 (1998)

Bluebook and ALWD Correct Examples for Practitioners

Hardy v. Bailey, 520 U.S. 118, 124 (1992)
Jackson v. Emerson Inc., 109 Wis. 2d 99, 104, 691 N.W.2d 145, 150-51 (1994)
Jackson v. Emerson Inc., 691 N.W.2d 145, 150-51 (Wis. 1994)
Steven Mills, *Bankruptcy Law*, 31 Stan. L. Rev. 308, 314-15 (1998)

Note that whereas *The Bluebook* requires one to drop repetitious digits for page spans, the *ALWD* approach is optional so that all digits may be retained if desired, as in 314-315.

6. Quotations (*Bluebook* Rule 5; *ALWD* Rules 47-49)

The approach to presenting quotations is nearly identical in *The Bluebook* and in *ALWD*.

- Quotations of forty-nine words or fewer are enclosed in double quotation marks (" ") and placed in the narrative portion of your text. Always put periods and commas inside your quotation marks. Quotations within quotations are shown by single quotation marks (' ').
- Quotations of fifty words or more are indented left and right, justified, and appear without quotation marks (quotation marks within this block should appear as they do in the original). Place the citation at the left margin on the line immediately following the quotation and not within the block.
- Use an ellipsis (. . .) to show an omission in the middle of a quoted sentence. Do not start a sentence with an ellipsis (*Bluebook* Rule 5.3; *ALWD* Rule 49.3(b)); instead, use brackets, as in "[N]oncompetition agreements must be reasonable." If the omitted matter includes the end of a sentence, add another period to the ellipsis (. . . .).
- Use brackets ([ ]) to show a minor alteration in a quotation, such as a change from uppercase to lowercase. Use the signal "[sic]" to show a misteak [sic] in the original material.

Note that *ALWD* provides that if a quotation is at least fifty words *or* exceeds four lines of typed text, it should be presented as a block quotation. *The Bluebook* approach does not refer to lines of text but provides only that if the quotation is fifty words or more, it should be presented as a block quotation.

7. Short Forms

Short forms may be used for most citations once the citation has been given in full in the document. The treatment of short forms is much the same in *The Bluebook* and in *ALWD*.

- Use *id.* to send the reader to the most immediately preceding legal authority, no matter what the preceding authority is. *Id.* may be capitalized or not, depending on its location in a sentence.
- Use the form "*id.* at __" to send the reader to a different page within the preceding citation.

Bluebook Correct Example for Law Review Footnotes

First reference: Thomas v. Murphy Bros., 520 U.S. 118, 124 (1995)
Second reference: *Id.* at 128-29.

- Do not use the word "at" before a section symbol or paragraph symbol (*Bluebook* Rule 3.3). *ALWD* requires the use of "at" before the symbols (*ALWD* Rule 11.3).

Correct Example *(Bluebook)*

First reference: 42 U.S.C. § 101 (2006)
Second reference: *Id.* § 114

Bluebook. Use one of the following forms to send a reader to a preceding case that is not immediately preceding:

Correct Examples for Practitioners

First reference: *Geary Bros. v. Levy Ass'n,* 521 U.S. 16, 19 (2001)
Later references: *Geary,* 521 U.S. at 23; or
                     521 U.S. at 23;
                     In *Geary,* the Court also held . . . . (*See* Rule 10.9(c)), which allows a reference to a case by one of the parties' names without any further citation if the case has been cited in full in the same general discussion.)

ALWD. Use the following forms to send a reader to a preceding case that is not immediately preceding:

First reference: *Ryan v. O'Leary,* 521 U.S. 118, 122 (1999)
                     Later references: *Ryan,* 521 U.S. at 124; or
                     521 U.S. at 124;
                     In *Ryan,* the Court also held . . . . (*ALWD* Rule 12.20)

■ Use the signal *supra* (meaning *above*) to send a reader to a previous secondary authority that is not the immediately preceding authority. The signal *supra* cannot be used to send a reader to a case, statute, constitutional provision, or regulation. *Supra* always appears with the name of an author or the title of a work (*Bluebook* Rule 4.2 and Bluepages B8.2; *ALWD* Rule 11.4). Thus, *supra* is used primarily to send readers to a previously cited book or law review article.

Bluebook Correct Example for Law Review Footnotes

First reference: SUSAN GRAY, DUE PROCESS § 12 (1999)
Later reference: GRAY, *supra* note 4, § 14

Bluebook Correct Example for Practitioners

McCarthy, *supra,* at 177.

Correct *ALWD* Example

Davis, *supra* n. 41, at 16. (Note that *ALWD* Rule 11.4 states that *supra* cannot be used unless a document has footnotes or endnotes.)

■ The first reference to a statute must give the full citation. Later references may use any short form that is understandable to the reader.

■ Although *The Bluebook* and *ALWD* clearly require a year and a reference to the publisher (unless the set is official) for citations for statutes, almost all practitioners omit the parenthetical.

Correct *Bluebook* and *ALWD* Example: 15 U.S.C. § 1051 (2006)

Example in Common Use: 15 U.S.C. § 1051

G. Differences Between The *Bluebook* and *ALWD*

Although the basic methods of citation are much the same in *The Bluebook* and *ALWD*, there are some notable differences, including the following:

■ **Parallel Citations for U.S. Supreme Court Cases.** *The Bluebook* (Bluepages B4.1.3 and Table T.1.1) does not permit parallel citations for U.S. Supreme Court cases. *ALWD* does (*ALWD* Rule 12.4(c)).

■ **Case Names.** The abbreviations used in case names are different in the two citation systems. *See Bluebook* Table T.6 and *ALWD* Appendix 3. Moreover, the current fourth edition of *ALWD* allows variation in the presentation of some abbreviations in case names. Thus, the word "Department" may be shown as *Dep't* or as *Dept.*, and "Association" may be shown as *Ass'n* or *Assn.* *The Bluebook* never allows variation in abbreviations of words in case names. Additionally, if the United States is a party, *Bluebook* Rule 10.2.2 requires reference to *United States*. *ALWD* allows either *United States* or *U.S.* (*ALWD* Rule 12.2(g)).

■ **Treatises and Dictionaries.** The publisher of a treatise or dictionary is not included in the parenthetical with the date under *The Bluebook* approach (Rule 15) but it is under the *ALWD* approach. Also, the placement of a volume number for a set of books varies.

■ **Districts and Departments.** *The Bluebook* does not allow one to indicate which district or department within a court decided a state case unless the information is particularly relevant (Rule 10.4(b)). *ALWD* requires this information (Rule 12.6(b)).

■ **Pinpoints.** When giving page pinpoints, *ALWD* allows one to retain all digits (example: 914–916) or to drop repetitious digits (example: 914-16). *The Bluebook* requires one to drop repetitious digits (example: 914–16).

■ **Capitalization.** Capitalization of headings in court documents differs slightly. *Bluebook* Rule 8 states that prepositions of four or fewer letters should not be capitalized (unless they begin the title or follow a colon). *ALWD* Rule 3 states that no prepositions should be capitalized (unless they begin a title).

Bluebook Example: Punitive Damages Are Recoverable Under the Act

ALWD Example: Punitive Damages Are Recoverable under the Act

Challenge	?	Citation Form

Using either *The Bluebook* or *ALWD*, correct the following citations. You need not include punctuation after the citations. You may need to make up information, such as volumes, pages, and so forth.

1. Andrews v. Smithson Company, a 2009 case from the United States Supreme Court, located in volume 450 at page 395, with a quotation from pages 399 through 401.
2. Hall Brothers versus the Securities and Exchange Commission, a case from the Third Circuit Court of Appeals, located in volume 205 at page 100, with a quotation from pages 105 through 107.
3. Shaw Association v. the United States of America, a 2010 case from the Southern District of Texas, located in volume 103 at page 990.
4. Frank and Susan Kimball versus Taylor Incorporated, a 2009 case from the Missouri Court of Appeals, appearing in volume 409 of the relevant reporter (Second Series), beginning on page 677.
5. Engineering Technology Co. versus Bradford, a 2008 case from the Georgia Supreme Court. Assume court rules require you to include parallel citations.
6. Section 404 of Title 35 of the United States Code.
7. New York Employers Liability Law Section 10004.
8. Section 404 of the second edition of a book written by Ellen Edwards and James Bennett, volume 3, entitled "Insurance Defense Litigation."
9. A 2010 law review article written by Timothy L. Stewart, III, entitled "Negotiating Arbitration Clauses" and appearing in the Indiana Law Journal.
10. Restatement of Contracts, Second, Section 312.
11. Give the short form citations for the Andrews case. Assume the pincite is page 405.

appendix B

English as a Second Language

StyleLinks

http://owl.english.purdue.edu/owl/resource/678/01
Purdue University's Online Writing Lab offers resource pages, handouts, information on spelling and grammar, and quizzes for ESL learners.

www.esldesk.com
ESL Desk provides numerous resources, tools, and quizzes for ESL learners.

www.english-at-home.com
This site provides games, quizzes, tests, and other tools for ESL learners.

www.eslcafe.com
This excellent website provides numerous links to ESL resources as well as handouts on grammar and usage and quizzes.

www.rongchang.com
This site provides links to numerous ESL websites and offers a wide variety of quizzes, games, and learning materials.

www.babelfish.com
The Babelfish site offers translations to and from various languages.

A. Introduction

If English is your second language, you have probably already noticed a number of oddities and contradictions in English and in legal writing. Some are purely linguistic differences and others are cultural differences. This appendix provides a very brief overview of some common trouble spots for legal writers learning English as a second language ("ESL").

B. Grammar

A number of grammar issues cause confusion for nonnative speakers of English, including word order, placement of adjectives and adverbs, the use of prepositions, verb tense, and determining the correct article to use before a noun.

1. Standard Word Order

In English, unlike many languages, word order is important in sentences and significantly affects meaning. Generally, the standard sentence structure in English is subject-verb-object, as in *John mailed the document,* whereas in many other languages, the verb is placed first. Follow the standard English sentence structure in most instances because English readers are often confused by deviation from this expected pattern.

Moreover, a simple change in word order may change a direct statement to a question. Consider the following:

Statement: *The brief was filed today.*
Question: *Was the brief filed today?*

Each sentence contains the same words; however, a slight change in word order results in a completely different meaning.

2. Adjectives

In English, adjectives usually appear before the nouns they modify or describe. Consider the following example: *Elena is preparing for a difficult trial.* The adjective is *difficult* (because it describes something about the trial), the noun is *trial,* and the adjective is placed before the noun.

Some adjectives, however, appear after linking verbs. A *linking verb* is a verb, often of the senses, that does not show action, such as *seem, feel,* and the forms of the verb *to be,* such as *is* and *was.*

Correct Examples: *The attorney <u>seemed nervous</u>.*
The music <u>sounds haunting</u>.
The ice cream <u>tastes cold</u>.

3. Adverbs

Adverbs (words that modify or describe verbs) may appear either before or after the verb they describe but they should be placed as close to the verb as possible.

Poor	Better
The judge stated that there would be no continuance of the trial <u>angrily</u>.	The judge <u>angrily</u> stated that there would be no continuance of the trial. or The judge stated <u>angrily</u> that there would be no continuance of the trial.

4. Prepositions

Prepositions (*at, by, for, from, in, of, to, with,* and so forth) link nouns to other words and show relationships in sentences. Some prepositions show time relationships (*after, before, during, since*); some show place relationships (*at, below, in, on, to*); and others show manner relationships (*for, of, with*). Prepositions come before nouns and pronouns. Although Romance languages (such as Spanish, French, and Italian) also use prepositions, using prepositions in English is difficult because of their many idiomatic uses. An *idiom* is a phrase or expression whose meaning cannot be understood from the ordinary meanings of the words, as in the use in English of the phrase *give in* meaning *to yield* or *to surrender.*

Following are some prepositional expressions commonly used in legal writing:

according to	*innocent of*
appeal to	*liable for*
comparable to or *comparable with*	*on the contrary*
consistent with	*opposed to*
dependent on or *dependent upon*	*refer to*
different from	*regardless of*
familiar to or *familiar with*	*relevant to*
guilty of	*reliance on* or *reliance upon*
in contrast	*responsible for*
in light of	*similar to*

Remember from Chapter 4 that many prepositional phrases are wordy and can be replaced by single words. For example, replace *with regard to* with *about* or *regarding.* See Figure 4-2. Chapter 4 also includes a list of common idioms in legal writing.

5. Pronouns

In English, any noun may be replaced by a pronoun. Thus, *the attorneys* can be replaced by *they* or *them, the plaintiff* can be replaced by *he, she,* or *it,* and *the corporation* can be replaced by *it.*

6. Tense

Tense refers to *when* action takes place. Generally, English verbs have six basic tenses. Verbs change form to indicate whether an action takes place in the past, present, or future.

Tense	Form	Use	Examples
Present	Singular	Shows action happening now	I am happy. She argues the case today.
Past	Often ends in -ed	Shows action that happened in the past	I was happy. She argued the case last month.
Future	Often used with *will*	Tells about action that will happen	I will be happy. She will argue the case next week.
Present Perfect	*Has* or *have* used with main verb	Tells about a past action that continues or is complete at the time of the statement	I have been happy. She has argued the case every day thus far.
Past Perfect	*Had* used with main verb	Tells about past action that was completed before another past action or speculates about something that did not happen	The witness had practiced his testimony before the trial. If she had argued with me, I would have responded.
Future Perfect	*Will have* used with main verb	Tells about action that will take place before another future action	The trial will have ended by Tuesday. By the time the month is over, she will have argued the case five times.

The *progressive* tenses indicate continuing or progressive action. They consist of a form of *to be* together with an *-ing* form, as in *The attorney is concluding* or *The judge will be listening* for hearsay evidence.

English uses simpler tense forms than many languages, and often nonnative speakers will use progressive and perfect tenses rather than the simpler present, past, and future tenses that are most common in legal writing.

Remember to discuss the following in the past tense:

- Acts that occurred in the past, as in *The accident <u>occurred</u> on May 18, 2013*.
- The procedural history of a case you are discussing, as in *The court below <u>dismissed</u> the plaintiff's complaint and the plaintiff <u>appealed</u>*.
- The holding of a case you are discussing, as in *The court <u>held</u> that failure to hold an annual shareholders' meeting <u>was</u> a violation of law*.

Use the present tense when you are discussing a current statute or a rule of law, as in *The rule in this state <u>is</u> that punitive damages are recoverable upon a showing of reckless and willful misconduct*. Avoid shifts in tense.

Helping or Auxiliary Verbs

Helping or auxiliary verbs accompany main verbs. Some common helping verbs include *could, do, may, might, shall, should, will, would,* and any form of the verb *to be*. ESL learners frequently have trouble distinguishing the meanings of the following helping verbs:

- **Can** shows ability or possibility, as in *She can file for damages because of the breach of contract* or *She can fail this class if she does not study.*
- **Could** shows past ability or possibility, as in *She could play the piano before she was injured.*
- **May** shows permission or possibility, as in *She may file the claim so long as the statute of limitations has not expired* or *You may be liable for copyright infringement.*
- **Might** shows possibility, as in *Your motion might be denied by the court.*
- **Must** indicates obligation or requirement, as in *You must file the brief today.*
- **Shall** indicates obligation (although it is a slightly more legalistic word than *must*) and is often used in statutes, as in *An injured party shall provide notice to . . . .*
- **Should** shows advisability, as in *You should pay the rent early this month.*
- **Should have** indicates advice that was not taken or expectations not met, as in *You should have notified the insurance company as soon as you were injured.*
- **Will** shows future action, as in *We will select the jury next week.*
- **Would** indicates intention or a request or a possibility, as in *We told Maria that we would prepare her lease for her review* or *Would you like to interview the candidate?*

7. Nouns

There are two primary difficulties for ESL learners with regard to noun use: forming plurals of certain nouns and using the correct article or determiner before a noun. The use of articles (*a, an, the*) can be particularly difficult for nonnative speakers because many languages do not use articles.

a. Plurals of Noncount Nouns

Most nouns form plurals by adding *s* to the singular form as in *plaintiff-plaintiffs*. But some nouns, usually called *noncount* nouns (because they name something that cannot be counted in English, such as *wealth, democracy, intelligence,* or *evidence*), do not form plurals. Thus, you cannot write *the evidences of the plaintiff* no matter how many separate exhibits, documents, and other pieces of evidence a plaintiff introduces at trial.

b. Use of Articles: *A, An,* and *The*

Native speakers of English can often rely on their "ear" or intuition for determining the article that should be placed before a noun. Nonnative speakers often have more difficulty with articles because many languages do not use articles.

English has three articles: *a, an,* and *the*. Use *a* before words that begin with a consonant sound (such as *a brief, a court, a hand*) or a "you" sound (as in *a uniform*), and use *an* before words that begin with a vowel sound (such as *an attorney, an opening argument, an hour, an honest mistake*). Remember to focus on the sound a word makes and not its initial letter. Thus, write *a union* because the letter *u* sounds like a *y* consonant and *a one-page memo* because the letter *o* sounds like a *w* consonant.

When you write about a topic, use *a* or *an* with a noun when the reader has not yet been introduced to the topic or the noun you mention. Once you have introduced and described the noun, you can then introduce it with *the*. For this reason, *a* and *an* are called *indefinite articles* and *the* is called a *definite article*.

Correct Example

Sarah was asked to prepare <u>a memorandum</u> on nuisance law. After Sarah prepared <u>the memorandum</u>, she placed <u>a copy</u> in her files. <u>The copy</u> was later lost.

You can also use *the* when referring to an institution or entity that will be known to the reader, as in *File the brief with <u>the court</u>*.

Some other rules about using articles are as follows:

- Plural nouns require a definite article; they are never preceded by an indefinite article. Thus, you would write *I filed <u>the briefs</u> today* and not *I filed <u>a briefs</u> today*.
- The articles *a* or *an* generally do not precede a noncount noun. Thus, you would not write *A confidence is an appealing trait*.
- Some noncount nouns may not require any articles at all. Thus, *Biology is my field of study*, not *<u>The biology</u> is my field of study* or *<u>A biology</u> is my field of study*.
- Articles generally do not precede a proper noun. Thus, write *President Obama delivered the speech*, not *The President Obama delivered the speech* (there are some exceptions to this rule, as in *the United States, the Obamas, the New York Yankees, the Sahara desert*).

c. Demonstrative Pronouns

In addition to the articles *a, an,* and *the,* other words that are placed before nouns can be confusing. Nonnative speakers often have difficulty selecting the right demonstrative pronouns (*this, that, these, those*) to place before a noun. Consider these rules:

- Use *this* and *these* for items that are near in space or time, as in *this pen on my desk, this morning's newspaper,* and *these exhibits that we reviewed.*
- Use *that* and *those* for items that are far in space or time, as in *that courthouse, those cars in the accident,* or *those Justices on the Court.*
- Use *this* and *that* for singular nouns, whether they are count nouns or non-count nouns, as in *this client* and *that knowledge.*
- Use *these* and *those* before plural count nouns, as in *these documents* and *those footnotes.*

Some Troublesome Words

- **Few** can mean either *not many* or it can mean *some.*

  Correct Examples: *Few lawsuits go to trial* (meaning *not many lawsuits go to trial*).

  A few shareholders attended the meeting (meaning *some, but not many, shareholders attended the meeting*).

- **Little** can mean *not many* or it can mean *not enough.*

  Correct Examples: *There is little time left to appeal* (meaning there is *not much* time to appeal).

  He gave me a little help with cite-checking (meaning *he gave me some, but not much, help with cite-checking*).

- **Much** is used with a noncount noun. Thus write *Much evidence was admitted,* not *Many evidence was admitted.*
- **Many** is used with count nouns. Thus, write *Many shareholders attended,* not *Much shareholders attended.*

C. Spelling and Vocabulary

Spelling in English is often illogical and is not always phonetic. Thus, the letter group *ough* is pronounced differently in each of the following words: *cough, tough,* and *though,* and there are more than twenty ways to spell the "oo" sound (as in *too, two, to, blue,* and *stew*). Similarly, the words *defendant* and *dependent* sound much the same yet are spelled differently. You will need a good dictionary if you are a nonnative speaker (as do most native speakers). *Merriam-Webster's Collegiate*

Dictionary, now in its eleventh edition, is an excellent dictionary. *Merriam-Webster's* website, www.merriam-webster.com, offers a free, online dictionary, thesaurus, word games, and a word of the day. Review Chapter 3 of this Handbook for rules and tips on spelling. Nevertheless, you will simply have to memorize the spelling of certain words.

If you learned English outside of the United States, you will have to learn the American spellings of some words. Many dictionaries will use *Brit.* to indicate that a spelling is a British one.

British Spelling	American Spelling
judgement	judgment
colour, labour, behaviour	color, labor, behavior
grey	gray
centre, metre, theatre	center, meter, theater
analyse, criticise, organise	analyze, criticize, organize
specialise	specialize
catalogue, dialogue	catalog, dialog
counselling, signalling	counseling, signaling
banque, cheque	bank, check
defence, licence	defense, license

Build your vocabulary with websites or daily tear-off calendars that offer a "word of the day" lesson. Ask for help. Ask friends and colleagues to help you if you mispronounce a word or have difficulty finding the right word.

D. Some Cultural Comments About Legal Writing

England and America are two countries separated by a common language.

Usually attributed to George Bernard Shaw

The American legal system is often called an *adversarial system,* meaning that its defining feature is that two sides are pitted against each other. Similarly, lawyers are often called *advocates* because they are meant to argue fiercely for a client's position. Thus, much legal writing is frankly partisan and may often take an approach that readers in America would view as direct and entirely appropriate but that some ESL readers would view as blunt and rude.

Consider the following general comments about American legal writing.

1. Adopting the Right Style

In America, the favored legal writing style is plain English, which emphasizes simple, direct, everyday language. In many cultures, a more elaborate writing style is not only common but is expected. Such a manner of writing would reflect well on the writer's intelligence and thoughtfulness. In American legal writing, a premium is placed on being direct and adopting a straightforward readable style. It is the writer's responsibility to ensure that the reader understands the writing.

2. Being Concise

Because a reader's time is valuable, legal writers tend to "get to the point" rather quickly in a document. Long-winded openings and introductions are frowned upon. Thus, in a letter, generally no more than one sentence is devoted to an introduction (for example, *As you requested, I obtained a copy of the employment agreement . . .*). The legal writer will then proceed to address the issue.

Because many legal topics are complex, legal writing that makes a difficult subject easy to understand is valued. Moreover, because readers are often impatient, legal writers tend to move immediately into their central argument. Finally, the recent trend of courts to impose page and word count limitations has forced legal writers to become direct. Thus, avoid lengthy introductions or general explanations of an area of law and move directly to the substance of the document. For example, if a brief addresses whether silent prayer in public schools is prohibited under the First Amendment to the U.S. Constitution, a long overview of the history of the First Amendment, the intent of the drafters of the Constitution, and quotations from the Framers of the Constitution are unneeded. The judge reading the brief will be familiar with the law and will skip over such a digression anyway. In some cultures, exploration of this side topic might be considered a useful introduction or an illustration that the writer is highly knowledgeable about this area of the law. In America, such a long-winded introduction might be considered either an ineffective digression or perhaps padding and might make a reader think that there is no substance to the argument.

3. Being Too Direct

Although legal writing in America prizes directness, in some instances, one can be too direct, leaving an impression of rudeness. Consider softening requests or instructions with *please*. Thus, rather than write *You must come to our office to sign your will*, write *Please call me to make an appointment so you can come in and sign your will*. Almost all readers bristle when they see the words *you must*; replace with *you should*, if applicable.

4. Giving Advice

In some situations, such as office memoranda, assigning attorneys want and expect recommendations as to strategy and tactics. They want more than a summary of cases; they want and need a candid discussion as to how these cases apply to the client and, if the cases are unfavorable, how obstacles can be overcome. Similarly, legal professionals are expected to give their opinions as to the value of a case, how discovery should progress, and whether a witness seems credible. In some cultures, giving advice to a senior attorney would be considered brash and impertinent. Thus, you may need to discard any innate reluctance to give your opinion, particularly when it is part of your assignment.

5. Including Analysis

Because the American legal system is based on the concept of following precedents, every assertion made in a legal document must be supported by adequate authority. Even a commonplace truism such as *One who breaches a contract is liable for damages caused by the breach* must be supported by a citation. Thus, readers will expect the writer to prove each and every point and expertly guide the reader through each step in the analysis. Although case law can be interpreted in a light most favorable to the client, it is unethical to mischaracterize a legal authority. Furthermore, you must include citations to all authorities relied on. If you rely on a legal authority, give the citation. If you quote from an authority, give the citation. Finally, although responding forcefully to an adversary is expected, make sure that your response is aimed at the adversary's argument, not at the adversary personally.

6. Asking for Help

Ask your colleagues to review your writing for the tone and style of the document. Be aware of the differences in cultures and understand that the style of writing you may have learned may need to be revised for a different legal audience. For example, if your language does not use the articles *a, an,* or *the,* review for their correct use. Read legal newspapers, memos written by your colleagues, court opinions, and briefs filed in court to get the flavor and feel for American legal writing.

Challenge ?	Make corrections to the following passage.

Our client, the Delaware resident, has asked us to prepare an one-page memoranda on a statute of limitations for malpractice actions. In Delaware, a action for medical malpractice must have been brought within two years from the date the injury was occurred. Nevertheless, if the injury was not known to and could not in the exercise of reasonable diligence should be discovered by the injured person, the action may be brought within three years from the date such injury occurred. In no event may an action be brought or damage recovered after three years from the date a injury occurred. In fact, much courts grant motions for summary judgement if any action is filed in Delaware greater than three years from a date of injury.

appendix C

Sample Appellate Court Brief

[Note: This brief is located at the following website and is reproduced exactly as filed with the U.S. Supreme Court: http://www.americanbar.org/content/dam/aba/publications/supreme_court_preview/briefs/11-697_petitioner_amcu_powells_et-al.authcheckdam.pdf]

No. 11-697

IN THE

Supreme Court of the United States

SUPAP KIRTSAENG, D/B/A BLUECHRISTINE99,

Petitioner,

v.

JOHN WILEY & SONS, INC.,

Respondent.

ON WRIT OF CERTIORARI TO THE UNITED STATES
COURT OF APPEALS FOR THE SECOND CIRCUIT

BRIEF OF *AMICI CURIAE* POWELL'S BOOKS INC., STRAND BOOK STORE, INC., HALF PRICE BOOKS, RECORDS, MAGAZINES, INC., AND HARVARD BOOK STORE INC. IN SUPPORT OF PETITIONER

MARK A. LEMLEY
Counsel of Record
JOSEPH C. GRATZ
DURIE TANGRI LLP
   217 Leidesdorff Street
   San Francisco, CA 94111
   (415) 362-6666
   mlemley@law.stanford.edu

Counsel for Amici Curiae

242686

COUNSEL PRESS
(800) 274-3321 • (800) 359-6859

i

TABLE OF CONTENTS

ii

TABLE OF CITED AUTHORITIES

Page

CASES

STATUTES

iii

Cited Authorities

OTHER AUTHORITIES

iv

Cited Authorities

1

INTEREST OF THE *AMICI CURIAE*[1]

Amici are among the nation's best-known independent booksellers.

Powell's Books, based in Portland, Oregon, is the world's largest independent used and new bookstore. It was founded in 1971.

The Strand Book Store, founded in 1927, stocks more than 2.5 million used and new books. In the 1970s, George F. Will wrote, "the eight miles worth saving in this city are at the corner of Broadway and 12th Street. They are the crammed shelves of the Strand Book Store."

Half Price Books began in a converted Dallas laundromat in 1972, and has grown to 115 locations in sixteen states. Those stores buy and sell new and used books, magazines, comics, records, CDs, DVDs and collectible items.

Harvard Book Store is an independently run bookstore serving the greater Cambridge area. The bookstore is located in Harvard Square and has been family-owned since 1932. It is known for its extraordinary selection of new, used, and bargain books and for a history of innovation.

---

1. Counsel for the parties have consented in writing to the filing of this brief. Pursuant to Rule 37.6, no counsel for either party had any role in authoring this brief in whole or in part, and no party other than the named *Amici* has made any monetary contribution toward the preparation and submission of this brief.

2

Amici regularly buy and sell used as well as new books. We have no relationship with the parties and no direct stake in the outcome of this case, but we have a strong interest in ensuring that the marketplace for books remains robust in the digital era.

SUMMARY OF THE ARGUMENT

For centuries the free movement of goods has been a fundamental principle of American law. Restraints on alienation are strongly disfavored because they interfere with the workings of a free market. Over a century ago, this Court held that a bookseller could not control the price at which its books were resold. Once the copyright owner sold copies "in quantities and at a price satisfactory to it[, it] exercised the right to vend," exhausting that right with respect to the particular copies sold. *Bobbs-Merrill v. Straus*, 210 U.S. 339, 351 (1908). That principle was enacted into the Copyright Act the following year. Copyright Act of 1909, ch. 320, § 1, 17 U.S.C. § 41 (1946) ("nothing in this Act shall be deemed to forbid, prevent, or restrict the transfer of any copy of a copyrighted work the possession of which has been lawfully obtained"). It was reaffirmed in the 1976 Act. 17 U.S.C. §109(a). And it has been a fundamental part of copyright law for the past two centuries.

In the modern world, traffic in ideas and goods is international. Books first published in the United States are frequently manufactured abroad. Books first released abroad are sold over the Internet everywhere in the world. Buyers of books also travel, and frequently resell their books in a different place from where they bought them.

3

Unfortunately, the Second Circuit has held in this case that the venerable principle of exhaustion of rights has no applicability when goods cross national borders. The practical effect of that decision is to make it more difficult for struggling bookstores to sell used books. A bookstore has no way of knowing whether the used books it buys were first sold in the United States or not. But under the Second Circuit's ruling, bookstores could be sued at any time for offering books that turn out to have been lawfully sold by the publisher on the wrong side of a border. The Second Circuit's decision imposes a practical restraint on alienation that is inconsistent with the long-standing principle of copyright exhaustion, and this Court should reject it.

ARGUMENT

I. Copyright Exhaustion Has Long Been a Central Feature of Copyright Law

The copyright exhaustion doctrine arose from the common-law aversion to restraints on alienation.[2] It was well-established in the Nineteenth Century that "inseparably with the transfer of the title in any copy of the work must go the right of alienation, so far as the peculiar protection of the copyright statutes is concerned." *Henry Bill Pub. Co. v. Smythe*, 27 F. 914 (C.C.S.D. Ohio 1886). *Henry* described exhaustion upon first sale as a "doctrine running through all the cases." *Id.* at 923.

---

2. For a discussion of this history, see, e.g., Jason P. Schultz & Aaron Perzanowski, *Digital Exhaustion*, 58 UCLA L. REV. 889 (2012); Molly S. van Houweling, *The New Servitudes*, 96 GEO. L.J. 885, 897-98 (2008); Zechariah Chafee, Jr., *Equitable Servitudes on Chattels*, 41 HARV. L. REV. 945, 982 (1928).

4

Accord Harrison v. Maynard, Merrill & Co., 61 F. 689
(2d Cir. 1894); *Doan v. American Book Co.*, 105 F. 772,
776-77 (7th Cir. 1901).

This Court took up the exhaustion doctrine in *Bobbs-
Merrill v. Straus*, 210 U.S. 339, 351 (1908). There, the
copyright owner had sold a book with a notation that it
was not to be resold for less than a dollar. The defendant
bought copies of the book at wholesale and sold them at
retail for 90 cents. When the plaintiff sued for copyright
infringement, this Court held that the lawful first sale
exhausted any control over the defendant's subsequent
sales. It explained that the point of the copyright laws
was to prevent the making and distribution of new copies,
not to put limits on commerce in existing copies. *Id.* at
347 ("it is evident that to secure the author the right to
multiply copies of his work may be said to have been the
main purpose of the copyright statutes."). As a result,
this Court said, "one who has sold a copyrighted article,
without restriction, has parted with all right to control the
sale of it. The purchaser of a book, once sold by authority
of the owner of the copyright, may sell it again, although
he could not publish a new edition of it." *Id.* at 349-50.

While the Court described the question as one of
statutory construction, that statutory construction
occurred against a backdrop of common-law principles
permitting free alienability of goods. While the statute in
that case gave the copyright owner the exclusive right to
"vend" the works, the Court refused to read that language
as controlling all sales rather than merely the first sale:
"What the complainant contends for embraces not only the
right to sell the copies, but to qualify the title of a future
purchaser." *Id.* at 351. Thus, the Court applied the common
law doctrine of exhaustion of rights upon first sale to limit

5

what might otherwise have been argued to be the plain language of the statute.

The same common-law principle can be seen in this Court's interpretations of the Patent Act. In *Bauer & Cie v. O'Donnell*, 229 U.S. 1, 18 (1913), the Court faced the same issue as in *Bobbs-Merrill*: whether a patentee could control the price of resale of a patented good after a lawful first sale. Noting the close kinship between patent and copyright law on this very point,[3] the court emphasized the common-law disdain for restraints on alienation: "this court from the beginning has held that a patentee who has parted with a patented machine by passing title to a purchaser has placed the article beyond the limits of the monopoly secured by the patent act." *Id.* at 18. That common law principle retains its vitality today. In its most recent opinion on the issue, this Court adhered to the "longstanding principle that, when a patented item is once lawfully made and sold, there is no restriction on [its] use to be implied for the benefit of the patentee." *Quanta Computer v. LG Elecs.*, 553 U.S. 617, 630 (2008).

The principle of exhaustion upon first sale, then, has been a feature of the patent and copyright laws as long as we have had such laws. *See* Jason P. Schultz & Aaron Perzanowski, *Copyright Exhaustion and the*

---

3. *Id.* at 12-13 ("While [the copyright] statute differs from the patent statute in terms and in the subject-matter intended to be protected, it is apparent that, in the respect involved in the present inquiry, there is a strong similarity between and identity of purpose in the two statutes."). Both statutes at the time granted the exclusive right to "vend" copyrighted or patented works; today, the patent statute has replaced "vend" with "sell," while the copyright law has replaced "vend" with "distribution of copies to the public."

6

Personal Use Dilemma, 86 MINN. L. REV. __ (forthcoming 2012), available at http://papers.ssrn.com/sol3/papers. cfm?abstract_id=1925059. That principle does not spring from an accident of statutory drafting. To the contrary, this Court has read exhaustion into the law even when interpreting words like "sell" or "vend" that seem to contain no first sale limitation.

Congress has repeatedly acceded to this Court's application of the exhaustion doctrine in copyright cases. Only a year after *Bobbs-Merrill*, Congress added the exhaustion doctrine to the new Copyright Act of 1909, ch. 320, § 1, 17 U.S.C. § 41 (1946) ("nothing in this Act shall be deemed to forbid, prevent, or restrict the transfer of any copy of a copyrighted work the possession of which has been lawfully obtained"). When it embraced *Bobbs-Merrill*, Congress made it clear that it did "not intend[ ] to change in any way existing law." H.R. Rep. No. 60-2222, at 19 (1909), *reprinted in* E. FULTON BRYLAWSKI & ABE GOLDMAN, 6 LEGISLATIVE HISTORY OF THE 1909 COPYRIGHT ACT (1976). That "existing law" was the common law exhaustion principles articulated by the courts.

Similarly, the 1976 Act adopted a first sale doctrine in 17 U.S.C. § 109(a). Like the 1909 Act, the legislative history of the 1976 Act indicates Congressional intent to "restate[ ] and confirm[ ]" the first sale rule "established by court decisions." H.R. Rep. No. 94-1476, at 79 (1976), *reprinted in* 1976 U.S.C.C.A.N. 5659, 5693. Congress, then, did not think it was abolishing or limiting the exhaustion principle in the 1976 Act. To the contrary, it intended to codify that common law principle as set out in this Court's decisions.

7

II. Bookstores Have Long Relied on the Exhaustion Doctrine, and Continue To Do So

Bookstores, including *amici*, have relied on the copyright exhaustion doctrine for centuries to permit the sale of used books. *Amici* have been operating under this legal principle since as early as 1927, and other bookstores have been selling used books for centuries longer. Indeed, the sale of used books which had been printed abroad and imported without the authority of the publisher was a widespread practice since before our nation's founding. *See generally* MADELEINE B. STERN, ANTIQUARIAN BOOKSELLING IN THE UNITED STATES (1985).

Given the long history and widespread nature of the importation of books for the purpose of further distribution, the interpretation Wiley advances would have made pirates even out of our Founding Fathers. In the 1730s and 40s, Benjamin Franklin operated a bookstore on Market Street in Philadelphia stocked primarily with books imported from British dealers. STERN at 22. If Franklin opened his bookstore today, on Wiley's view, virtually every sale he made would be an infringement of copyright, since each such sale would constitute distribution of books manufactured abroad.

In the 1820s, Thomas Jefferson worked closely with Boston bookseller William Hilliard to build a collection of books for the newly-founded University of Virginia, consisting in large part of the importation of books purchased abroad from book dealers and at auction. STERN at 7-8. If Jefferson did so today, under Wiley's

8

interpretation of the law, he would need to secure the permission of each publisher each time a book was lent.[4]

The Founding Fathers recognized, as *amici* do, the critical role that second-hand bookstores play in the literary life of the nation.

Selling used books helps spread knowledge to those who might not otherwise be able to afford it, and it promotes reading. The sale of used books from abroad, in particular, helps American readers broaden their world view, as they are not limited to those books which have been published in the United States. Books published abroad are frequently not distributed in the United States by their publishers. Without used book stores, those books would be unavailable for purchase by American consumers. A clear and untrammeled first-sale rule has served the reading public well since the founding era, providing unique benefits to booksellers and readers alike.

The Second Circuit's decision threatens to destroy those benefits. In the modern world, books – like any other goods – cross borders. Books may be released by a U.S. publisher but manufactured abroad and shipped into the United States. They may be released at different times in different countries but sold online to a worldwide audience. Readers may order a box of used books from Amazon. com without knowing from where the books originally came. Publishers may release different versions of books

---

4. While 17 U.S.C. §602(a)(3) would excuse the act of *importing* books for a non-profit university library, under Wiley's reading of the statute those books are not "lawfully made under this title" under section 109(a) despite the legality of their importation, and so the act of lending them would violate section 106(3).

9

in different countries, and fans may acquire the version they prefer from abroad. *See, e.g.*, Alan Cowell, "Harry Potter and the Magic Stock," N.Y. TIMES, Oct. 18, 1999 ("Many American children and their parents, in fact, know Harry and his fellow students at the Hogwarts School of Witchcraft and Wizardry from the British versions they have bought over the Internet – books that use different art, different typography and in some cases different spelling and vocabulary than their American cousins."). Readers may purchase books in one country and move to another country, shipping their books along with them.

Each of these perfectly ordinary transactions is threatened by the opinion below. Consider a reader who buys a handful of copies of the British version of a *Harry Potter* book on the Internet for her book club, or a traveler who brings home a gift for a friend from Shakespeare and Company in Paris, or a professor of literature who brings his books when he moves to the United States and then donates his collection to the university library upon his retirement. Under the Second Circuit's interpretation of the Copyright Act, all those readers are infringing copyright even though they paid the copyright owner for the book. That fact itself should give us pause; it seems unlikely Congress really intended to make those benign acts illegal.

For bookstores that sell used books, however, the problem caused by the Second Circuit's rule is more than an inconvenience: it is an existential threat. Stores like Powell's Books purchase used books in bulk to sell in the store. Powell's may look at 5,000 used books at a time, making almost immediate decisions whether to buy a book or not. There is no realistic way for a bookstore

10

to tell whether a particularly copy of a book is one first sold in the United States or first sold in England. But if it was first sold in England, under the Second Circuit's rationale, both the customer's sale of the book to Powell's and Powell's subsequent sale of the book to a new reader violate the Copyright Act.

The Second Circuit's cramped reading of the law, then, puts bookstores in an impossible position. To comply with the law, they would for all practical purposes have to stop buying and selling used books in bulk, and could buy only those books which, upon close examination, indicate that they were printed in the United States. (Eventually, the proportion of books manufactured domestically would dwindle, given the incentive that Wiley's interpretation would give publishers to move book manufacturing abroad.)

And it is no answer to say that Wiley (or other reputable publishers) are unlikely to sue the bookstores. There are enough copyright owners out there – and enough crazy copyright lawsuits – that it is not always reasonable to rely on forbearance by copyright plaintiffs. *See, e.g.*, *In re BitTorrent Adult Film Copyright Infringement Cases*, CIV.A. 11-3995 DRH, 2012 WL 1570765 (E.D.N.Y. May 1, 2012) (decrying "a nationwide blizzard" of dubious lawsuits seeking quick settlements). In any event, no one should be put to the choice of violating the law and hoping they don't get caught or losing their business.

11

CONCLUSION

Selling used books has always been legal. And Americans have always imported some of the books they read. Congress did not intend to change that. An interpretation of the Copyright Act that makes impossible a practice that has been widespread since the early days of the Republic, one that promotes the progress of science, is an interpretation this Court should be reluctant to credit.

The judgment of the Court of Appeals should be reversed.

Respectfully submitted,

MARK A. LEMLEY
  Counsel of Record
JOSEPH C. GRATZ
DURIE TANGRI LLP
  217 Leidesdorff Street
  San Francisco, CA 94111
  (415) 362-6666
  mlemley@law.stanford.edu

Counsel for Amici Curiae

appendix D

Answer Keys to Challenges

Readers: Note that for some challenges, other answers may be acceptable. Correct or suggested answers are shown in italics. In some instances, alternative answers are provided.

Section One: The Mechanics of Writing: Grammar, Punctuation, and Spelling

Chapter 1

Challenge: Sentences

Rewrite the following to correct them.

1. Tell the deponent to review the transcript, it must be reviewed by Friday.
   Tell the deponent to review the transcript. It must be reviewed by Friday.
   Tell the deponent to review the transcript; it must be reviewed by Friday.

2. His argument was too long. At least in my opinion.
   In my opinion, his argument was too long.

3. Adam drafted the agreement. Which included a nondisclosure provision.
   Adam drafted the agreement, which included a nondisclosure provision.

4. I am not attending the meeting, Susan is.
   I am not attending the meeting. Susan is.

5. The corporation is insolvent, it cannot pay its debts.
   The corporation is insolvent. It cannot pay its debts.
   The corporation is insolvent; it cannot pay its debts.

6. The dividend payment was unlawful. According to Steven.
   According to Steven, the dividend payment was unlawful.

Challenge: Subject-Verb Agreement

Select the correct word.

1. Although both attorneys were delayed, neither **was**/were apologetic.
2. Either the printer or the editors has/**have** misplaced the files.
3. Neither the defendants nor the plaintiff are/**is** present.
4. Each of the firm's offices have/**has** its own ethics policies.
5. Several of the firm's offices **have**/has their own ethics policies.
6. Everybody was asked to silence their/**his or her** cell phone.
7. More than one exhibit **is**/are missing.
8. More than five exhibits is/**are** missing.
9. The committee meet/**meets** on Monday.
10. No one in their/**his or her** wildest dreams could have predicted an acquittal.
11. General Electric **has**/have decided to cancel **its**/their lease.
12. The agreement, as well as the exhibits, display/**displays** careful drafting.

Challenge: Modifiers

Rewrite the following.

1. Having argued the case, the threat of a mistrial was disturbing.
   Having argued the case, I (or he or she) found the threat of a mistrial was disturbing.

2. Studying the evidence, the decision was clear.
   After studying the evidence, the jury was clear on its decision.
   The decision was clear to the jury after it studied the evidence.

3. At the age of three, doctors diagnosed Luke with autism.
   When Luke was three, the doctors diagnosed him with autism.

4. The suspect was found hiding behind a tree armed with a gun.
   The suspect was found armed with a gun, hiding behind a tree.

5. Carter agreed to deed his home to Beth after his death.
   Carter agreed that upon his death, his home would be deeded to Beth.

6. After complaining of pain, Alex was transported to the hospital in an abundance of caution.
   After Alex complained of pain, and in an abundance of caution, he was transported to the hospital.

Challenge: Pronoun Use

Rewrite or select the correct pronoun.

1. Him/**He** and Jen argued the case.

2. Everyone is waiting for their/**his and her** security clearances.

3. I and Stella prepared for the meeting.
   Stella and I prepared for the meeting.

4. The judge called David to the bench, and he looked concerned.
   The judge called David to the bench, and the judge looked concerned.
   The judge called David to the bench, and David looked concerned.

5. To who/**whom** is the document directed?

6. For who/**whom** will you vote?

7. **Who**/Whom shall I say asked for Ms. Bennett?

8. You can video me and my opponent.
   You can video my opponent and me.

9. Only one in four candidates **favors**/favor the resolution.

10. Just between you and I/**me**, I think the judge ruled incorrectly.

11. Meg and myself/**I** will draft the interrogatories.

12. It was the committee who/**that** voted to approve the new hire, and **its**/their/it's vote was unanimous.

13. The trial presented a great opportunity for **me**.

Challenge: Gender-Linked and Special Pronouns

Correct the following or select the correct word.

1. A surgeon should offer his patients a copy of their records.
   Surgeons should offer their patients copies of their records.
   A surgeon should offer patients copies of their records.
   A surgeon should offer his or her patients copies of their records.

2. A teacher always wants her students to do well.
   Teachers always want their students to do well.
   A teacher always wants his or her students to do well.

3. I'm depending on **his**/him arguing the case tomorrow.

4. He resents me/**my** appearing at the meeting.

5. The judge asked **us**/we plaintiffs to attend the settlement conference.

6. I know you better than him.
I know you better than he does.
I know you better than I know him.

Challenge: Conjunction Junction

Punctuate correctly or correct the following.

1. He likes drafting and to edit briefs.
He likes drafting and editing briefs.
He likes to draft and to edit briefs.
He likes to draft and edit briefs.

2. Lily stayed for two hours. And then decided to leave.
Lily stayed for two hours and then decided to leave.

3. The judge not only admonished the attorney and also sanctioned her.
The judge not only admonished the attorney but also sanctioned her.

4. Either Mark or Martin **has**/have the transcript.

5. Either she must attend the meeting or prepare for the consequences.
Either she must attend the meeting or she must prepare for the consequences.

6. The board neither wanted to merge nor to consolidate.
The board wanted neither to merge nor to consolidate.
[Notes for Questions 5 and 6: When using correlative conjunctions, you must ensure that the structures joined by the correlative conjunctions are mirror images or parallel to each other.]

Chapter 2

Challenge: Punctuation

Punctuate the following sentences correctly, correct the punctuation errors, or indicate if the sentence is correct.

1. He plans to have lunch with Ben and Grace and I will be on vacation at that time.
He plans to have lunch with Ben and Grace, and I will be on vacation at that time.
He plans to have lunch with Ben, and Grace and I will be on vacation at that time.

2. Whether or not the weather will cooperate, is open to debate.
Whether or not the weather will cooperate is open to debate.

3. The only question the judge asked was when the motion would be heard?
The only question the judge asked was when the motion would be heard.

4. "You then turned left, didn't you"?
   "You then turned left, didn't you?"

5. I am responding to your July 10, 2012 report.
   I am responding to your July 10, 2012, report.

6. On Thursday, we will travel to Chicago.
   On Thursday we will travel to Chicago.
   (Note that some individuals would place a comma after "On Thursday." Placement of the comma after such a short introductory phrase is optional.)

7. After the judge left the courtroom there was a mass exodus.
   After the judge left the courtroom, there was a mass exodus.

8. Robert is a diligent conscientious worker.
   Robert is a diligent, conscientious worker.

9. The trial began in March and it is expected to last more than six weeks.
   The trial began in March, and it is expected to last more than six weeks.

10. Sandra Allen the public defender was appointed defense counsel.
    Sandra Allen, the public defender, was appointed defense counsel.

11. The exhibits were marked but they were not introduced into evidence.
    The exhibits were marked, but they were not introduced into evidence.

12. The judge instructed the jury and left the courtroom.
    This sentence is correct.

13. The bailiff, called the court to order.
    The bailiff called the court to order.

14. The witness stated I don't remember.
    The witness stated, "I don't remember."

15. The witness stated that he didn't remember.
    This sentence is correct.

16. I researched the law but I was unable to find any cases on point.
    I researched the law, but I was unable to find any cases on point.

Challenge: Apostrophes

Punctuate the following correctly or indicate if they are correct.

1. The 1970s were a turbulent decade.
   This sentence is correct.

2. Arkansas revenue decreased last year.
   Arkansas's revenue decreased last year.

3. The four investors objections were noted.
    The four investors' objections were noted.

4. Mr. Cox' briefcase was searched and all of it's contents removed.
    Mr. Cox's briefcase was searched and all of its contents removed.

5. The fundraiser will be held at the Willis home.
    The fundraiser will be held at the Willises' home.

6. Ms. Willis deposition transcript was lost.
    Ms. Willis's deposition transcript was lost.

7. Whose/**Who's** attending the hearing?

8. The company just filed its annual report.
    This sentence is correct.

9. The three citizens complaints were ignored.
    The three citizens' complaints were ignored.

10. Chris calendar showed a conflict.
    Chris's calendar showed a conflict.
    (Note that many individuals would show this as *Chris' calendar showed a conflict.* Both approaches are correct, but most experts prefer *Chris's* to *Chris'.*)

11. Our clients, the Foxs, have paid their retainer.
    Our clients, the Foxes, have paid their retainer.

12. The Foxes check was cashed yesterday.
    The Foxes' check was cashed yesterday.

13. The FAQs on the website were helpful.
    This sentence is correct.

14. In three week's, I will be given two months severance.
    In three weeks, I will be given two months' severance.

15. Phil's and Monica brief was persuasive.
    Phil and Monica's brief was persuasive.

16. Mr. Baileys will was amended.
    Mr. Bailey's will was amended.

17. The Christmas card was signed "From The Smith's."
    The Christmas card was signed "From the Smiths."

18. Meg and Steve's wedding was in August.
    This sentence is correct.

Challenge: Punctuation

Correctly punctuate the following.

1. Susan was asked to: draft the brief, cite-check it, and file it.
   Susan was asked to draft the brief, cite-check it, and file it.

2. The defendant stated his plea in unequivocal terms, "not guilty".
   The defendant stated his plea in unequivocal terms: "Not guilty."
   The defendant stated his plea in unequivocal terms: "Not guilty!"

3. The officers at the meeting included the following. Ted Davis, president, Rachel Porter, treasurer, and Brian Nelson, secretary.
   The officers at the meeting included the following: Ted Davis, president; Rachel Porter, treasurer; and Brian Nelson, secretary.

4. Lindsey has excelled in her job; for example she was promoted twice last year.
   Lindsey has excelled in her job. For example, she was promoted twice last year.
   Lindsey has excelled in her job; for example, she was promoted twice last year.

5. The bailiff barked, Silence in the courtroom.
   The bailiff barked, "Silence in the courtroom!"

6. The attorney said that "he would move for a mistrial."
   The attorney said that he would move for a mistrial.

7. Were you the witness, asked Ryan.
   "Were you the witness?" asked Ryan.

8. File your motions, the judge stated, and do so promptly.
   "File your motions," the judge stated, "and do so promptly."

9. Susan asked "whether she could attend the hearing."
   Susan asked whether she could attend the hearing.

10. Susan asked May I attend the hearing?
    Susan asked, "May I attend the hearing?"

11. Are you familiar with the doctrine of "res judicata?"
    Are you familiar with the doctrine of "res judicata"?

Challenge: Parentheses, Hyphens, and Other Marks

Correct the following.

1. I have paid all funds to take my all inclusive vacation to Mexico.
   I have paid all funds to take my all-inclusive vacation to Mexico.

2. My uncle kept a pre Revolutionary musket.
   My uncle kept a pre-Revolutionary musket.

3. I resent the fact that you resent my message to Lauren yesterday.
   I resent the fact that you re-sent my message to Lauren yesterday.

4. He was the chief operating officer, CEO, from 2007—2009.
   He was the chief operating officer ("CEO") from 2007-2009.

5. She is a quick witted attorney whose quick wit charms others.
   She is a quick-witted attorney whose quick wit charms others.

6. All documents are due by Monday (this is the first day of the new term of the court).
   All documents are due by Monday. (This is the first day of the new term of the court.)
   All documents are due by Monday, which is the first day of the new term of the court.

7. It was James, not his brother, who was married last year.
   This sentence is correct; however, it may also be shown as follows:
   It was James (not his brother) who was married last year.
   It was James—not his brother—who was married last year.

Chapter 3

Challenge: Spelling

Select the correct word.

1. We cannot **accommodate**/accomodate your request.
2. The defendant has acknowldged/**acknowledged** liability.
3. The **existence**/existance of the contract is not in dispute.
4. The **omission**/ommision of Exhibit B was **inadvertent**/inadvertant.
5. I will **precede**/preceed her in entering the courtroom
6. The **pro-Italian**/proItalian group will testify on Monday.
7. We will **reestablish**/re-establish contact next week.
8. The judge will **ensure**/insure that they do not **withhold**/withold evidence.
9. The brief had ten **separate**/seperate exhibits, which I **definitely**/definately felt were too many.
10. The computer program is **user friendly**/user-friendly.
11. The user friendly/**user-friendly** computer program was installed on Friday.
12. The **publicly traded**/publicly-traded stock of Facebook, Inc. is offered on NASDAQ.

Challenge: Capitalization and Abbreviations

Correct the following.

1. She has alleged a violation of her Constitutional/**constitutional** rights.
2. Our federal/**Federal** constitution/**Constitution** guarantees us freedom of speech.
3. This **winter**/Winter was harsh in the **East**/east.
4. To change the law, **Congress**/congress will need to pass a **congressional**/Congressional amendment.
5. In this action, the **Defendant**/defendant filed his second amended answer/**Second Amended Answer**.
6. In the case *Roe v. Wade*, the Defendant/**defendant** was the **attorney general**/Attorney General of the state/**State** of Texas.
7. Generally, state Codes/**codes** address residency requirements for divorce.
8. **Five**/5 years ago, the defendant was acquitted.
9. The witness is in her **seventies**/'70s.
10. U.S./**United States** law requires strict adherence to **statutory**/statuary formalities.
11. The meeting will begin at 10:00 a.m. (Omit second period at end of sentence.)

Section Two: Features of Effective Legal Writing and Organization

Chapter 4

Challenge: Word Choice

Select the correct work or rewrite to improve meaning.

1. Senior government officials and their wives will attend the conference next week.
   Senior government officials and their spouses will attend the conference next week.

2. Writing for the majority, Chief Justice Roberts felt the statute should be invalidated.
   Writing for the majority, Chief Justice Roberts stated/held the statute should be invalidated.
   Chief Justice Roberts wrote for the majority, which held the statute should be invalidated.

3. We have not yet had a chance to conversate about the document production.
   We have not yet had a chance to discuss the document production.

4. The issue will need to be addressed at Monday's meeting.
   _____*[Specify the issue] will need to be addressed at Monday's meeting.*

5. The exhibit binder is comprised of three sections.
   The exhibit binder consists of/comprises three sections.

6. Making payments on a mortgage helps equitize ownership interests in real estate.
   Making payments on a mortgage helps increase equity ownership interest in real estate.

7. The human resource department has been tasked with locating workmen with the right competencies.
   The human resources department has been asked to locate workers with the right skills.

8. There are some documents that are missing.
   Some documents are missing.

9. Nick is currently officing out of his house.
   Nick is currently working out of his house.

10. Kate is known as a pushy advocate.
    Kate is known as a confident advocate.

Challenge: Elegant Variation

Rewrite the following statements. [Note that in many instances it is not necessary to repeat a word; a pronoun may replace a repeated noun, or sentences may be combined in such a way to avoid repetition.]

1. The congressman from Texas introduced legislation last week that would change the tax code. The politician's proposed law would increase taxes on dividends. Moreover, the statesman's proposal relating to distributions would decrease the tax rate for corporations.
   The Texas congressman introduced legislation last week that would change the tax code. The congressman's proposed law would increase taxes on dividends and decrease the corporate tax rate.

2. Under the terms of the contract, the defendant was obligated to deliver the goods to the plaintiff. The agreement also provided that the materials should be insured. Finally, the parties' understanding was that the items should be delivered within ten days.
   Under the terms of the contract, the defendant was obligated to deliver the goods to the plaintiff within ten days. The agreement also required that the goods be insured. [or The agreement also required that the defendant insure the goods.]

3. Benefits for senior citizens will increase in July. The elderly will see an increase of five percent in their monthly payments. Aged citizens need not take any action to receive the increase.
   Benefits for senior citizens will increase in July. Senior citizens will see an increase of five percent in their monthly payments and need not take any action to receive the increase.

4. Many students learn better by listening than reading. These pupils report improved comprehension. Learners likewise report less eyestrain when they hear rather than read material.

   Many students learn better by listening than reading. These students report improved comprehension and less eyestrain when they hear rather than read material.

5. The attorneys filed the petition for a writ of certiorari. The lawyers then filed the well-researched brief with the court. Their diligence was rewarded when the court ruled for the advocates' client.

   The attorneys filed the petition for a writ of certiorari and then filed their well-researched brief with the court. Their diligence was rewarded when the court ruled for their client.

Challenge: Negative Expressions

Rewrite the following negative expressions.

1. Individuals other than the claimant may not receive these funds.
   Only the claimant may receive these funds.

2. I do not find it implausible that there is no trademark infringement in this case.
   It is possible that no trademark infringement exists in this case.
   It may be that there is no trademark infringement in this case.
   Trademark infringement is unlikely in this case.

3. He has failed to comply with the ban against smoking.
   He has violated the ban against smoking.

4. The judge did not accept the argument that the two amendments were not the same.
   The judge rejected the argument that the two amendments were different.

5. I am not able to determine if the proposal is not unlike others that the plaintiff has refused to accept.
   I am unable to determine if the proposal is similar to others that the plaintiff has rejected.

Challenge: Word Order and Active Voice

Rewrite the following.

1. The judge scheduled a settlement conference on Friday.
   On Friday, the judge scheduled a settlement conference.
   The judge scheduled a settlement conference to be held on Friday.

2. Responding to the interrogatories was a task given to Beth.
   Beth was given the task of responding to the interrogatories.

3. Asking difficult questions is part of the job of an attorney.
   Part of an attorney's job is to ask difficult questions.

4. Oral argument was scheduled by the clerk of the court.
   The clerk of the court scheduled oral argument.

5. Changes to the tax code are likely to be met with vigorous opposition.
   [Legislators/Consumers] are likely to vigorously oppose any changes to the tax code.

6. The directors were informed that corporate revenues had declined.
   _____ informed the directors that corporate revenues had declined.

7. An increase in executive compensation was approved by the shareholders.
   The shareholders approved an increase in executive compensation.

8. A dividend was declared by the corporation.
   The corporation declared a dividend.

9. A proposal to the buyer to make a counter offer was issued by the seller.
   The seller invited the buyer to make a counter offer.
   The seller proposed that the buyer make a counter offer.

Challenge: Parallel Structure

Correct the following.

1. The directors set three goals for the year: increasing revenue, acquiring another company, and a decreased reliance on foreign energy sources.
   The directors set three goals for the year: increasing revenue, acquiring another company, and decreasing reliance on foreign energy sources.

2. I found her to be charming, witty, and I also thought she was affectionate.
   I found her to be charming, witty, and affectionate.

3. The treasurer's duties are to maintain payroll records, prepare the yearly report, and to attend all board meetings.
   The treasurer's duties are to maintain payroll records, prepare the yearly report, and attend all board meetings.
   The treasurer's duties are to maintain payroll records, to prepare the yearly report, and to attend all board meetings.

4. Either you should begin to prepare for trial or conduct settlement negotiations.
   You should either begin to prepare for trial or conduct settlement negotiations.

5. Samuel's approach to drafting the agreement was better than her.
   Samuel's approach to drafting the agreement was better than hers.

6. The office has room for a new conference table but not storage.
   The office has room for a new conference table but not for storage.

7. I objected that the question was hearsay and also on the grounds of irrelevancy.
   I objected that the question was hearsay and irrelevant.

Challenge: Nominalizations and Legalese

Rewrite the following.

1. The brief gives an analysis of the business judgment doctrine and offers an explanation of it.
   The brief analyzes and explains the business judgment doctrine.

2. The committee issued a report that offered a suggestion to produce an increase in sales.
   The committee's report suggested ways to increase sales.

3. We will conduct an investigation into the allegation that the defendant issued a denial of any fraud.
   We will investigate the allegation that the defendant denied any fraud.

4. Enclosed herewith is the most recent addendum to the contract, which is dated the fourteenth of August. We would appreciate your reviewing and executing the same in the spaces designated for such and transmitting it to us.
   Enclosed is the most recent addendum to the contract, dated August 14. Please review it, sign it, and return it to us.

5. We are writing this letter to remind you to maintain all pertinent corporate documents so that the company does not face an assertion of spoliation in the instant case at bar.
   Please maintain all pertinent corporate documents to ensure the company is not accused of spoliation (willful destruction of documents) in this case.

6. At all times herein mentioned, Plaintiff was a resident of Texas and was possessed of three patents.
   Plaintiff is a Texas resident and owns three patents.

7. We intend to provide a full and complete disclosure of all materials that were the subject of our earlier discussion.
   We will disclose all materials that we discussed.

8. We opine that the new trust document eliminates and reduces prolix provisions.
We believe the new trust reduces unnecessary language.

Challenge: Keeping Subjects and Verbs Close

Rewrite the following.

1. The tenant, who had previously complained about the leaky roof and the lack of security at the premises, began to withhold rent in January.
The tenant had complained about the leaky roof and lack of security at the premises. Thus, he began withholding rent in January.

2. The contract's provision that proposed arbitration rather than litigation in the event of disputes, and under which the prevailing party would be entitled to attorneys' fees, was valid because it was freely agreed to by the parties.
The contract proposed arbitration rather than litigation in the event of disputes and provided for payment of attorneys' fees to the prevailing party. This provision was valid because it was freely agreed to by the parties.

3. Holders of Common A and Common B stock will be entitled to receive on each payment date, to the extent funds are available therefor, a distribution.
Common A and Common B stockholders will receive a distribution on each payment date if funds are available.

Challenge: Transition Words

Rewrite the following to make them smoother.

1. Shareholders are not usually liable for corporate obligations. Failing to respect that the corporation is a separate entity may lead to shareholder liability. Two acts are commonly seen. They may justify imposing liability on shareholders for corporate obligations. They are commingling of personal and corporate funds or failing to observe corporate formalities.
Shareholders are not usually liable for corporate obligations. Nevertheless, if they fail to respect the corporation as a separate entity, they may face liability. Two commonly seen actions may justify imposing liability on shareholders for corporate obligations: commingling of personal and corporate funds and failing to observe corporate formalities.

2. Patent law was significantly reformed in 2011. The America Invents Act changed patent law. No longer will a patent be awarded to the first to invent. The United States will award a patent to the first to file a patent application. This should reduce disputes over inventorship. It harmonizes U.S. law with that of most foreign countries.

Patent law was significantly reformed in 2011 with the passage of the America Invents Act. Under the Act, a patent will now be awarded to the first to file a patent application rather than to the first to invent. Consequently, disputes over inventorship should be reduced. Moreover, the Act harmonizes U.S. law with that of most foreign countries.

Challenge: Shifts in Verb Tense

Rewrite the following.

1. The company's trade secret protection program called for using encryption technology and also employed iris scanners.
   The company's trade secret protection program called for using encryption technology and iris scanners.
   The company's trade secret program used [or uses] encryption technology and iris scanners.

2. The board of directors formed a nominating committee to assist in finding candidates and an audit committee whose responsibilities included oversight of financial reporting.
   The board of directors formed a nominating committee to assist in finding candidates and an audit committee to oversee financial reporting.
   The board of directors formed a nominating committee to assist in finding candidates and an audit committee whose responsibilities include oversight of financial reporting.

3. The court held that the extension of the period of duration of copyright protection was valid. The court further notes that under the Constitution, Congress has the power to regulate copyright law.
   The court held that the extension of the period of duration of copyright protection was valid. The court further noted that under the Constitution, Congress has the power to regulate copyright law.

4. The plaintiff alleged fraud, which arises out of an omission of a material fact.
   The plaintiff alleged fraud, which arose out of an omission of a material fact.
   The plaintiff alleged fraud arising out of an omission of a material fact.

Challenge: Conciseness

Select a more concise word or phrase for the following.

- previous to   *before*
- half of   *half*
- period of time   *period, time*
- collaborate together   *collaborate*

- adversely impact   *hurt*
- afford an opportunity   *allow, let*
- as prescribed by   *under*
- temporary reprieve   *reprieve*
- preliminary to   *before*

Rewrite the following to make them more concise:

1. The will has been entirely and completely revised, altered, and modified.
   The will has been revised.

2. The motion, which was recently filed, was granted.
   The recently filed motion was granted.

3. The defendant arrived at the trial by means of automobile.
   The defendant arrived at the trial by car/automobile.

4. The board of directors has appointed and named Ellen Edwards as treasurer.
   The board of directors has appointed [or named] Ellen Edwards as treasurer.

5. Anthony served as chair for a period of two years.
   Anthony served as chair for two years.

6. Once the pleadings are filed, we will proceed forward with discovery.
   Once the pleadings are filed, we will proceed with discovery.

7. It is incumbent upon the employees to act in accordance with company rules and policies.
   Employees must follow company rules [or policies].

8. The defendant's defenses are few in number and arise from the same identical fact pattern.
   The defendant's defenses are few and arise from the same fact pattern.

Chapter 5

Challenge: Position and Voice

Rewrite the following from a defendant's point of view.

1. The defendant failed to deliver the goods to the plaintiff.
   The plaintiff did not receive the goods. The goods were not delivered.
2. The defendant repeatedly engaged in verbal attacks on colleagues in the workplace.
   A number of workplace disputes occurred.

3. Contrary to the terms of the employment agreement, the defendant disclosed proprietary information to others.

The alleged proprietary information was known by others.

4. The defendant failed to pay rent to the landlord.

Rent was not received by the landlord.

Defendant's obligation to pay rent was excused due to the plaintiff's conduct.

Section Four: Postwriting Steps and Document Design

Chapter 11

Challenge: Proofreading

The letter "F" appears seven times in this sample.

> **Proofreading Exercise**
> **Count every "F" in the following example:**
> FRANK FILED THE RE-
> SULTS OF HIS STUDY OF SCIENTIFIC
> PRINCIPLES TOGETHER WITH
> THE LAB RESULTS OF HIS FINAL
> PROJECT.

Challenge: Proofreading

Correct the errors.

In general, all securities offered in the **United** States must be registered with the SEC or must **qualify** for an exemption from the registration requirements**.** The securities to be issued by the corporation are **usually** in the form of equity securities (stock representing **ownership** interest in the corporation) or debt securities (bonds representing money owed by a corporation to a creditor).

The generally **accepted** test used to determine if a "security" is being issued hinges **on** whether the person is investing money in a common enterprise and is **led** to expect any profits from the **[omit second "the"] managerial** efforts of others. If so, a security is being offered and, unless exemptions exist, the issuer must comply with the Securities Act of 1933.

The form of **registration** statement provided by the SEC is **Form** S-1. The SEC has adopted regulations requiring the use of "plain

English" in the registration form so that **it** is clear and understandable to the average investor. Since 1993, registration forms must be filed **electronically** with the SEC through its **EDGAR** (Electronic Data Gathering and Retrieval) database. The main part (or Part I) of the registration statement is called the prospectus. The prospectus describes the **securities** being sold, provides background information about the issuing corporation and its directors and officers, and describes the investment so that all **investors** can fully evaluate the potential risks involved **in** purchasing the security. **Part** II of the registration statement includes "additional information" about the company and the offering and **remains** on file with the SEC for public inspection.

Appendix A

Challenge: Citation Form

Note: *The Bluebook* forms shown below show the appropriate format for practitioners. For law review or academic format, the answers are the same with the following exceptions:

- Full case names would not be italicized.
- The following would be shown in LARGE AND SMALL CAPS:
  - The state statute in Question 7
  - The authors and title of the book in Question 8
  - The name of the periodical "Ind. L.J." in Question 9
  - The name of the Restatement in Question 10

Note also that answers are in accord with the Nineteenth Edition of *The Bluebook* and the Fourth Edition of *ALWD*.

1. Andrews v. Smithson Company, a 2009 case from the United States Supreme Court, located in volume 450 at page 395, with a quotation from pages 399 through 401.
   Andrews v. Smithson Co., 450 U.S. 395, 399-401 (2009)
   (ALWD would permit parallel citations to S. Ct. and L. Ed.)

2. Hall Brothers versus the Securities and Exchange Commission, a case from the Third Circuit Court of Appeals, located in volume 205 at page 100, with a quotation from pages 105 through 107.
   Hall Bros. v. SEC, 205 F.3d 100, 105-07 (3d Cir. 20xx)
   (ALWD would allow the pincites to be presented as "105-107" or as "105-07.")

3. Shaw Association v. the United States of America, a 2010 case from the Southern District of Texas, located in volume 103 at page 990.
   Shaw Ass'n v. United States, 103 F. Supp. 2d 990, xxx (S.D. Tex. 2010)

(*ALWD* would allow either *Ass'n* or *Assn.* and would allow either *United States* or *U.S.*)

4. Frank and Susan Kimball versus Taylor Incorporated, a 2009 case from the Missouri Court of Appeals, appearing in volume 409 of the relevant reporter (Second Series), beginning on page 677.
   Bluebook: Kimball v. Taylor Inc., 409 S.W.2d 677, xxx (Mo. Ct. App. 2009)
   ALWD: Kimball v. Taylor Inc., 409 S.W.2d 677, xxx (Mo. App. ___ Dist. 2009)

5. Engineering Technology Co. versus Bradford, a 2008 case from the Georgia Supreme Court. Assume court rules require you to include parallel citations.
   Engineering Technology Co. v. Bradford, xxx Ga. xxx, xxx S.E.2d xxx (2008)
   (If this case were cited as a "stand alone," *The Bluebook* would show the case name as *Eng'g Tech. Co. v. Bradford*. *ALWD* would show the case name as *Eng'g Tech. Co. v. Bradford* or as *Engg. Tech. Co. v. Bradford*.)

6. Section 404 of Title 35 of the United States Code.
   35 U.S.C. § 404 (2006)

7. New York Employers Liability Law Section 10004.
   Bluebook: N.Y. Empl'rs Liab. Law § 10004 (Publisher Year)
   ALWD: N.Y. Emplrs. Liab. Law § 10004 (Publisher Year)

8. Section 404 of the second edition of a book written by Ellen Edwards and James Bennett, volume 3, entitled "Insurance Defense Litigation."
   Bluebook: 3 Ellen Edwards & James Bennett, *Insurance Defense Litigation* § 404 (2d ed. Year)
   ALWD: Ellen Edwards & James Bennett, *Insurance Defense Litigation* vol. 3, § 404 (2d ed., Publisher Year)

9. A 2010 law review article written by Timothy L. Stewart, III, entitled "Negotiating Arbitration Clauses" and appearing in the Indiana Law Journal.
   Timothy L. Stewart, III, *Negotiating Arbitration Clauses*, xxx Ind. L.J. xxx (2010)

10. Restatement of Contracts, Second, Section 312.
    Bluebook: Restatement (Second) of Contracts § 312 (Year)
    ALWD: Restatement (Second) of Contracts § 312 (Year)

11. Give the short form citations for the Andrews case in Question 1. Assume the pincite is page 405.
    Id. at 405.
    Andrews, 450 U.S. at 405.
    450 U.S. at 405.
    Andrews (if case is cited in full in the same general discussion)

Appendix B

Challenge

Make corrections to the following passage.

> Our client, **a** Delaware resident, has asked us to prepare **a** one-page **memorandum** on the statute of limitations for malpractice actions. In Delaware, **an** action for medical malpractice must **be** brought within two years from the date the injury [**omit** *was*] occurred. Nevertheless, if the injury was not known to and could not in the exercise of reasonable diligence [**omit** *should*] be discovered by the injured person, the action may be brought within three years from the date such injury occurred. In no event may an action be brought or **damages** recovered after three years from the date **an** injury occurred. In fact, **many** courts grant motions for summary **judgment** if any action is filed in Delaware **more** than three years from **the** date of injury.

appendix E

Glossary of Terms

Abbreviation: A shortened form of a word or a symbol used in place of a word, as in the abbreviation *Mr.* for the word *Mister*.

Acronym: An abbreviation that spells out a pronounceable word, such as *AIDS* or *NATO*.

Active voice: A style of writing in which the subject of the sentence performs the action, as in *The corporation held its meeting*.

ALWD: A reference to ALWD & Darby Dickerson, *ALWD Citation Manual* (4th ed., Aspen Publishers 2010), a guide to citation form.

Antecedent: The noun to which a pronoun refers.

Appeal brief: Written document seeking reversal, affirmance, or some modification of a lower court's action.

Appositive: A word or phrase that explains the noun it follows, as in *James, the first witness, was tall*.

Auxiliary verbs: See *Helping verbs*.

Block quotation: A quotation of fifty words or more that is justified and indented from the regular text and set without quotation marks.

Bluebook: A reference to *The Bluebook: A Uniform System of Citation* (Columbia Law Review Ass'n et al. eds., 19th ed. 2010), a guide to legal citation form.

Boilerplate: Standard language in a document, such as a contract.

Brainstorming: A method of outlining in which the writer lists all words related to a project.

Brief: A document submitted to a court that includes legal argument; a summary of a case, namely, a *case brief*.

Certificate of compliance: A document that verifies compliance with court rules.

Certificate of service: A document attached to a court pleading that verifies that the pleading has been served on all parties.

Clause: A group of related words containing a subject and a verb.

Clustering: A visual method of outlining that shows relationships among ideas.

Collection letter: A type of letter seeking to collect money for a client from a debtor.

Collective noun: A noun that stands for a group of people or things, such as *jury* or *committee*.

Comma splice: A run-on sentence caused by a comma that joins two main clauses.

Compound predicate: A sentence with one subject and two verbs joined by *or* or *and*, as in *The defendant went home and ate dinner*.

Compound sentence: A sentence with two independent clauses, usually joined by a conjunction such as *but* or *and*, as in *The defendant went home, and the jurors were released for the day*.

Compound subject: A subject made up of more than one word, as in *The jurors and the bailiffs were relaxing in the hallway*.

Compound word: A word composed of two ideas or words, such as *well-intentioned* or *keyboard*.

Conjunction: A word that joins together words or groups of words.

Connotation: The suggested meaning of a word.

Coordinating conjunction: The words *for, and, nor, but, or, yet,* and *so* (the "FANBOYS") that join together words or groups of words.

CRAC: An acronym for Conclusion, Rule, Application, and Conclusion; a method of analyzing legal authorities.

CREAC: An acronym for Conclusion, Rule, Explanation of Rule, Analysis/Application of Rule, and Conclusion; a method of analyzing legal authorities.

Dangling modifier: A modifying phrase that does not include a subject and does not modify any word or group of words in a sentence, as in *Driving down the road, the brakes failed*.

Defined term: A label associated with a name or a term in a legal document, which must be used consistently.

Definite article: The word *the*, which identifies a definite, known noun.

Demand letter: A type of letter demanding some form of action, such as the payment of money.

Dependent clause: A clause that cannot stand on its own (also called *subordinate clause*).

Elegant variation: The practice of substituting one term for another in a document to avoid repetition of a term.

Ellipsis: Three periods separated by spaces and set off by a space before the first and after the last period (. . .), used to show omissions from quotations.

ESL: English as a Second Language; a reference to the use of English by nonnative speakers of the English language.

Font: Typeface, such as Times New Roman.

Freewriting: A method of outlining in which the writer writes without stopping for a short period of time.

Full justification: See *Justification*.

Fused sentence: A run-on sentence caused by a lack of punctuation between two main clauses.

Gerund: A verb form that ends in *-ing* and that functions as a noun, as in *pleading* or *drafting*.

Helping verbs: Verbs that accompany and precede main verbs, such as *can, must,* and *will,* as in *You must file the appeal by May 18* (*must* is the helping verb and *file* is the main verb).

Idiom: An expression the meaning of which cannot be determined by its actual wording, such as *come up with a remedy.*

Indefinite antecedent: An antecedent that does not refer to any specific person or thing, such as the use of the words *anyone* or *everybody.*

Indefinite article: The articles *a* and *an,* which introduce a noun that has not been introduced previously.

Independent clause: A clause with a subject and a verb that expresses a complete idea and can stand on its own (also called a *main clause*).

Indirect question: A question that indicates what someone asked but not in the exact form of a question, as in *Mother asked me whether I was going* (also called an *indirect quotation*).

Infinitive: The word *to* plus a verb, as in *to argue.*

Inverted sentence: A sentence in which the verb precedes the subject, as in *There is an attorney present in the room.*

IRAC: An acronym for Issue, Rule, Analysis/Application, and Conclusion; a method of analyzing legal authorities, especially in examinations.

Jargon: The specialized language of a profession.

Justification: The appearance of margins on a page; full justification refers to a margin in which all words begin and end at the same location in each line.

Legalese: A style of jargon used by legal professionals that uses archaic, stuffy, and unfamiliar terms rather than plain English.

Legend: A notation or warning on a legal document, such as a notation that a letter is subject to the attorney-client privilege.

Linking verb: A verb that connects its subject to the material or description following in the sentence; linking verbs include forms of the verb *to be, seem, appear,* and other words that refer to a state of being.

Litotes: An expression that makes an assertion by denying its opposite, as in using *not unprepared* to mean *prepared.*

Main clause: See *Independent clause.*

Memorandum: A research document that analyzes a legal problem in an objective manner; usually for interoffice use only.

Memorandum of law: A written argument submitted to a court in support of a certain position; may be called a *brief.*

Misplaced modifier: A modifier that is located in the wrong place in a sentence.

Modifier: A word that limits, qualifies, or describes another word or group of words.

Monospace: Typeface in which every letter takes the same amount of horizontal space.

Motion: A request that a court enter an order in favor of a party.

Nominalization: Conversion of a verb into a noun, which weakens the verb (as in *decide—issued a decision*).

Nonrestrictive clause: A clause that adds information but is not essential to the meaning of a sentence and is set off with commas, as in *The corporation, which had merged, filed its papers with the SEC.*

Notice pleading: The current pleading philosophy that a pleading must be sufficiently clear as to notify another party of the nature of one's claims or defenses.

Open punctuation: A style of punctuation that uses fewer punctuation marks than more traditional approaches to punctuation.

Opinion letter: A type of letter providing a legal opinion; usually provided to clients.

Parallel structure: Correct writing style of using the same pattern of words or phrases in sentences or lists, such as starting all items in a list with a word ending in -*ing*.

Paraphrasing: Using one's own words to summarize or present another's thoughts or writings. Paraphrasing in legal writing must be attributed to the original source.

Phrase: A group of words that lacks a subject, a verb, or both, and cannot stand on its own.

Pinpoint citation: A reference to the specific page on which material, often a quotation, appears; required in citation form; also called a *pincite*.

Plagiarism: Taking another's ideas, writings, or expressions and representing them as one's own.

Plain English: A writing movement that calls for straightforward and clear expression rather than legalese.

Pleading: A document, such as a complaint or answer, filed by a party in a pending court action.

Prayer: The ending of a pleading, often a complaint, that requests relief.

Pronoun: A word that takes the place of a noun, such as *he, she,* or *it.*

Proper noun: The name of a particular person, place, or thing, such as *Justice Kennedy, Lake Huron,* or *the Washington Monument.*

Proportional spacing: Use of a typeface in which letters take up different amounts of horizontal space; Times New Roman is a proportionally spaced typeface.

Protection clause: Clause in a letter used when information is incomplete to protect the writer; also called a *savings clause.*

Ragged edge: Reference to a margin, usually the right margin, in which words end at different locations in different lines, producing a ragged-looking edge to the page.

Recitals: Clauses in agreements that identify the nature and purpose of the document.

Redlining: The technique of using a computer's "track changes" feature to show changes in a document, usually one that is prepared collaboratively; changes appear in red on the computer's screen.

Reflexive pronoun: The *-self* pronouns, such as *myself* and *herself*, that are used to refer back to another noun, as in *Mary asked herself that very question.*

Restrictive clause: A clause or phrase that restricts or limits the word it modifies by giving essential information, as in *The case that the defendant cited is on point*; it is not set off by commas.

Reverse outlining: A method of outlining in which the outline is prepared after a document is drafted and then used to analyze the project's structure.

Sans serif: A typeface that does not use decorative strokes at the edges of letters.

Sentence fragment: An incomplete sentence; a sentence lacking a subject and a verb.

Serial comma: The last comma in a series of three or more items, as in *Our flag is red, white, and blue*; required in legal writing.

Serif: A typeface in which small decorative strokes are added to the edges of letters.

Slash: A diagonal line used in punctuation that means *or*; also called a *solidus* or *virgule.*

Solidus: See *slash.*

Split infinitive: An infinitive that is divided by one or more words between the word *to* and the verb, as in *to quickly run*; avoid when possible.

Squinting modifier: A modifier that can refer to the word before it or after it.

Subordinate clause: See *Dependent clause.*

Subordinating conjunction: Words such as *after, although, because, before, if,* and *when* that are used to join dependent or subordinate clauses to main clauses, as in *Although she testified, she was not an effective witness.*

Tabulation: The listing of items.

Tense: The form of a verb that shows the time of action. For example, *I run* is in the present tense, and *I ran* is in the past tense.

Thesis statement: An assertive introductory statement in a writing project that provides a preview of the analysis to follow; sometimes called an *umbrella statement.*

Topic sentence: The sentence in a paragraph (usually the first sentence) that announces the theme or subject for the information to be presented in the paragraph.

Transactional document: A document, often a contract, that specifies parties' rights, duties, and obligations.

Transitional expressions: Words or phrases that connect parts of sentences, such as *however, for example,* and *therefore,* or sentences that connect paragraphs and sections.

Virgule: See *slash.*

Handle them carefully, for words
have more power than atom bombs.
Pearl Strachan Hurd

appendix F

Glossary of Usage

StyleLinks

http://grammar.about.com/od/words/a/UsageGlossary.htm
About.com provides an excellent glossary of usage with 200 sets of commonly confused words.

http://grammar.ccc.commnet.edu/grammar/faq.htm
This site provides an excellent list of commonly confused words.

http://public.wsu.edu/~brians/errors/errors.html#errors
This excellent site lists and explains hundreds of commonly confused words.

www.bartleby.com
This site offers direct linking to numerous writing resources, including reference materials such as dictionaries and thesauri, which will help in selecting the correct word.

Introduction

Because words change meaning over time and because many words and phrases sound alike, writers can easily become confused when selecting words. This Glossary of Usage identifies troublesome words and phrases that are commonly confused in legal writing.

A, an: The sound of a word, not its spelling, dictates whether the article **a** or **an** will be used before it. Use **a** before all consonant sounds, including a sounded *h*, a long *u*, and the sound of *w*, as in *one*. Thus, say *a brief, a historic event, a one-day event, a union.* Use **an** before any vowel sound (except a long *u*) and words beginning with a silent *h*, as in *an appellant, an hour, an heir, an IRS ruling.*

Accept, except: **Accept** means *to receive something* or *agree to it.* **Except** usually means *other than. I will accept all of the contractual revisions except the most recent one.*

Adverse, averse: **Adverse** means hostile or difficult, as in *The adverse party* or *adverse circumstances.* **Averse** means having a strong feeling against or reluctant, as in *We are averse to meeting at the employer's office.*

Advice, advise: **Advice** is a noun meaning *help* and **advise** is a verb meaning *to give help. I advise all my clients to take my advice on trial strategy.*

Affect, effect: **Affect** usually means *to influence* and is a verb, and **effect**, usually used as a noun, means *result. I was affected by John's testimony, which had the effect of changing my opinion.* **Effect** can also mean *to cause.* **Tip:** If these words cause confusion, do not use either of them. Use their synonyms (*to influence* for **affect** and *to bring about, result,* or *produce* for **effect**).

Also: Many writers object to sentences starting with **also.** Use *additionally, moreover,* and similar words.

Alternate, alternative: An **alternate** is a *substitute,* as in *The court selected an alternate juror* (although it can also mean *one after another,* as in *black alternates with white in this diamond pattern*). Conventional authorities state that **alternative** should be used only when referring to two choices (as in *You have the alternative of making the opening statement or the closing statement*). The more modern approach is that **alternative** means one of several choices or options.

Although: See *While.*

Alude, elude: **Allude** means to refer to something indirectly, as in *She alluded to some marital problems but was not specific.* **Elude** means to escape or evade, as in *She managed to elude her bill collectors.*

Ambiguous, ambivalent: **Ambiguous** means *having more than one meaning,* as in *the lease is ambiguous as to when rent is due.* **Ambivalent** means *having conflicting feelings,* as in *I was ambivalent toward the third juror.*

Among, between: **Among** is typically used when referring to three or more items or people. *The damages were divided among all six plaintiffs.* See *Between.*

Amongst: Avoid this British usage for **among**.

Amount, number: Use **amount** for quantities in bulk that cannot be counted. Use **number** for individual items that can be counted. *The amount of suffering experienced by the plaintiffs cannot be overestimated. We have a large number of pending class actions.*

Ampersand (&) symbol: Do not use the symbol for *and* (called an *ampersand*, a corruption of the phrase *and per se and*) rather than the word *and* in legal writing unless a company or firm name shows this presentation, as in *The law firm of Reed & Smith is located downtown.*

And: **And** is a coordinating conjunction and is generally used to connect words or groups of words. Most legal writers avoid starting sentences with coordinating conjunctions (*for, and, nor, but, or, yet, so*), although such usage is commonly seen in informal writing.

And/or: The use of the expression **and/or** is confusing. It means *one or the other or both.* Write *The employer or the employee, or both, may terminate the contract* rather than *The employer and/or employee may terminate the contract.*

Ante-, anti-: **Ante-** means *before*, as in *antebellum.* **Anti-** means *against*, as in *anti-American.*

Appraise, apprise: **Appraise** means *to estimate value* and **apprise** means *to inform. I will apprise you when I have received the property appraisal.* Avoid possible confusion by using *inform* rather than **apprise**.

Arbitration, mediation: Although both **arbitration** and **mediation** are methods of alternative dispute resolution, in **arbitration** a binding decision is usually rendered by an impartial third party. In **mediation** a neutral third party attempts to help the disputing parties resolve their differences and no decision is rendered. *If mediation does not produce a satisfactory resolution, the parties will proceed to binding arbitration.*

As: Do not use **as** in place of **because**. Thus, write *She could not sue because the statute of limitations expired* rather than *She could not sue as the statute of limitations expired.*

As, because, since: Do not use **as** in place of **because** or **since**. Write *She was expelled from the partnership because she embezzled funds.* Do not write *She was expelled from the partnership since she embezzled funds.* See *Since.*

As follows: Use **as follows** (not *as follow*) to introduce a list. *The directors attending the meeting were as follows: Adams, Baker, and Carey.*

As, like: Use **as** for most comparisons, as in *She looks as if she is angry* rather than *She looks like she is angry.* The word **like** is a preposition. Write, *She argues like* *an experienced advocate.* Use *as* when what follows it is a clause with a verb. If no verb follows, use *like.*

Assure: See *Ensure, insure, assure.*

As to whether: Substitute the word *whether* in place of this awkward phrase. *The issue is whether the contract was induced by fraud.*

As yet: Substitute the word *yet* in place of this phrase. *The documents have not arrived yet.*

Bad, badly: Write or say *I feel bad the settlement was rejected.* The only way a person feels badly is if his or her hands are damaged. Just as you wouldn't write *I feel sadly,* don't write *I feel badly.* Use *bad* to describe a state of being, as in *Sally felt bad that she hurt Dan's feelings.* Use *badly* to describe an activity, as in *Sally swam badly.* Linking verbs (forms of *to be* and verbs such as *feel, appear, and look*) are usually followed by adjectives and not adverbs. Thus, *Lee looked sad and felt bad* is correct.

Being that: Do not use **being that** as a substitute for **because.** *Because I was in Ohio, I could not serve on the jury* (not *Being that I was in Ohio, I could not serve on the jury*).

Beside, besides: **Beside** means *at the side of,* as in *Come sit beside me.* **Besides** means *in addition to,* as in *Besides the directors, the officers also attended the meeting.*

Between: Typically and traditionally, between is used when referring to two items or people. *The treaty was entered into between Canada and France. The profits will be divided among the four partners.*

Between you and me: The phrase **between you and me** is correct. Do not write *Between you and I.*

Bi-, semi-: **Bi-** means *two*; **semi-** means *half* or *somewhat.* Thus, a *bimonthly meeting* occurs every two weeks (or, according to some dictionaries, every two months) and a *semi-annual checkup* occurs every half-year or six months. Because of the confusion in using these prefixes, avoid them. Write *The meeting will be held every other month.*

Bring, take: If movement is toward you, use *bring.* If movement is away from you, use *take,* as in *Bring me my new pen and take away this old one.*

But: The word **but** is redundant with *doubt* and *help.* Thus, write *I have no doubt that he is guilty* (not *I have no doubt but that he is guilty*). Avoid starting sentences with **but** (see *And*).

By contrast, in contrast: When comparing and contrasting cases, use the expression **in contrast** rather than **by contrast.**

Can, may: Use **can** to show *ability* and **may** to show *permission* or *possible action. He can introduce the evidence* (meaning he is able to introduce the evidence). *The witness may step down* (meaning that the witness has permission to step down).

Cannot: Spell **cannot** as one word when you mean *unable to* or *forbidden*. Do not spell as *can not*.

Capital, capitol: **Capital** means *money* or *the city that is the seat of a government*. **Capitol** (with an *o*) is *the building in which a governmental body meets. The capital of our nation is Washington, D.C. Tours of the capitol building are given daily.*

Case law: Use **case law** rather than *caselaw*.

Cite, citation, sight, site: Use **citation** rather than the less formal **cite** to refer to *legal authorities*, as in *His brief included four citations to case law.* **Sight** refers to *ability to see* or *the thing seen*, as in *The moon was a beautiful sight.* **Site** refers to a place, as in *the site of the accident.*

Compare to, compare with: **Compare to** is used to show similarities and is used less frequently than **compare with**, which is used to show similarities and differences between like kinds. *Compared to me, she is tall. Compared with his opening statement, his closing argument lacked force.*

Compose, comprise: **Compose** means *to make up*, as in *The contract is composed of four sections.* **Comprise** means *to include* or *to consist of*, as in *The corporation comprises four separate divisions.* It is correct to say *consists of* or *composed of*, but it is not correct to say *comprised of*. **Tip:** When using *comprise*, place the "whole" item first and then place the "parts" item second, as in *America comprises 50 states.*

Continual, continuous: **Continual** means *frequently repeated*. **Continuous** means *without interruption. Counsel was continually interrupted by objections. The music from the party next door was continuous.* The distinction between these two words is subtle, and you may wish to use *periodically, routinely,* or *intermittently* in place of **continually**.

Council, counsel: A **council** is a *governing body. The city council enacted the ordinance.* **Counsel** means *advice, advise,* or *lawyer. My counsel gave me good counsel when she suggested that I should draft a new will. I will counsel the client.*

Criteria, criterion: **Criteria** is the plural of **criterion**. *There are three criteria for proving a breach of contract case.*

Data, datum: **Data** is the plural of **datum**. The singular form **datum** is seldom used, and **data** is commonly used as a singular and a plural word. *The data supports your theory.*

Discreet, discrete: **Discreet** means *careful* and *cautious*, as in *The witness was discreet about his whereabouts on the day of the murder.* **Discrete** means *distinct from others* and *separate*, as in *There were four discrete parts to the pleading.*

Disinterested, uninterested: **Disinterested** means neutral, as in *The arbitrator is a disinterested party*. **Uninterested** means bored, as in *The jurors seemed uninterested in the testimony*.

Due to: Use **due to** only when you mean *caused by*. **Due to** appears only after a linking verb (such as *is, was,* or *seemed*). Thus, it should not be used to begin a sentence. Don't use **due to** as a substitute for *because of*. Thus, the following examples are correct: *The plaintiff's injury was due to Mr. Lee's negligence. Because of the holiday, the trial was postponed*.

Effect: See *Affect*.

E.g.,: This abbreviation for *exempli gratia* (meaning *for the sake of an example*) is not italicized in legal writing when it is used to introduce an example; however, it is italicized or underscored when it is used as a signal to introduce a supporting legal citation (see Rule 1.2 of *The Bluebook*; Rule 44.3 of *ALWD*). The citation signal **e.g.,** should always be followed by a comma according to *Bluebook* rules (and the comma is not underscored or italicized), but is not followed by a comma according to *ALWD*. Consider using the phrase *for example* in legal writing rather than **e.g.,** when introducing an example. *He suffered numerous injuries, for example, cuts, bruises, and broken bones*. Do not confuse **e.g.,** with **i.e.,** an abbreviation that means *that is*.

Elude: See *Allude, elude*.

Eminent, imminent: **Eminent** means *distinguished*, as in *He is an eminent jurist*. **Imminent** means *about to happen* as in *Her appointment to the bench is imminent*.

Ensure, insure, assure: **Ensure** means *to make definite* or *guarantee* as in *We must ensure that the rent is paid promptly*. **Insure** means *to protect against loss*, as in *You should insure your jewelry for at least $50,000*. **Assure** means *to make a person sure*, as in *I assure you the trial will not be delayed*.

Et al.: This abbreviation for *and others* should be italicized or underscored when used in legal writing to refer to additional people. *The plaintiff sued Anderson, Baker, Levy et al*. Do not use **et al.** in citations of case names (Rule 10.2.1(a) of *The Bluebook*; Rule 12.2(c) of *ALWD*).

Etc.: Do not use this informal abbreviation for *et cetera* (meaning *and other things*). Use the expression *and so forth*, as in *In contracts class, you will learn about offer, acceptance, consideration, and so forth*.

Explicit, implicit: **Explicit** refers to *something stated expressly*. **Implicit** refers to *something implied. He left explicit instructions in his will. She gave me implicit consent to draft the agreement*.

Fact: A **fact** is *something that has occurred* or *something that can be verified*. Use the word **fact** only when describing an event or something proved. *It is a fact that* *the plaintiff has blue eyes. It is not a fact that a defendant is guilty until a court or jury says so.* **Fact** is often used in long-winded phrases such as *Due to the fact that.* Substitute *Because* for such phrases.

Farther, further: **Farther** refers to *physical distance*, as in *I can throw the ball farther than I thought.* **Further** refers to *time, quality, or additions*, as in *I will discuss this matter further tomorrow.*

Feel: **Feel** refers to *emotion* or *touching*. Courts do not feel. Courts reason, state, rule, or hold. Avoid the use of the wishy-washy expressions *I feel* or *the court felt* in legal writing.

Fewer, less: **Fewer** refers to *objects or people that can be counted*, as in *The plaintiff took fewer depositions in fewer days than planned.* **Less** refers to *quantity and things that cannot be counted*, as in *Ellen has less compassion and less patience than Bill does.* **Less** is also used to describe time, money, and distance, as in *The defendants paid less than $10,000.*

Finding, holding: In the strictest sense, a court makes **findings** on questions of fact and issues **holdings** on questions of law.

First, firstly: Use **first, second, third** rather than the more archaic *firstly, secondly, thirdly.*

Forgo, foregoing: **Forgo** means *to give up*, as in *She was forced to forgo her third cause of action.* **Foregoing** is an adjective meaning *preceding*, as in *As provided in the foregoing paragraph, the goods shall be delivered on June 3, 2013.*

Former, latter: **Former** refers to *a first item or person* and **latter** refers to *a second item or person.* Consider using labels such as *The Seller sold the property to the Buyer* rather than *The former party sold the property to the latter party.*

Good, well: **Good** is used as an adjective, as in *She is a good judge.* **Well** is used as an adverb or to refer to health, as in *He performed well today* or *I feel well.*

Guilty, liable: Use **guilty** to refer to *criminal wrongdoing.* **Liable** refers to *responsibility for a civil wrong. Defendant Smith is guilty of robbery whereas Defendant Jones is liable for damages for breach of contract.*

Hanged, hung: **Hanged** is the past tense of *hang* only for an execution. *He was hanged at dawn.* **Hung** is used for all other meanings and usually means *suspended. We framed and hung the photos in the gallery.* Informally, you may refer to a *hung jury.*

Have to: Do not use this informal phrase. Use **must.** *We must file the complaint by Monday.*

Holding: See *Finding.*

Hopefully: Use **hopefully** to mean *in a hopeful manner: The victim waited hopefully for the verdict.* Although **hopefully** is often used to mean *I hope* or *it is hoped* *that,* many experts object to such usage. Thus, avoid writing *Hopefully, the jury will render its verdict soon.* Write instead, *I hope the jury will render its verdict soon.* In 2012 the Associated Press *Stylebook* stated that it approved the use of *hopefully* to mean *it is hoped* or *we hope.* When the *Washington Post* reported this change, it received more than 700 comments, most of which disagreed with the *Stylebook* decision.

However: Many experts object to using **however** to begin a sentence when it is used to mean *nevertheless.* Better placement is in the middle of a sentence, as in the following two examples: *The jury that was selected, however, was diverse. Donna was anxious about testifying; however, she was an effective witness.*

i.e.,: This abbreviation for *id est* (Latin for *that is*) is used to introduce further explanation, as in *The defendant was a partnership, i.e., an association of two persons.* The abbreviation **i.e.,** is always followed by a comma and appears in Roman type, not in italics or underscoring. Do not confuse **i.e.,** with **e.g.,** which introduces an example.

Illegible, unreadable: **Illegible** means *handwriting that cannot be read or deciphered,* as in *The testator's handwritten will was illegible.* **Unreadable** refers to content that is unclear, as in *The judge stated the brief was so poorly written it was unreadable.*

Impact: Many experts recommend using this word only as a verb to mean *a collision,* as in *His car impacted mine.* Avoid using **impact** as a noun in place of *affect.* Thus, write *My actions affected your decision* (not *My actions impacted your decision*).

Implicit: See *Explicit.*

In contrast: See *By contrast.*

Innocent, guilty: A defendant pleads or is found *guilty* or *not guilty.* A defendant does not plead *innocent* and is not found *innocent;* however, a defendant is presumed *innocent* until proven *guilty.*

In regards to: Avoid this nonstandard phrase. Use *about, concerning, regarding* or *in regard to* (or possibly *as regards,* although that phrase is somewhat stuffy). *I am writing you regarding your lease. I have some concerns about your trial brief.*

Irregardless: **Irregardless** is a glaring nonstandard form of *regardless.* It may be a combination of *regardless* and *irrespective.* Always use *regardless,* as in *Regardless of her alibi, she was found guilty.*

Is when, is where: Do not use these terms in giving a definition. Thus, write *A guaranty is a promise to perform another's obligation* (not *A guaranty is when a person promises to perform another's obligation*).

Its, it's: **Its** is the possessive form of the word it and means *belonging to it.* The only meaning of the contraction **it's** is *it is* (or possibly *it has*). *The corporation held* *its meeting last week. It's a Fortune 500 corporation listed on the New York Stock Exchange.* Contractions (such as **it's** for *it is*) are seldom used in legal or formal writing. There is no such word as *its'*.

-ize: Words ending in **-ize** (*monetize, colorize, strategize*) are often "made up" words borrowed from modern business settings and are usually too informal for legal writing. Avoid such words unless they appear in a standard dictionary.

Judicial, judicious: **Judicial** refers to courts, as in *A review showed no abuse of judicial discretion.* **Judicious** means *using good judgment*, as in *A judicious use of graphs makes a document visually appealing.*

Kind of, sort of: Use *somewhat* or *rather* in place of these informal terms, as in *She was somewhat reluctant to testify.*

Lay, lie: **Lay** means *to put* or *place something* and its forms are *lay, laid, laying,* and *lays.* **Lie** means *to recline* and its forms are *lie, lay, lain, lying,* and *lies.*

    Correct: *I lay the document in the folder. I laid it there last Monday.*

    Correct: *I will lie down and nap when I have a moment. I lay down yesterday for a brief rest.*

Lead, led: **Led** is the past tense of the verb **lead**. Write *I usually lead the team of defense counsel but yesterday Ann led the team.*

Lend, loan: **Lend** is a verb and **loan** is a noun. *I will lend you money because you need a loan. Yesterday I lent money to Steven.* Informal usage permits either **lend** or **loan** as verbs. Thus, you may see *She loaned me the money.*

Less: See *Fewer.*

Lessor, lessee: Do not spell as *leasor* or *leasee.*

Liable, libel, slander: **Liable** means *responsible for some civil wrong*, as in *She is liable for damages caused by her negligence.* **Libel** is written defamation, as in *His newspaper article libeled the plaintiff by calling her a crook.* **Slander** is oral defamation, as in *She slandered me in her speech yesterday.*

Like, as: **Like** is a preposition. Use as follows: *We need another expert like Dr. Harris.* As is usually a conjunction and introduces a clause with a verb. Use as follows: *She acted as if she didn't know me.* See *As.*

Literal, literally: The word **literal** (meaning *in fact* or *actually*) is often used incorrectly to show exaggeration. It would be incorrect to write *When the client received the bill, he literally exploded.* Use *almost* or *nearly* in such cases.

Loose, lose: **Loose** means *not tight*, as in *Her clothing was loose.* **Lose** means *to misplace* or *not win*, as in *Did you lose the document?* or *Never tell clients they cannot lose a case.*

Lots, a lot of: Avoid using these informal expressions. Use *many* or *significant,* as in *The defendant had significant resources.*

Manner: Avoid writing *in a ___ manner.* Thus, write *She walks awkwardly* rather than *She walks in an awkward manner.*

May: See *Can.*

Maybe, may be: **Maybe** means *possibly,* as in *Maybe the defendant will not appear at the hearing.* **May be** is a verb. Use as follows: *She may be the court clerk, but I am not sure.*

Media, medium: **Media** is the plural of **medium** and should be used with a plural verb, as in *The media have distorted my client's record.* **Media** and other similar words (such as *agenda, criteria, data*) are often used in common parlance as singular words. See *Data.*

Mediation: See *Arbitration.*

Memoranda, memorandum: The word **memoranda** is plural and refers to *several documents.* **Memorandum** is a *single document.* Use as follows: *He prepared all six memoranda. The first memorandum was the most persuasive.*

Might of: This is the incorrect and nonstandard use of *might have.*

Moot, mute: **Moot** means debatable or theoretical, as in *His argument was moot because the case had just settled.* It rhymes with *boot.* **Mute** means silent, as in *She stood mute, unable to speak.* It rhymes with *cute.*

More important, more importantly: **More important** is often used at the beginning of a sentence to mean *what is more important,* as in *More important, the statute of limitations had expired.* **More importantly** means *in a more important manner,* as in *The scheduling of the deposition was treated more importantly than it deserved.* Consider avoiding these expressions as they are often overused to signal a reader, "What I'm about to tell you is important. Pay attention." Use strong writing to convince a reader, not gratuitous instructions.

Must: See *Shall, must, will.*

Myriad: **Myriad** means *numerous* or *many* and traditionally should not be followed by *of.* Thus, prefer *There were myriad contracts to be reviewed* (not *There were a myriad of contracts to be reviewed*). The use of **myriad** as a noun is now accepted by many dictionaries. Thus, *I have a myriad of friends* is acceptable to many.

Not guilty: See *Innocent.*

Number: See *Amount.*

Of, have: It is incorrect to use the preposition **of** in expressions such as *could of* or *might of.* The correct uses are *could have* and *might have,* as in *I could have attended the conference.*

On, upon: Use **on** rather than the stuffier **upon**, as in *On discovering the defect, the tenant sued the landlord.*

Oral, verbal, written: **Oral** means *something spoken,* as in *Her oral testimony at trial confirmed her earlier deposition testimony.* **Verbal** means *a communication in words* and can refer to either *written* or *spoken communication.* Thus, the statement *We had a verbal agreement* is confusing because it could refer either to a written agreement or to a nonwritten agreement. To avoid confusion, use **oral** or **written** and avoid the use of **verbal**.

Overrule, reverse: A court **overrules** earlier decisions in its jurisdiction. *In 1954, the Supreme Court case* Brown v. Board of Education *overruled the 1896 case* Plessy v. Ferguson. A court **reverses** the very case before it on appeal and changes its result, as in *The defendant in* State v. Thomas *was found guilty. He appealed his conviction, and the appellate court agreed and reversed the trial court's decision.*

Passed, past: **Passed** is used as the past tense of the verb *to pass,* as in *The defendant passed the truck in the right-hand lane.* **Past** usually refers to a *former time* or *age,* as in *My past caught up with me.*

People, persons, parties: Use **people** to refer to a group of individuals collectively, as in *The people summoned for jury duty have arrived.* Use **persons** to refer to small numbers of specifically identified individuals, as in *The persons responsible for the negligence have been sued.* Generally, however, the word **people** sounds more natural in most contexts and is more commonly used. Use your ear. The word **parties** is used to refer to the individuals or entities involved in litigation, as in *The parties have settled the case.*

Per: Generally, use *a* or *an* rather than the Latin **per**, as in *The firm bills $200 an hour* (not *The firm bills $200 per hour*).

Percent, percentage: Spell **percent** as one word and use only after a specific number, as in *Interest was assessed at five percent.* **Percentage** is used when no fixed number is given, as in *A significant percentage of new businesses fail.*

Plead, pleaded, pled: The correct past participle of the verb **plead** is **pleaded**, as in *The defendant pleaded guilty.* Avoid the less preferred but commonly used **pled**.

Plus: Do not use the informal word **plus** when you mean *moreover* or *additionally.* *The defendant was old; moreover, he was sickly.*

Practicable, practical: **Practicable** usually means *feasible,* as in *It is not practicable to learn the meaning of every Latin phrase.* **Practical** means *useful* or *sensible,* as in *It is not practical to structure the business as a partnership.*

Precede, proceed: **Precede** means *to come or go before,* as in *The clerk will precede the judge into the courtroom.* **Proceed** means *to continue* or *to go ahead,* as in *You may proceed with the cross-examination.*

Precedent, precedence: A **precedent** is a previous judicial decision, as in *The court followed its earlier precedent in reaching its decision.* **Precedence** means *priority* or *the act of coming or going before,* as in *Working on the brief takes precedence over all other matters.*

Prescribe, proscribe: **Prescribe** means *to order,* as in *The doctor prescribed complete bed rest.* **Proscribe** means *to forbid* or *to prohibit* as in *Iowa laws proscribe littering.*

Principal, principle: **Principal** means *a supervisor at a school, a dominant item,* or *a sum of money.* **Principle** means a *fundamental rule.* Match the *le* in *principle* with the *le* in *rule.*

Correct: *The principal rang the opening bell of school.*
             The principal office of the corporation is in Los Angeles.
             You must repay the principal amount of the debt.

Correct: *The principles of physics are complex.*

Procedural, substantive: **Procedural** refers to legal procedures, such as the rules for pleading and other similar practical matters. **Substantive** refers to the law itself. For example, a law requiring a complaint for medical malpractice to be filed within one year of the wrongful act is a matter of substantive law. A court rule requiring the pleading to be filed on white, opaque paper is a matter of procedural law.

Protection clause: A clause in a letter or document that protects the writer (often from a claim of legal malpractice); also called a *savings clause.*

Proved, proven: Use **proved** as a past participle of **prove**, as in *The attorney proved his case.* **Proven** is an adjective, as in *The proven facts were clear.*

Quotation, quote: Use **quote** only as a verb, as in *Don't quote me on this.* Use **quotation** as a noun, as in *The decision included several quotations from the U.S. Supreme Court.*

Raise, rise: **Raise** means *to lift* or *bring up* and requires a direct object, as in *The plaintiff raised a serious objection* or *The foundation will raise the funds for diabetes research.* **Rise** means *get up* or *move upward* and is not used with an object: *They will rise at 6:00 a.m.* or *You must rise to the occasion.*

Reason is because, reason why: Avoid the redundant expressions **reason is because** and **reason why.** Replace **reason is because** with *reason is that.* Write *The reason the partnership dissolved was that the general partner died* (not *The reason why the partnership dissolved was that the general partner died*).

Rebut, refute: **Rebut** means *speaking or writing against something,* as in *The defendant's opening statement rebuts the plaintiff's opening statement.* **Refute** means *to disprove something,* as in *How will you refute the claim that you breached the contract?*

Recur, reoccur: **Recur** means *to happen repeatedly,* as in *Her recurring dream was to win the lottery.* **Reoccur** refers to *something happening a second time,* as in *If the leaks reoccur, contact the landlord.*

Regardless: Use this word to mean *notwithstanding,* as in *Regardless of his protestations of innocence, he was found guilty.* Never use *irregardless,* which is not a word. See *Irregardless.*

Reluctant, reticent: **Reluctant** means *hesitant,* as in *I am reluctant to hire him.* **Reticent** means *tending to be silent,* as in *Amy is reticent and shy at meetings and seldom speaks.*

Respectfully, respectively: **Respectfully** means *with respect* and is a commonly used closing in a document, as in *Respectfully submitted, Mary Harris.* **Respectively** means *in a certain order,* as in *The three landlords were Smith, Allen, and Madison, respectively.*

Sanction: This word has two meanings, so it is often confused. When used as a noun, **sanction** usually means *a penalty,* as in *The judge imposed sanctions against the plaintiff for failing to appear in court.* When used as a verb, **sanction** usually means *approved,* as in *The fundraiser was sanctioned by the governing board.*

Savings clause: See *Protection clause.*

Seem: Avoid this weak word whenever possible. For example, avoid the following: *Your letter did not seem to include the invoice.* Write instead, *Your letter did not include the invoice.*

Shall, must, will: **Shall** is generally used only in legal documents or in statutes and refers to *mandatory action,* as in *The tenant shall pay rent on the first of every month.* **Will** refers to *future action,* as in *Ted will attend the shareholders' meeting next month.* **Must** is becoming more commonly accepted as a replacement for **shall** in legal writing, as in *The seller must convey the property to the buyer.* Because **shall** is somewhat archaic, consider using **must** in place of **shall.**

Sight, site: See *Cite.*

Since, because: Avoid using **since** as a substitute for **because;** otherwise, ambiguity may result, as in the sentence *Since the tariffs were lifted, trade has increased.* It is not clear in this sentence whether **since** means *after a period of time* or whether it means *because.* To avoid confusion, use **since** to refer to the *passage of time,* as in *It has been four weeks since we filed the appeal* and use **because** to show *causation,* as in *Because the jury was improperly charged, the judgment was reversed.*

Sometime, some time: **Sometime** means *at some time in the future,* as in *The trial will be scheduled sometime soon.* **Some time** means *a period of time,* as in *It has been quite some time since the defendant was arraigned.*

Supposed to, used to: Avoid these informal expressions, but if you use them, always include a *d* in the verb. Consider using *should* or *accustomed to,* as in *You* *should have attended the deposition* (rather than *You were supposed to attend the deposition*) and *He has become accustomed to his client's tardiness* (rather than *He is used to his client's tardiness*). Never write *He was suppose to attend the deposition* or *He use to be careful.*

Sure and, sure to: Use **sure to**, not *sure and*, as in *Be sure to argue forcefully.*

Take: See *Bring, take.*

Than, then: Overenunciate these words to select the correct one. **Than** is used to refer to *comparisons*, as in *I have been practicing law longer than Sue has.* **Then** refers to *time*, as in *The plaintiff argued and then the defendant responded.*

That, which: Use **that** to introduce essential material, as in *The brief that I filed last week was missing an exhibit.* **That** is not set off by commas. Use **which** to introduce nonessential material, as in *The lease, which he signed, was entered into evidence.* A clause beginning with **which** is usually set off by commas.

That, who: **That** may be used to refer to people, things, or animals. Thus, all of the following are correct: *They are the attorneys that we hired; The brief that we filed was missing an exhibit,* and *The dog that barked was vicious.* **Who** may be used to refer to people or named animals, as in *Maria is the woman who called* and *Daisy is a dog who is clever.* Many experts prefer using *that* only for objects and would not use *that* to refer to people.

Therefor, therefore: **Therefor** means *for that*, as in *He agreed to donate funds to build the school and to donate the land therefor.* **Therefore** is used *to show causation*, as in *The defendant infringed the plaintiff's trademark. Therefore, damages were awarded to the plaintiff.*

Thus, thusly: Use **thus** instead of the more archaic word **thusly**.

Till, until: Both **till** and **until** are correct, although **until** is preferred in legal writing. Do not use the informal *'til.*

Tortious, tortuous, torturous: **Tortious** refers to *acts that give rise to civil actions*, as in *She sued for tortious interference with contract.* **Tortuous** means *full of twists and turns*, as in *We climbed the tortuous path.* **Torturous** refers to *torture or pain*, as in *I have a torturous toothache.*

Toward, towards: Americans use **toward**. The British use **towards**.

Treble, triple: These words mean the same but **treble** is often used in statutes to refer to *the tripling of damages*, as in *The court awarded treble damages because of the willfulness of the defendant's conduct.*

Try to, try and: Use **try to**, not **try and**, as in *Try to keep your argument brief.*

Ultimate, penultimate: **Ultimate** means *the last* and **penultimate** means *next-to-last.*

Unique: This word means *one of a kind* and should not be modified. Thus, write *The defendant's argument was unique* (not *rather unique, somewhat unique,* or *very unique*).

Unreadable: See *Illegible*.

Usage: **Usage** refers to *a customary practice* or often *a customary way of using words*, as in *The correct usage of "whom" is confusing to most people*.

Use, utilize: Prefer **use** to **utilize** in most instances. **Use** means *to put into action, make use of*, or *to employ*, as in *Use your main argument first*. **Utilize** often suggests *a practical purpose* or *making use of a utensil*, as in *Utilize a black marker to make the exhibits more noticeable. Use a black marker . . .* is also acceptable and is simpler.

v., vs.: In case citations, use a lower case *v* followed by a period, as in *Smith v. Jones*. In other instances, including court pleadings, **vs.** may be used.

Verbal: See *Oral*.

Verbiage: The word **verbiage** generally means *wordiness* and is usually used in a critical manner, as in *The document's verbiage made it impossible to read*.

Void, voidable: A contract or act that is **void** has *no effect*. A contract that is **voidable** *is effective until a party (with cause) declares it void*, as in *The agreement will be voidable at the option of either party after sixty days*.

Where: **Where** refers to a *location* or *place*. It is not a substitute for *when* or *in which*. Use as follows: *Oregon is where the defendant was convicted* (not *State v. Jackson is a case where the defendant was convicted*).

Whether, whether or not: Generally, the phrase *or not* is redundant and can be omitted, as in *The issue is whether the defendant acted recklessly*.

Which: See *That, which*.

While: Traditionally, **while** has meant *during the time that*, as in *While the defendant was in jail, he confessed*. In more modern usage, **while** has come to be an accepted substitute for *although*, as in *While the contract was long, it was readable*. To avoid ambiguity, consider using *although* at the beginning of a sentence to show contrast and using **while** when you mean *concurrently* or *during the time that*.

Who's, whose: **Who's** is a contraction meaning *who is*, as in *Who's the witness?* **Whose** is the possessive form of *who*, as in *Whose client pleaded guilty?*

Will: See *Shall, must, will*.

Willful, wilful: Prefer the first spelling, which is the American spelling, to the second spelling, which is the British spelling.

Sample Case Brief

StyleLinks

www.4lawschool.com/conlaw/conlaw.htm
This site offers more than one thousand sample case briefs posted by law students.

www.lib.jjay.cuny.edu/research/brief.html
This site provides instructions on preparing case briefs.

Introduction

Formats for case briefs vary from person to person. Following is a suggested format for a typical case brief.

Cobaugh v. Klick-Lewis, Inc., 561 A.2d 1248 (Pa. Super. Ct. 1989)

Procedural History

Plaintiff Cobaugh sued an automobile dealer to compel delivery of a car offered as a prize in a golf tournament. The trial court entered summary judgment for the plaintiff, and the defendant appealed. The Pennsylvania Superior Court affirmed.

Statement of Facts

Amos Cobaugh, a golfer playing at a golf tournament, observed a car and a sign at the ninth tee stating that a hole-in-one would allow a golfer to receive a car as a prize. Cobaugh made a hole-in-one and attempted to claim his prize. The car dealership refused to deliver the prize, stating that the car had been offered as a prize for an earlier golf tournament and that it had neglected to remove the car and the posted sign prior to Cobaugh's hole-in-one.

Issue

Does an offer to award a prize in a contest constitute an enforceable contract?

Answer

Yes. An offer to award a prize in a contest will result in an enforceable contract if the offer is properly accepted by appropriate performance prior to revocation of the offer.

Reasoning

When a promoter of a contest makes an offer and another party acts on the offer before it is withdrawn, the promoter must perform his promise. A person reading the sign at the golf course would reasonably understand that he or she could accept the offer and win the car by performing the feat of shooting a hole-in-one. There was thus an offer that was accepted when Cobaugh shot a hole-in-one. Moreover, the defendant benefited from the publicity generated by the contest. This was adequate consideration to support the contract. Additionally, there was no mutual mistake such as would make the contract voidable. When a mistake is not mutual but is due to the negligence of one party (in this case, the defendant's failure to remove the sign), rescission of the contract will not be granted. Finally, a contest to award a prize to a golfer for a hole-in-one is not illegal gambling because some skill is involved.

Index